Advance Praise

Tom Sheehan dissects the life of everyman, for in peace and war and all the trauma and joy in between, he has known everyman. He masters the details of memory, in sight, sound, smell and feel, so that memory becomes memorable. He is Dos Passos reincarnated. The man touches our hearts and drives a story into our souls as if it were an old Buick Roadmaster.

-Alan Lupo, columnist, *Boston Globe*

Be advised that memories are not docile, helpless objects, for, indeed, they respond as they are being gathered and leave their marks on those who choose to gather them—these marks, poignant, touching on painful, yet endlessly rewarding—bringing us as they have a fresh, moving heightened vision of Saugus, our Saugus, your Saugus, for us to know it, as the poet said, "for the first time."

-John Burns, Co-editor of *A Gathering of Memories, Saugus 1900-2000*

Tom Sheehan is a national treasure. A true writer in the purest form of the word, Sheehan gives us prose and poetry that spans decades of experience with not only intelligent insight, but with a deep and abiding love of life and people that has no match. His language thrills and his creative dynamic is a wonder in itself. Living life fully is not for sissies, and Sheehan shows us humanhood at its most majestic.

-Beverly A. Jackson, Editor-In-Chief/Publisher, Lit Pot Press, Inc.

These life stories Tom Sheehan memorably unfolds are not those of an outside observer, but are from one who has lived them, someone who has connection with the people on the gritty and piquant streets of Charlestown and Malden in the hard years, and the idyll that was Saugus back then. And it is the communities and the people found in this book that is its essence. A Saugonian-in-exile in Maine, I read the stories and know these people. Most I have never met but am able to see them clearly today, as if I have known them forever. They live forever in these stories, Sheehan's gift to them, not being forgotten, yet they would be if not cast up here, they'd just be gone, forever. I rekindle my connection to my home town, the gathering of memories that leave their marks on me, reminding me that it is not just my hometown but is for all who have something of Tom Sheehan's Saugus in them. Whether they've lived there or not, they will find it so.

-Tom Weddle, geologist, State of Maine

Author of *This Rare Earth & Other Flights* and *Death for the Phantom Receiver*, and numerous publications online and in print, Tom Sheehan is the inveterate writer of fiction and poetry of our times. It would be easy to fall back on one's laurels, bask in the glow of retirement and reflect upon the past with a fond, dewy eye; but, this is not the Tom Sheehan I know. Tom is a friend to all mankind; and, what is mankind, if not everything we believe in? Composed of kindness to the past and present, our collective experiences, struggles and triumphs that elevate existence beyond the simple pleasures of reading, we live and relive in Sheehan's writing that no one may be forgotten. I have literally cried, laughed, dined and fallen down countless times with the heroes in

Tom's many stories. Tom is a friend to the reader. *A Collection of Friends* is a recollection, if you will, about the town of Saugus, Massachusetts, its longtime residents, ghosts, heroes, and families. It's often said that one can never go back home, but Sheehan's Saugus remains a safe harbor for its dearest friends: for those who have chosen to stay, those who have passed on, Sheehan has been faithful to their memories.

-Mia, Editor, *Tryst*

Tom Sheehan is not only an accomplished wordsmith, he is also a master story-teller. His compositions bridge the boundaries of space and time to trace images and feelings on the readers' soul. The pieces included in *A Collection of Friends* evoke the whole range of emotions and re-kindle long-dormant memories. Mr. Sheehan's roots are every American's roots, and he has been blessed with the skills to make the reader say, "Yes! I remember!" Thank you, Mr. Sheehan!

-Bart Brady Ciampa, www.bartsmusic.com

A Collection of Friends

Thomas Sheehan

Pocol Press

POCOL PRESS

Published in the United States of America
by Pocol Press
6023 Pocol Drive
Clifton, VA 20124
www.pocolpress.com

Publisher's Cataloguing-in-Publication

Sheehan, Thomas.
    A collection of friends / Thomas Sheehan. – 1st ed. – Clifton, VA : Pocol Press, 2004

        p. ; cm.
        ISBN: 1-929763-17-4

        1. Sheehan, Thomas. 2. Authors, American--Massachusetts—20th century—Biography. 3. Authors, American—Massachusetts—20th century—Anecdotes. 4. Saugus (Mass.)—Anecdotes. I. Title.

PS3619.H444 C65 2004
813.6–B–dc22   0409

Preface

We celebrate in many way those people met in life who refuse to let go. They are the ones who continue to fall into step with us as we move along in our own time, whose breaths hang evermore at our shoulders. They direct or challenge us, often reminding us which way to go or what might have been. And, they nurture ideas, dialogue, and a sense of conjunction.

This collection is a mix of nostalgia, reflections, images and ideas such people have spawned. Through them this man carries with him a host of memories and reveries always accompanied by a spill of the marvelous characters that have shaped him the way he has come. Celebrated here are the heroes of mighty deeds, comrades from the combat zones, as well as down-trodden folk, the lost and the lonely, those beset by life yet are textured by the hopes that another life might have been theirs, or one exists elsewhere for them to find.

Enduring, memorable, these people have filled my life, and they are found here in this book. They are: Johnny Igoe, whose voice still sounds like Yeats's voice; my mother and father I hear yet knocking on the tomb; and my brother James I came to know when he went away and stayed away. Inside are dear sisters by the handful; hospice nurse wife, sons and daughters; my fishing companions and teammates; dear friend Eddie LeBlanc afflicted by a dreaded muscle disease; and Parkie who, like Lazarus, arose from the deadly sands of WWII Sahara, caught in a chamber he and his comrades can never forget, thrust into an accord they cannot let go of. There's our dusty coalman of The Forties who for bare moments dodged the death of his son; Skink, harmless town drunk, eventually celebrated in beer and bombast by an infantry squad in Korea just before a night of terror; the watchful poolroom attendant who saw us grow; and Wingsy, a clumsy but elegant boyhood friend, comrade, going down in the middle of Korea, remembered always.

Here are the memories of a young life at early labors, then knowing family departures and family growth, and the incessant dreams of a writer coming into a sense of balance in life through the people he has known.

Piecemeal, as entities, in my ear, clapping me on the back, giving me a push when needed, they have caused this book. I am indebted to them, those who have given my life all its savage joys.

Perhaps for a short time of reading, they might live again for new friends under a soft lamp or the keen morning light.

-Thomas Sheehan
Saugus, MA
September 2004

Dedication

For those who have passed through Saugus, those comrades who bravely walked away from home and fell elsewhere, and the frailest imaginable soldier of all, frightened and glassy-eyed and knowing he is hapless, one foot onto the soil at D-Day or a statistical sandy beach of the South Pacific and going down, but not to be forgotten, not here.

Photograph Acknowledgments

The author and publisher gratefully thank the following individuals for their usage of photographic material.

Cover photo © James F. Harrington – Saugus Photos Online. Riverside Cemetery, Saugus, Massachusetts.

Rich Garabedian, Global Visual Communications (GVC). Author on rear cover in Saugus baseball cap.

Jongseuk Lim. Title page. Korean War Memorial, Washington, D.C.

Acknowledgments

The author wishes to acknowledge the following publications in which these stories, sometimes in slightly different form, first appeared.

The Dumpmaster's Boy	The Paumanok Review (Pushcart nomination)
The Great God Shove	Small Spiral Notebook Magaera
The Boy Who Got Stuck Under the Warren Avenue Bridge	Showbound (Keikomedia)
The Bill Collector	Electric Acorn Slow Trains Nuvein
Falling-down Jack, A Study	3amMagazine Tryst
Orion's Belt	Bias Onus Nuvein
The Day Titanic Drowned	AJP Poor Mojo
Fred Rippon's Mushroom House	The Paumanok Review
Assault on Mount Carmel	Muse Apprentice Guild Nuvein
Parkie, Tanker, Tiger of Tobruk	Stirring Poet's Haven
Wingsy	Tryst
The Quiet, Empty Bedrooms of Saugus	A Gathering of Memories

The Hermit of Breakheart Woods   Small Spiral Notebook
Magaera

A Toast to Skink   3amMagazine
Tryst (Pushcart nomination)

The Three Fishermen   Eastoftheweb
(Nonfiction Composition
winner)

It's All in the Maul   The Paumanok Review

The Ghosts of Lily Pond   The Paumanok Review
(Pushcart nomination)

This Old House   The Paumanok Review

Eddie Smiledge, Houseman   The Saugonian
The Paumanok Review

My Hometown, Saugus,   The Saugonian
Massachusetts   North Shore Sunday

Table of Contents

Early Years
The Dumpmaster's Boy   1
The Great God Shove   15
The Boy Who Got Stuck Under   32
    the Warren Avenue Bridge
The Bill Collector   40
Falling-down Jack, A Study   48
Orion's Belt   63

Adolescence
The Day Titanic Drowned   78
Fred Rippon's Mushroom House   83
Assault on Mount Carmel   93

War Stories
Parkie, Tanker, Tiger of Tobruk   103
Wingsy   117
The Coalman   134
The Quiet, Empty Bedrooms of Saugus   144

Misanthropes
The Hermit of Breakheart Woods   150
A Toast to Skink   164
Eddie Smiledge, Houseman   184

Reflections
The Three Fishermen   192
It's All in the Maul   198
The Ghosts of Lily Pond   206
Johnny Igoe, Spellbinder Remembered   216
This Old House   225
My Hometown: Saugus, Massachusetts   231

The Dumpmaster's Boy

Ears I had, and eyes, and I used them well.
Before I walked by the group of men on the corner,
bringing my Grandfather's lunch to the city dump
where he worked, I knew they'd be talking about me.
We had moved from Charlestown. We'd move back for
sure, a game with landlords and cold water flats. Even
at six years of age, in 1934, there were certainties. It
was the time of day, before the sun was up straight. The
way they lounged. Who they were. How their clothes
hung on them the way visitors come from out of town
or right from ships. It was the clatter of their voices,
snappy as a swung bag of clothespins.

At times their teeth clicked a harmony. It could
be measured. Ancient Irish men made noises that were
music to my ears. My Grandfather made music. He was
Irish. One of them said one day, in a whisper I could
hear, that my Grandfather was sick. That's when I got
the worry. Even at six years of age, there were
certainties, and uncertainties, and the unknown. I had
become a worrier.

"Oosh," or "Ach," they'd say as I walked by, or
"Arrah" in the old tongue, their teeth clicking on briars,
the old Irishmen gathered outside Clougherty's bar in
the west end of Malden, Massachusetts. The Depression
made a living taste about us, Prohibition afoot, and the
things that rose with us at breakfast, what there was of
it, were set with the absence of a late snack.

Clicking still, the men were as dark as the
insides of that holy place behind them I hadn't been
inside of yet. Their jackets and pants were harsh to the
touch, and their dark gray caps sat jaunty on their heads.

Squat pipes, teeth-bitten, twirled smoke up
under the brims. Jaws set like anchors for those who
were shaven, white-forested for those not. Any other

1

place in the world they'd be sitting out front of a mine shaft or a gas works, far from home, "Ochone" keening from their lips, the grief. They'd be sitting on wooden boxes, milk crates, or odd scrounged chairs, with Clougherty's, a temple of mystery behind them, behind a dark, dark door.

Even short of my seventh birthday, I'd know the air around them even before I saw them. My nose would be up proper, testing. The coal-cut of gas slid over on its covering wing from the gas works back of Commercial Street. It is a smell lingering to this day, a smell that comes back, as though it's on reminder visits. I know it whenever gasoline is being pumped at a station or being spouted into a lawn mower. I know it when I see an old and odd coal car now and then sitting like a fossil along little-used railroad tracks. I know it in the depths of an old cellar when coal dust, fine as crushed days telling of fieldstone and time, waits to be found by a nose like mine.

The smell was so strong it allowed the creation of games when I'd hold my breath. I'd pretend the Kaiser's freeking men were after me with their bags of green-awful gas. I'd puff my cheeks, waiting for G-8 or Nippy or Bull Martin, my pulp heroes, to come to my rescue. My face would get brick red and my chest would heave against itself. Behind my eyes I'd see the rotters with their gas bags knocking down the way from Highland Avenue or The Fellsway, coming at me. There were times when I could let Hell break loose.

The old Irishers' voices would bring me back, voices that later I would stamp as high-pitched Yeatsian tongue in poetic treble. In time the memories of them would bring me a new music, hearing The Man on record, hearing it "in the deep heart's core," knowing the haunt of it forever.

"That's for sure Johnny Igoe's boy acarryin' his lunch to the dump. Now that's a good lad for his

Grandfather altogether, won't you know." Pipe smoke would rise, a hand held in half salute.

They were not knocking the dump. For too many of us at that time it was hardware store and haberdashery, all-around supplier of used goods. It had endless yield and my Grandfather, dumpmaster, city employee, was the head picker. Johnny Igoe had first call, first dibs. All he had to do was point at something and it was his, the chair with only one leg missing, a still-shiny pot, a book with its cover nearly gone asunder, an iron fire engine or tin plane, the kind to keep.

As I passed the men, they'd be quiet a bit and let the smoke twirl up under their caps and their feet go still on the walkway. Amaze you they could, some of the older ones. They often played their shoes on the pavement like a soft shoe set, or a tambourine shushed and low. Some would nod their heads the way priests do when they look in your eye, heads cocked. Some looked like teachers my brother had at the school up on Pleasant Street. How they cocked their noses, as if they knew everything there was to know on the face of the Earth.

I watched their eyes, their hands, their feet, when I went by them on my errand. So many messages could be picked out of the air, so much understood about the long stretch of time. Gold chains across their vests, anchored to hidden watches, clutched inward a dazzle of daylight or sunlight. Occasionally one of them would work the shiny chain in his fingers. Twirling it, they'd cut the air in little loops, catching light rays, spilling seconds out of hours. Now and then a watch went into that small circle, in disdain of the flight or the compound of hours. It was noiseless, a sun around a fist, and, like the sun, silent in journey.

Someday I'd swing a watch or chain like that in small mechanics, the wrist pure and musical, time on the fly, sunlight all mine, or on its journey.

But then, entrusted to my hands, was the great sandwich in a line of great sandwiches. My Grandfather Johnny Igoe's lunch of a day I carried, two good fingers thick, and the bread crusty and thick, too. It was wrapped in brown paper and tied up in white string by my Grandmother, Mary Brennan Igoe. Out of her oven that very morning the bread had come, six loaves so golden and gleaming a mouth'd water for an hour or more. Sometimes a whole day if she ever got cross with you for *a poor deed, poor deed indeed.* You could be begging for a block of butter to drop into the hot wrap of it.

Her black stove flung itself across the kitchen back wall. It snapped noises only chimneys could catch hold of, mysterious crackling noises. They had an ultimate power that drove every one of us out of that room but her on any July or August day. She had her colors. The stains under her arms turned as dark as lakes, her hair white, the blue eyes deep as the ovens themselves. Only the back of her wrist would touch her brow, the gesture of relief that only comes to women. Especially to those who warm by the oven, their eyes closed in tiny relief, a look off into the distance before going back about their business.

Bake she was born for and bake she did, and having kids in her days. She was forever giving off tarts and slabs of pies and tasty things thick and chewy with gobs of cinnamon in them. Sugar trailed in every corner of the house and a wonder the little black ants didn't carry off the whole house of it.

"Suck on your tooth when you're done, Thomas. You might get another day out of it," the laugh in her throat like the bells at Mass in the right hands.

Mary Brennan Igoe was different from my father's mother, Mary Elizabeth King Sheehan right out of Cork. There was an elegant thirty-year widow for you. Tall and gracious, precise of language she was, with her little black widow's hat on her head and the shiny glasses on her nose. They'd be a bread roll or two in her pocketbook from whenever she supped outside her Somerville home. Her pocketbook was always black. It always shone the light around it. A touch of new leather at her hands as if a bargain had just been made.

At Ginn and Co. in Cambridge, she was a bookbinder, for more that sixty years eventually, and never baked a pie in her life it seems. Or baked bread. But she could wash your feet and scrub your back on a visit with her slender fingers and make you feel new all over. And she knew history and got books with broken covers or those which were not yet bound, geographies and histories and once in a great while there'd be poems. We'd get Amergin or Columcille or Donnchadh Mor O'Dala or Dallan MacMore or Saint Ita or Saint Colman, about Saint Patrick and Eileen Aroon and Fionn and Saint Brendan and Diarmaid and Grainne and a host of kings afoot on the very land itself. Much of it told to me, of course, though I was a reader, according to my Grandfather, long before some of his own children brought the pages home to comfort.

Grandma Igoe would stand beside that great stove or by the buffet in the front room where she stored her finished goods. The pies and tarts and cakes and cream puffs were so elegant you could steal but for the threat of the Lord hanging in the air over you. Her jelly rolls were historic, mounded and rolled and sugared. The sweet red line twisted its marble pattern you could only see from the end view, gathering inward until it disappeared, the way it could disappear *sure down that b'y's t'roat.*

Buffet drawers were crammed with her baked goods, the big ones at the bottom and the small ones at the top, and the cubbyholes behind doors at each end.

My Grandfather said she baked every day of her last thirty years. He said the memory of hunger in the old country hung its dark face at the head of the stairs, waiting to visit again.

"Jayzuz, bless the memory," he would say.

And I could hear her say, "Hunger," in that musical voice of hers, "'twill be a guest here if I ever once t'turn my back t'him."

Flour clung about her like weeds against a fence. It might have been atomized on her before the atomizer was thought of. Her arms were white with it, and her apron and the neck of her dress where her hands were always at work fixing herself as if something wasn't set right. As if she had an itch waiting on her. White was her hair, too, like snow left over from late March and April in the back yard. Yet patches of sweat, dark as plaster in a leaky ceiling, were squeezed under her arms and moved perilously on her large breasts. Sometimes, though I dared never tell her, but especially when she wore her blue dress, I'd pretend the patches of sweat were maps of parts of the world I wanted to visit. The maps I'd seen in the Atlas at the library with my Grandfather.

All of Russia came up, dark with its lakes and seas and strange names at the edges of oceans. The steamy Congo he told me about came also, plunked in the middle of Africa, with rivers and hidden lakes, and creatures that ate up little people in a single bite. Once, from the first moment, a deep stain was Brazil, down there under my feet. The country kept growing and growing. It grew with the pies and the cakes and the six loaves of bread. All morning it grew. She never knew how big that country got. That it might grow so ponderous geography books would have to be done over. The globe itself would tip on its side and bring her down.

In the lunch package I carried was also a pint

whiskey bottle, filled with coffee, dark and shoe-colored, crammed against the sandwich. The top of the bottle would be plugged with an old cork or a twist of paper. Grandma worked it down in as she turned the bottle in her floury hands. Sometimes it was from an old *Globe* or *Traveler* or *Transcript*, or a page out of the *Saturday Evening Post.* Or it might come from a copy of *G-8 and His Battle Aces* I'd already read, Nippy and Bull Martin done for that issue.

She always left a loop in the package's string. When my hand got tired of lugging the package near all the way to the dump, I could slip a finger in the loop. I'd swing it along with me, still safe for delivery.

Off to the Malden City Dump was I, *the little caterer* my Grandfather would say, carrying his lunch. "As long as the weather is *dacent,*" his only rule. He'd raise one pointed finger over his head, taking the deep blessing of the Lord on its tip for all that were bound by such high appointment. That was as much anointment as ever I understood.

And my reward would come, once I got there. Once I got past Commercial Street and Medford Street. And past the factories that could spill people out of them some hours the way Fenway Park did at game's end.

Once I got past Mulcahy's Bar and my Uncle Johnny squinting out the back window at me with his burning eyes on the sandwich pack. *Sticks* they called him ever since he came back from France and *The Big Stink.* That's what he called World War One. His legs still brought him a pain only the pint could cure. Crutches, more likely than not swiped from the Malden Hospital, were jammed up under his armpits. Foul air still held out in his chest from the freekin' Kaiser's gas. And his mouth always watering for one of Grandma's sandwiches she only made for those in the work.

Often I got past the pub with no name out front

but which I called Uncle Dermott's Place. He could be found there of an evening. Or a morning. Or an afternoon, with the sun out over Medford and still in the trees or splashing like ducks in the Mystic River. Or when his last job was into its second or third day and *his pain* became too real to ignore. Sometimes I didn't get past him.

A pair of uncles I had in them! War heroes from *The Big Stink*, carrying the pain yet. France and Germany never far away from them. Their eyes were dark, their cheeks high and thin, their wrists coming out of jacket sleeves thin as morning gruel.

Once I got past Dinty Mulligan's house with his white Chow bigger than his bark and mean as nails, I'd be real close. Once past there, and all the other obstacles a boy had, I'd get my reward. I never thought that anyone would trouble me on my errand, like kidnapping or knocking me down and stealing the lunch. No, not Johnny Igoe's boy, not the dumpmaster's boy, not the boy with two heroes for uncles. Nobody would bother an Irish lad bringing lunch to the dumpmaster who never ate it, who gave it off to the drunks who crowded around him. They were the drunks who came every night to prop their cold feet up on the ring of his great monger's stove. They were the drunks whose hands went fishing in that brown package like birds' beaks did to suet in the backyard feeder. Their skinny little hands had nails for fingers and wrists thin as death itself, and their eyes almost *gone over*. Some of them for sure also carried the pain of all of France as baggage.

Nobody in the world would hurt Johnny Igoe's boy. "A sharp eye, lad, a sharp eye is all you'll need, and a brain to match the work of it."

At the last, I'd hurry to see if he was still there, waiting for me as I crossed the railroad tracks after looking and listening both ways. I'd strain to see if he was still sitting on his bench, alive. I'd look for his pipe

8

lit and smoking up under his gray cap, his back against the little house he made out of scraps. It was an elegant little house that could have saved lives in the old country and saved them here. A lean tin chimney sprouted out of the top like a Jack o' the Beanstalk thing.

Now he leaned on the little house, waiting.

I'd catch the rich, ripe smell of the dump, dense as a bag over my head. Foul old stuff. Damp. Liquid stuff. Food gone bad. Old wet blankets falling apart. Horses in there someplace, perhaps pieces of them, their shit anyway from the milk barns and the milk companies. The manure coming to life again from Hood's and Whiting's delivery barns. Cluttered newspapers came thicker with water, ink blobbing in clumps, words going downhill like sundown. Squashes rotted to the last seed of hope. Plaster dust drowned in puddles, houses going away. Wood going so sour it would melt in your hands. Once a week, it seemed, a cat or dog was caught on the wrong side of life.

Proof of the senses was shared with my street comrades then, my friends who roamed alleys with me. Blindfolded we could tell where we were if we had been there before. We knew alleys that could run right out from under our feet and go down a drain. Alleys that wore continuous walls of sweat, even in winter. Alleys that taught us what veneer meant even before the word came into our vocabulary. We knew family backyards because of their discards, what they threw out, in what quantity, in what kind of container. What was one family's poison, was the same to another family. And that was rot within the hour of being tossed out onto a pile of yesterday's leavings.

Smells, like those of the dump, were living things, were markers, were signposts. Paying attention was necessary, for we were survivors as well as scavengers.

9

The dump smell itself was a livable smell. It was compost. Things could grow in it, get green again. Not like the coal gas smell that cut down into you sharp as a knife in the hands of a wacky doctor or a charlatan. Not at all like the gas works, the way its smell penetrated everything, wall and roof and window. Into the church even and you on your knees trying to get away from it. You swore black dust was sprouting things on you, and growing its own little meanness.

He'd be there at the shack, my Grandfather, at last, not gone anywhere, not undone, waving across the dump. Here was the little man whose magical voice rang down the days. It leaped alleys and lanes and railroad tracks that came across the centuries from Italy and Greece and Denmark and other dark places. Those were the places he swore the horsemen of the Central Plains of Europe rode through on their long route to Ireland. To the last end of Europe itself.

And even from England, for all of the stories. Whole poems came out of that man's mouth. Whole poems! Whole poems without a stumbling pause and never repeated until I might ask for one. That so many poems fit in such a small man was the end of amazement. He must have filled his arms and legs and the whole of his chest besides his white-haired head, with the poems. On he'd go, on and on, magic on top of magic. The Argo watery and wind-driven, the waves crashing on rocks. Perhaps Beowulf about in the land, or Grendel, or The Red King or Righ Seamus (King James). All of a Saturday afternoon he'd give off Brian Merriman's *The Midnight Court* at the Feekle, without a stop. Unless your eye began to blink and head nod and the fill coming on you sooner than counted on.

Oh, sometimes he was daft with a poem that took a long time to learn, and so easy with others that came with music right into them, like

The pale moon was rising above the green mountains,
The sun was declining beneath the blue sea,
When I stray'd with my love to the pure crystal fountain
That stands in the beautiful vale of Tralee.

She was lovely and fair as the rose of the summer,
Yet 'twas not her beauty alone that won me,
Oh, no, 'twas the truth in her eyes ever beaming
That made me love Mary, the Rose of Tralee.

About his eyes the crinkles would fair light up
with Billy Mulchinock's poem. And he'd push me with
his roughed hand as though words were being pressed
into place for ever, his pipe chomped in his teeth. But
then, when his eyes darkened, when his lips set like
steel as though a curse was about to form, I'd know a
change was coming. It was so when he started *Lament
for the Death of Owen Roe O'Neill*:

"Did they dare, did they dare, to slay Eoghan Ruadh
O'Neill?"
"Yes, they slew with poison him they feared to meet with
steel."
"May god wither up their hearts! May their blood cease to
flow!
May they walk in living death, who poisoned Eoghan
Ruadh!"

"Though it break my heart to hear, say again the bitter
words."
"From Derry, against Cromwell, he marched to measure
swords:
But weapon of the Sacsanach met him on his way,
And he died at Cloch Uachtar, upon Saint Leonard's
day."

I never knew, of course, from one day to the
next, who last had his ear. Or what sword struck him,
what knife still at stab from Roscommon, with its *grief*
calling. Or whose words he last sang. Or if the words,
the weight of the words, had brought him down. It was

11

not the same game that came with the sweaty maps of my Grandmother's blue dress. It was the worry of the *little caterer*.

Nearing him across the dump, I'd wave to him my joy. His cap would signal back a joy. Before I ran the last yards I'd look for the day's pickings, to pray for his little successes. And for the whole family. They'd be stacked at the near end of the dump where Goldberg's junk wagon could come in from the lane for the pick-up.

Iron and tin and pipes of all classes in one pile, pieces of stoves and car parts. There'd be unknown black objects as much mystery as Russia and all its lakes and rivers. Pots and pans came another mound of salvage, silvery and coppery and throwing off pieces of the sun on good days.

There'd be doubled-over and tripled-over sheets of lead from wrecks of houses and roofs and downed chimneys. Roofing tar black as ever still clutched at edges old as scabs, thick now in their pressings as slabs from a pine. I'd think about grabbing off a few sheets and melting them and pouring the melt into the casting molds to make more lead soldiers. My lead soldiers stood as an army at home, by the hundreds. Kaiser's men and Doughboys and Tommies and Washington's sore troopers and some from a place called Balaclava in their giddy uniforms.

The army of soldiers was in the cellar near the coal bin where Uncle Lew's beer can hung on a nail. Grandma wouldn't let him drink upstairs in the house proper.

My Grandmother would say, "You'll not drink up here, Lewis, the day of any day, and the b'y needs more sojers like I need a hole in me head." But Grandfather would smile and wink a soft wink she daren't see even if she did. And we'd have more soldiers coming from clumps of lead he'd bring home another day.

Sojers. But not Lewis drinking in the house proper. Or Uncle Johnny or Uncle Dermott or Uncle Tim or Uncle Tom.

Alongside the pile of pots and things tin and iron, and brassy bits, shining like bits of gold, knockers and hinges and old bells with a *dacent sound still lodged in them*, would be a pile of rags. He'd already have been through the pile searching for sweaters and jackets and pants and towels and dresses and things worn whose names I didn't know.

The good things!

The good things would be set aside again, and I'd get my choice of a pair of pants or a shirt or a sweater. It might be a belt I'd have to cut down to my size and use a nail to drive new holes in. And now and then, like a family store, there'd be a pair of boots for me. Once I found a new jackknife still in the boot pocket, the little leather scabbard my right hand could drop to and touch. The laces were made of real rawhide and came near to the knee. His eyes twinkled and he nodded and said, "For me little caterer."

The good things would be brought home and doled out, the dole coming over on the ship I understood. Sometimes it would go to family and sometimes to neighbors. The good things elicited not a sneer or a twisted head or a frown. A proud boy or girl would look lovely in a new dress or a jacket or a pair of pants that Johnny Igoe had rescued from oblivion. A boy in an old worn green shirt forever would be one day in a blue or red one. It would have come from the Malden City Dump at the hands of Johnny Igoe who'd not let the world go to waste, or anything in it.

The Dumpmaster. My Grandfather.

I wondered then, more often than not, how long would such a man live, carrying the weight of all his words.

It wasn't going to be forever, though you couldn't tell me so.

But that was my worry all the while.

He hung on until he was ninety-seven through one of his wars and four of ours.

I never knew until much later that the words were heavy, but the poems were not, except the one poem of his own, and the lines:

> Though adopted by Columbia
> I am Erin's faithful child.

The Great God Shove

I awakened slowly and the first reality that hit me was not the chill in the small bedroom of the cold water flat, not the faded and dingy surroundings, not the fact that there was no school for the day. I shivered. Reality was my arch tormentor. A boy nicknamed Shove, in the sunshine of a new day, waited to tease, pester, and plague me. Charlestown, MA and Shove, in 1935 when I was seven, were hard realities.

I shivered again. Shove the bully was relentless as well as real.

So was EAP, Edgar Allan Poe. Oh, I knew him young.

The fire in the kitchen stove was out. A bag of coal was needed from the store. I popped down the tenement stairs from the second floor. I was aware of the closed-in odors of urine nearly alive, cabbage cooking leftovers that met at your eyes, and damp plaster explaining a background of life. There was my father the robust Marine, my mother the iron of the family, and five children. I was the oldest at home.

And there was Shove.

In a side-saddle, bouncing gait I hit the bottom landing and burst out into the Saturday sunshine trying to warm the cobblestones of Bunker Hill Ave. I'd have to dare Shove again this day as all days. There always had to be some kind of display. It had been that way since the beginning.

A crisp and cool breeze, a late October breeze, whistled in from the Mystic River and the Charlestown Navy Yard. My father's Marine Barracks loomed over the wall. The breeze nipped at my ears. Pennies and nickels for a 25-pound bag of coal jingled in my pocket. I thought how soon the stovetop would be a mickey-brick red. And I could smell the cocoa my mother would make and the toast set on the stovetop for mere

15

seconds. Burnt was the way I liked it. Well done and filling the air with its burnt aroma. Aromas, in Charlestown, in 1935, had a strong place in the order of things. Especially aromas of food and distinct if minor creature comforts.

Charlestown itself was a yardstick for those who cared to calculate the measure of a thing. For me, at my seven years and a little wiser for my time than I should have been, it presented size. And it presented a kind of solid geometry that could not be shaken off too lightly. Perception of things for me began with the three- or four-decker tenements walling up around me and my little haunts. They hung over me sheer as cliffs. Often they closed in with their drab time-eaten gray paint, and a few revolutionary attempts by neighbors to spruce up. Now and then a corncob yellow or a pale green façade came into being. And passed just as quickly. We knew daydreams on a daily basis, an opiate in the air.

A drunk shivered and smelled in the doorway of No.2 Bunker Hill Ave. For him, I knew, there was no place to go. Locked into Charlestown gave you a certain grace for survival or a slow death. But it did not give great promise of escape. Escape came in the books I read. Escape was over the iron fence of the Navy Yard, high, iron wrist-thick and pointed at its top, and the harbor beyond. Like a medieval wall it was, that fence.

Before I turned the corner I looked behind me up the length of Bunker Hill Ave., past the cubic blocks of the tenements. The Bond Bread factory was made wholly of red mickeys and square as a prison face. St. Catherine's Church loomed as gigantic and ugly as any structure could be. I saw Hobie's little beanery stuck in between two tenements as if it were an afterthought, a stall for a pony in a Clydesdales' barn. The Ave. ran uphill and disappeared over the horizon. Out there the subway ran two ways out of Sullivan Square. One way went deep into downtown. The other headed off on a third-rail run to Everett and the places beyond. That's where trees grew in great clusters and fields leaped and the wind sang a different tune. Here upon me it shrieked around clapboard corners and up the slim alleys across which neighbors could touch each other.

The chill wind penetrated my felt jacket. Even before I looked I knew Shove was there in front of Halsey's Market on the corner of Chelsea and Ferrin Streets. I would have to run the gauntlet again, pass by him. Taunts there would be and perhaps more small pains he might inflict on me. Shove was nothing more than a bully. A seventeen year-old bully and I was his favorite target. To me it was surprising he didn't have a sloped forehead or a bulging jaw or a strange look in his eyes. I never heard that he was dropped on his head as a baby. Nothing said anything about him except what he did. And he bullied.

Hatless, blond, hands stuffed into dungaree pockets, wearing a denim jacket, he leaned against a brick wall. He was like a firecracker ready to go off, which is what I thought about him. Why he picked on me so much only he and I knew. It was a sort of mutual understanding that Shove would get as much of me as he could until the day of revenge came.

Shove thought it would never come. But I knew different. That promise was in the air.

He leaned against the wall in the superior way he had of imposing himself over most things around him. But a strange mixture he was to say the least. Shove was the neighborhood hero athlete, tall, lean in the middle, a super first baseman and long-ball hitter. He was also a driving high-knee action tailback that smelled the end zone, who cracked into daylight so often it was rote. They said he was a vicious tackler, had speed and punching power in each fist. They said he could arc a horseshoe into the air with the expectancy of hearing metal at its other end. Out of town, they said, Shove would have been a *ringer* in any game.

It was me he hated for a special reason. And that's why he always picked on me. It wasn't that he didn't pick on others, younger or older, but he made me out special.

The catalyst for all of this was my father, a striking figure in his dress blues, three stripes up and three stripes down. Six feet of leathered Marine was he with crayon-red hair even the wind deigned not move. Before Shove my father had been the athlete of most renown. He'd been a tough catcher who owned every pitcher he ever caught, a blocking back with the skills of a mercenary, a clutch candlepin bowler who excelled at Hi-Lo Jack. He'd been a seventeen letter high school athlete who had twisted the fate of many a gambler. And Shove was afraid of him. Shove and I shared that knowledge. It made him the bully he was and me his special consideration. Few people contested Shove's position as king of the hill. He had produced. In a big game with one leg near useless he dragged himself and two tacklers into the end zone with the clock running down. Hadn't he driven home the winning run in eleven straight games? Weren't the Braves interested in him? Didn't he stand back to back with a pal against a whole Jamaica Plain gang at a wedding once and beat some of them to a pulp?

Yet years before my father had done the same things, to this day being spoken of with awe, with reverence. Shove, most likely, went out of his way to taunt and tease me. He spoke to my father in that most unlikely fashion. I was seven years old and Shove was seventeen, but the disparity in age never entered his mind. Penny or nickel bottles he religiously kicked out of my hands. He punched bags of groceries I carried from the store. He intimidated me every way he could to dispel the mirrored image that existed between my father and him. At times he was so brutal that I cried in my bed at night.

But, in Charlestown in 1935, survival was a matter of self. That knowledge was all about me. As a result I told my father but once about the situation.

"He's always pushing at me, Dad. He trips me and knocks me over the barrels. He's always breaking my bottles outside the store and throws my comic books into Halsey's garbage bag. Once he grabbed my back pockets and yanked on them and split my pants right down the seam and laughed at me all the way home."

For righteous indignation I waited. For explosion I waited, awaited the crimson anger that could fill his face, his eyes. Waited the reality of him pounding Shove into unconsciousness, for the Irish to come out of the depths. My father, I knew, had the fists Harry Greb had.

That explosion lay like some quiet volcano, a mere simmer on the face of life. He looked down at me, eyes blue and warm, nose unbent and clean as if thugs had never gotten within his left jab. His hair was as red as bricks. The stiff collar of his dress blues blouse was opened as it was only at home. The hair on his chest peaked through. Those strong hands reached for me and what I was alert to were the veins sticking out on the backs of those hands. And one singularly bulbous vein arching down into one eyebrow, a throwback, he called it, to the Nicaraguan Campaign. His voice then was contradictory, at once steeled, and yet tender in its delivery.

"Sonny, I'll never chase him. I'll not disgrace the uniform. I'll never go looking for him, but if I ever turn a corner and he's there, he'll never belly up to you again."

Firm and ominous finality came with those words, and the one bulbous vein arching into the eyebrow, echoing all that I wanted to hear. I wanted to count again the ribbons on his chest.

In the same tone he continued to speak, aware of my understanding, sensing a nodding to each other had already taken place.

"What you have at hand is a problem."

He said *you* with the same firmness. It was not the first time I had been challenged, nor the first time my father had challenged me.

"You're only seven and he's seventeen. That's a pretty big difference, isn't it?"

The spider webs of lines running outward from his eyes seemed to ripple against one another.

I nodded a *yes*.

His eyes never wavered from mine for a second, but that vein was a still contradiction to the tone of his voice.

"You have every right in the world to protect yourself from him. I don't care if you use a bat or rock or a hunk of iron pipe, but don't get hurt by him. You've got half again as many smarts as most kids your age, so use them."

There it was! In the seven years of my life that had to be the greatest challenge thrown at me. My toes tingled. My ears buzzed. Ripples of an unknown charge surged through my fingertips. And a chill went up my back as if my shirt had been torn open on that backside. Half aloud I whispered, "Amontillado." I pronounced the word the way I figured old Georgio Rendici would pronounce it sitting on his milk crate in front of No. 7 Bunker Hill Ave. selling crabs for a nickel. The *As* in it were broad and thick.

Reaching out tenderly my father patted me on the head. There were times when words did not have to pass between us, but I was sure he had not understood that portentous word I had whispered. Off into the busy kitchen he walked, into an aura of hamburgers and mashed potatoes and stewed tomatoes that I sucked into my nostrils as sweet as any honey or candy. Revenge's delicious air came on stronger than the promised meal, even as my father stirred fried onions into the mix.

After the meal we had a glass of root beer. He ladled up a pint of beer from an open crock. He told us stories about Paris Island, Quantico, Nicaragua, Philadelphia, and his younger days in Charlestown. Entranced as usual, we sat in the kitchen of the second floor flat, the stovetop a dull red. Oblivious it seemed we were of the prison we were in, of the structure of the walls around us. Nested and happy we were for the grip of the moment, smiling and nodding to each other at an old story told anew. I did not know the strains of the dominant male were working their way across the face of my soul.

Later, going to bed, the image of Shove intruded in my last wakeful moments. The deep blue eyes leaped into mine. His open mouth was full of roar. His fist assumed monstrous proportions as it came sweeping at me in a huge arc from an endless orbit.

Then, with gravy and all the fixings, I dreamed of punishing him. Had I not been given license? Had not my father actually commissioned me to get Shove by any measure possible? Was I not the oldest of the brood at home? Would Shove, in his hatred and fear, next move toward my sisters? The dread things of survival in Charlestown I dreamed; the near misses, the near escapes, the vultures that floated about us, the Great God Shove kicking at me from some imperial throne with his mute cohorts standing tall as laughing columns.

The last moments told me I would get him. E. A. Poe had moved his spirit into mine. The mechanic of arch evil had given me some of his graces, had infused me. The God Shove, it was apparent, would bow before me. It was only right. Mean and evil things passed through me. He was dismembered at wrist and ankle. A Machiavellian enterprise crushed his eyes bloodless, made him a laughing stock of the Charlestown triangle. It ran from City Square to Sullivan Square to the Mystic Bridge and back to City Square along Chelsea Street and the huge black iron fence of the Navy Yard. Inside that triangle, long on one side, I would fix The Great God Shove forever.

The dreams were still with me as I approached Shove and his cronies sitting on Halsey's steps. I pulled the collar up around my neck to ward off the cold wind, knowing it was also producing ear defenders. Slurs and taunts would soon head my way. He held court with his young giants and I had to pass their gauntlet. In a superior and muscular grace they lounged, and I felt my own stature diminish. Shove's big hands pressed down on the granite step and he drew his heels in, the muscles bubbling at his thighs. Onto my eyes fell his eyes, the deeper blue taking on another hue, a telltale hue. I set my eyes back on his. The shared knowledge passed between us as secret as a note; the only person in the world Shove was afraid of was my father. Though his shoulders were wide, his jacket full at the chest, his waist thin as a pole, his hair blond from an Olympus touch, knowledge touched us. A short spark of electricity leaped in the air.

It burned me; it must have burned him.

"Well, look it now," he said, "it's the Jarhead's kid coming to do mommy's errands. Need to get another nipple for the growing family, baby Jarhead? Mommy and daddy got nothing else to do?"

Only when he laughed did his pals laugh. I went closer, my heart pounding, the last pain remembered. Closer I went for the purchase of the bag of coal; the pennies and nickels grasped in my fist still balled in my pocket.

"If you ain't the picture of the sweet little errand boy, I never seen one. Got your pennies locked up there in your hand, 'fraid the bogey man's going to take them?"

He guffawed loudly when he said, "Nipples are a dime a dozen this week for hot-pants Marines."

One of his pals slapped him on the back. Another pushed his finger into Shove's chest. It was like a celebration.

Shove saw the redness pushing in my face. "Jeezzus," he said loudly and with feigned puzzlement, "Wouldn't you think a Jarhead with all them goddamn kids running around the house would take his time coming home at night? But not his old man. The old redhead does the hundred in ten flat to get from that gate to that house."

He pointed to the Main Gate of the Navy Yard and the tenement where we lived, No. 3 Bunker Hill Ave. It wasn't much more than a hundred yards.

Buddha-like, Halsey sat behind the counter, his face gray, his eyes a pale and tired green, his cheeks smooth. The paunch of a belly hung over his belt like a comma out of place, distorting his skinny frame. Never once had I seen him outside the store. Bologna and cheese and mustard and quick sandwich smells filled the small room. Two bottle caps lay in the middle of the floor, checker pieces left over from a bigger game. I kicked one of them under the counter.

Halsey spoke a gutter dialect that said his name really wasn't Halsey. "Wuzzit?" He looked out the door at Shove looking in.

The pennies and nickels spread across the counter. "A bag of coal," I said, and pushed the coins at him. He counted each one and pointed to the back room. A bag hefted to my shoulder smelled like a gas pipe or as strong as the area of the railroad tracks on the other side of City Square. A film of coal dust sifted lightly onto my jacket.

Halsey hadn't moved at all, yet the pennies and nickels were out of sight. Very slowly his eyes moved toward the door where Shove's shadow loomed. He whispered, "Wunza time he getz catcha."

I looked at him from under the bag of coal. "I getz him catcha."

He motioned to the floor in front of the counter. "Wantza bazkid?" He shrugged his shoulders. It was a Charlestown shrug.

I grabbed a basket, stepped out the door and Shove punched the bag off my shoulder. It split on the sidewalk and spilled into the gutter.

"Damned if the Gyrene ain't got a butter-finger kid for an errand boy." He picked up a handful of anthracite pea coal and fired them, one by one, across the street. Four out of five hit the curbing and dropped onto the grating of the sewer drain.

I put the basket down and placed the half-empty bag in it and picked up the rest of the coal from the walk and the gutter. Halsey stared out the window at me. When they weren't looking he held up one finger, then hid it quickly. E.A. Poe had another fan.
Shove and his pals were hysterical with laughter. I ran to the corner with the basket and stepped into the hallway of No. 3 Bunker Hill Ave. Again, swift as a signature, the smell of cabbage and urine and wet plaster assailed me. I was overwhelmed for a moment. I hated cabbage. I hated drunks. I hated the landlord. But most of all, I hated Shove.

"Edgar," I said, "be my friend."

My hand fingered the pile of coal in the basket and found the one I wanted. It was good sized, round, graspable. It was rock-hard also. Into the street I stepped and went to the corner. They were still laughing. The piece of coal flew from my hand. Gracefully and easily, as if he were on the end of a super double play, Shove caught the hunk of coal in his hand and shouted back.

"Shit on you, kid. You and your father are both assholes!"

He tossed the piece of coal across Chelsea Street. It hit the curbing and fell into the mesh of the sewer drain. The laughter still echoes.

Up the long flight of stairs I lugged the coal, buried in a vault of misery, seeing no way out of all of it. Was there a way to get at Shove? The odors still came at me. Nausea came with it for a moment. It was a fate. We came into a place and would die in that place. All of it was prearranged. Karma called and done. Ashes unto ashes, dust unto dust.

And then it hit me!

Right then, in the middle of the long climb of stairs, it hit me. The whole grand and glorious scheme hit me right down to the last detail. I sat on the middle of the stairs with the basket of coal in my lap and drained off a large mystical draught of *Amontillado*. The *As* were still broad. I felt giddy. I felt glorious. I was akin to the gods of revenge. At the top of my voice I screamed, "I getz catcha, Shove! I getz catcha!"

The words ran up the walls of the hallway, went to the second floor and on up to the landing on the third deck. Just as swiftly they came echoing back from the gray ribbed metallic ceiling all touched by rust. I patted the cover of the trash can on the second floor landing, entered our flat, set about making a new fire, rolling *Globes* and *Heralds* and *Posts*, knotting them, laying on kindling.

Early next morning, after my father had left for the Barracks and a few others stirred in the building, I shook the ashes down from the stove grates. They gathered smoky in the coal hod, and the hod I carried carefully to the cellar. The law of the land, the code of the building, said that no ashes, hot or cold, were to be placed in the trash barrels on any upper floor. Fire, among the other dangers that faced us, presented a constant peril. Fire could leap up these stairs quick as any athlete, blocking off escape routes, forcing people to windows and long falls. Fire could leap from one building to the next in thin tongues of flame, seeking out dry rot and years of dust. Fire could crack and explode its ignition in a thousand places in every tenement building. A whole block could go up in minutes, a whole Fourth of July. Once I had seen a monumental fire engulf buildings in City Square. In a panic I had rushed home to warn my family when flames routed themselves along electrical overhead wires down Chelsea Street. The flames threatened to run their way right to our house, the burning insulation smoky and black and evil. For days afterward I remembered the hysteria that had filled me.

Down in the cellar I soaked the ashes with water and returned up the stairs with a heavier hod. Quietly I dumped the wet ashes into the trash barrel on the second floor, then returned to the cellar. Four times I repeated the trip with ashes wet from the trash barrels, filling the barrel on the second floor to within eight inches of its top. That done I scattered papers over the ashes, replaced the cover, pushing it securely in place.

With Edgar in attendance I waited the interminable time until nine o'clock came. The wait was spent in reveries of ultimate satisfaction, letting loose of my worries, and letting that *thing* in me build by slow degrees. The great God Shove would soon know a formidable adversary.

At a quarter to nine, sisters primped for the day, toast and hot oats and sugar under my belt, I started up Chelsea Street toward City Square. Never had I stolen from Halsey's or from Abie's Market or from Hobie's little shed where he baked beans and brown bread in the crudest of brick ovens. They were not fair game for theft. The Bond Bread factory, with its pies and cakes and tons of goodies, was fair game. They could afford it. So could all of the merchants in City Square. Unlike Halsey or Abie or Hobie, they never extended credit, never carried a family's lives on the books until the infrequent pay days came. Often they forgot to charge for little items that were so important to survival.

I clattered a stick against the iron fence of the Navy Yard, looking up and down the street for Shove. He was not in sight. The smell of the harbor, the full mixture of a sea salad, came over the wall beside the Barracks. It was crisp and clean and smelled vaguely like a treated wound. Behind me the iron wings of the Mystic Bridge sprang up against a Chelsea background. Ahead of me, standing on the shoulders of uniform ranks of ironclad stanchions, the lines of The El ran off to North Station and to Thompson Square. They ran off to the outlands, other places with other dimensions. It was an escape route that someday I would take.

In the drug store in City Square I nosed around the magazine rack, feigning interest in a dozen covers. I looked under piles for what I knew wasn't there. All I had to do was arouse a little suspicion. The clerk watched me for a while and came over.

"Looking for something special, kid?"

He was almost nodding to himself, having spotted another "lifter." I knew he hated kids who stole and sailors who drank, and he had seen plenty of each.

"My father's looking for the last issue of *G-8 and His Battle Aces*, but it's not here. He's got this one." I pointed to the current issue. "But he doesn't have the last one. Said this was the only place I could find it."

He bit all the way. "Let me look out back. Wait a minute." He left and I wasted no time. I dipped my hands into the adhesive tape box and scooped eight rolls inside my jacket. Eight, I figured, was enough.

The clerk returned with the magazine in his hand. "It's ripped a little on the cover." He was apologizing to me.

"I'll give you a nickel for it."

Another customer came into the store. The clerk raised his voice and said, "Aw, you can have it, kid. Go ahead, take it." The magazine was thrust into my hands as he smiled at the new customer. The customer smiled at the clerk and patted me on the head.

I ran down Chelsea Street. The song of the streets was not the thundering click-clack of the elevated cars leaning on the stanchions. Nor the ear-splitting shriek as metal wheels rode hard on curved rails. Nor the iron clad wheels of a milk wagon on the cobblestones. Nor a harbor whistle moaning far away. The new song beat its drums in my mind over and over, and the simple words leaped upon my ears.

"I getz catcha, Shove. I getz catcha. I getz catcha, Shove. I getz catcha."

The drums beat faster and my heart beat with them, pounding in my chest, putting an inner pressure at my ears.

It was a glorious new day and Charlestown was a glorious place. The Great God Shove was coming down from his mighty throne!

Later in the morning all was ready for the final confrontation. The battle plan was drawn. Never once did I waver in the plan or my determination to bring the bully down. Consequences did not bother me. I had been given license. After all, I was only seven years old and Shove was seventeen. Surely the whole world would side with me. It was only just to do so, and survival, ultimately, was the responsibility of the individual. I never had pitied the drunks sleeping in doorways. Each of them, if he had wanted to, could have had a different life. Of that I was so sure.

And I would not ever scramble in the gutter in front of Shove again.

At noon I was ready. I whiffed a great draught of Amontillado in the hallway and it killed all the odors I had come to hate so much. The sun hung out over Old Ironsides where my father had often baby-sat one or more of us. Shadows were short and square on Bunker Hill Ave. I prayed for Shove to be nearby. He was not on the Avenue. I could see way up past Abie's Market and he was not in sight. Time was important and I was worried. Around the corner I looked and my fingertips tingled. Shove was sitting in front of Halsey's with two of his pals. It was now or never, and the song began its drumbeat in my head.

Back inside the hallway, from behind the door I had set open with a stick, I retrieved five flat, smooth stones. It had taken hours to find them. Each was suitable for skipping across The Oily. That was the name we'd given to the Mystic River as it flowed its rainbows of colors out to sea. Each stone was balanced and true. David could have slung them.

At the corner I sucked in a huge gulp of air. Edgar and his Amontillado could not help me now. All the dreaming was done and the act of survival was at hand. I was alone on the corner.

I yelled. "Hey, Shove, you big bully." One stone was firmly gripped in the fingers of my right hand. The others were in my left fist. "Hey, Shove, you friggin' bully."

He moved off the steps and stood up. Like Goliath he looked.

"Screw you, kid," he yelled back at me.

In a high arc I heaved the first stone. Shove laughed as he easily caught it on the fly and heaved it back at me. It bounced on the sidewalk and skittered across the street. The arc of my second stone was not as high as the first one. He caught it, dropped it, picked it up and flung it back at me. I dodged it easily.

My third toss was a clothesliner. In its straight trajectory it flew at Shove's chest. He leaped sideways against the wall of the store and his pals jumped into the doorway out of sight. The stone smashed off the wall.

Fist raised, Shove screamed, "Why you scrawny little bastard you!"

And he started toward me, the fist still doubled. Ninety feet from me he started to walk faster, but his steps were measured, as though he were ready to leap sideways again. My heart echoed in my ears. I gulped for a last shot of air and heaved a last perfect shot. It hit out in front of him, skipped on its backside and took off. It hit him square on the shin and I could hear the *thunk* of it, like an ax hitting a board. Then Shove came. He came at a dead run. In two steps he was at top speed, his knees popping high, his stride as long as Paul Bunyan's.

"You little bastard, I'll kick your ass all over town!"

I darted around the corner, into the hallway and started up the stairs. Shove was screaming behind me, his steps getting closer, closing down the distance. In the middle of the long flight of steps I stumbled. My knees banged on the edge of the tread. The stab of pain took itself right into my hip. I still had time. Shove was not in the hall yet. Seventeen more steps and I was home. Fifteen more. Thirteen. Shove hit the wall in the hallway. He was right behind me! Nine more steps. Seven. Shove was on the steps! Five more steps. Three. He was pounding up behind me, still cursing and screaming. I leaped onto the second floor landing and over the barrel turned on its side. All the energy I ever wanted was in my arms and in my legs at that moment. I shoved the barrel off the landing and down the steps.

Eight complete rolls of adhesive tape were wrapped around the barrel, top to bottom, holding the cover in place. I was even able to make out the legend scrawled on one band of tape as the barrel started on its way. "I getz catcha!"

Both of us heard the barrel hit the first step in a dull, metallic and wooden thud. It hit the third step down a little sharper. The smashing sound was crisper, and more metallic. Shove's eyes ballooned in the dim light. They popped bigger than silver dollars. His hands came out in front of him in a pitiful gesture, half-beseeching, half-protecting. The barrel hit the steps again and I thought the whole tenement building shook.

The Great God Shove and the barrel met in the middle of the stairs. There was a sickening crunch at the collision. Shove screamed in pain and the scream flew up the walls of the hallway, up into the upper landings. They bounced off the metallic ceiling.

Shove crumpled on the steps three-quarters of the way down. The barrel, turned by the collision, went end over end and hit the door jam. It shook every flat in the building.

Above me a door opened and someone in a deep, demanding voice yelled out, "What was that? What the hell happened?"

Shove's two pals, framed in the doorway below, stood in a trance. Their mouths were open, their hands limp and helpless at their sides. Shove was crying. His leg was broken. When the police came he told them he was helping some kid carry the barrel and it had slipped.

I never saw Shove again.

At least not on *my* side of the street.

31

The Boy Who Got Stuck under the Warren Avenue Bridge

The only thing between me in Charlestown and Eddie Shore and the Bruins and the Boston Garden back there in 1935 was the Warren Avenue Bridge. It was a squat, short chunk of iron that stood in my way every time I snuck my way out of the borough to see No. 2 play in the Garden. When it came to hockey there was nobody like the rambunctious hitter. Years later he had his number cast up in those high and glorious fields of iron, the heavens of the old Garden. Later, per chance, there was Bill Russell and Bobby Orr and Larry Bird and a clutch of others who made my time and their times so memorable.

But in the beginning, for a seven year older playing hooky from the family, from the borough, from all the kids on Bunker Hill Ave. backed up by Ferrin Street, there was nobody else. On any evening from October on, there was nobody else. Just nobody like that opulent firecracker who was as good as he was mean. I thought life and all its vicissitudes in that tough environ I was growing up in was conquered the same way he played his game. It was nose and chin first and your eyes wide open for whatever might come back at you.

My ticket to that grand palace of hits and its swiftest of excitements was a drain pipe, a plain, old fashioned tin drain pipe. Some builder's laborer had mounted it so close to my bedroom window hanging over Ferrin Street that its invitation could not be refused. I was seven, agile and sublime. I thought I'd be seven always. Shod in sneakers from the Converse Rubber Company in Malden at a buck a pair. Legged in hand-me down corduroys most of the year. I knew that I would never be eight, would never grow up.

I was in no hurry. I was going to be a kid forever and wear sneakers all the time.

Being monkey was part of my being a survivor in those times. A survivor could climb up and down a slim drain pipe, could negotiate narrow sills, feared no height. This included all the upper floor entries of the Bond Bread factory where tasty pleasantries awaited the daring. Fire escapes, in comparison, were a breeze. It did not matter how they were constructed, or how high or how frail they were. Or how rust would eventually and seriously eat into them. But they were too noisy. They passed by windows. They were too well known as routes of passage—for whatever reason. The drain pipe, though, was secret. Under cover of any darkness, any bit of shadow or trace of evening shade, it provided the easiest and most illicit way out of an apartment. Any kid could slip past unsuspecting parents working both ends of the clock. It was also the way back in. There were five of us but I was the only climber.

I sneaked out of the house and sneaked into the Boston Garden in a variety of ways. All of them were dangerous, but all memorable. My mother would have had a bird if she had known what I was up to, the routes I dared, the climbs I made. My father was stationed at the Marine Barracks right across Chelsea Street in the Navy Yard. He wore three up and three down on his sleeve and was molded out of a harsher clay. He would have silently nodded. Somehow he would have hidden the smile tempting the corner of his lips. It was part of the times, part of the eternal scratch in growing up then in those uproarious and hounding Thirties. And a veritable hell was loose on the other end of the world!

City Square was generally cluttered with sailors and yard workers in their comings and goings from the Navy Yard. It was my first stop on the way. Its moving color often caught up my breath as I watched the total scene from a stoop or a piazza hung on the side of a building. Sometimes I watched from the edge of a roof I had gained. I knew lots of roofs in Charlestown. Few of them were entry-proof, few had to be. So there were many side shows and street scenes on my route. Many small adventures came my way. Many points of view made up the borough I lived in, smack against the river and the harbor. The small adventures were continual, a sort of tourist getting his money's worth. I wanted to see it all. And that's what took me underneath the Warren Avenue bridge one Saturday evening in late October.

And I had the life scared right out of me!

Curiosity had piqued me, and the little jolt hit home, a pellet or a Bee-Bee right on the mark. On a number of occasions I had seen the walk barricades come out. The bridge would swing itself open and I'd hear the deep mechanical groans underneath. It was as if freight cars, those massed on the other side of the square in the rail yard, were in agony. Then a rugged little boat would pass by, neat in its maneuvers, topside clean, heading out. There'd be a guy at the pilot wheel, and a girl in white shorts sitting beside him with a drink in her hands.

I was then, and still am, a rail hugger, a sidewalk supervisor. Watching a new or on-going activity was so gratifying. Curiosity was not just lurking in my genes, but fighting for satisfaction, scratching its way to the surface. Men's jobs, like the senses themselves, were so different. They made such varied demands, called for such special skills, allowed so much to happen. So it was not only the boats passing through or the mechanical groans rising up from that void that pulled me under the structure. It was who does what to which, where and when that drew me below that dark mass. A set of steel stairs, hung alongside the rail like a stiff appendage, took me down under. The near-feeble reach of a catwalk out over the dark water took me from one side of the bridge to the other. A handrail held onto my hand the whole length of the catwalk. Sea gull droppings were everywhere, like buckets of overripe whitewash tossed from above. The sodden and almost liquid mass appeared to move. Even as I looked at it, the thickness doubled the surface it lay on.

And all there was *was* a revelation! In one way it was similar to the high iron fields of the Boston Garden itself. That too was a massive display of braces and spans and purlins and girders. But here there were wheels, all connected to one another. And rust here, rust there, stained green here, stained green there, an ache of brown more felt than seen. It appeared a quiet but living monstrosity. Rivet eyes lurked everywhere, spotted with rust so they were red at times and closing on evil. Some looked like old half dollars nailed in place, some like the eyes of the just dead. Darkness and light seemed to fight each other at both ends of the bridge and in the overhead roadway span. There lamplight splashed on silver. Water practically touched everything with its salty tongue. I thought of Beowulf, and the monster Grendel loose in Charlestown. I was the only one to know who was at hand.

All the pieces of iron I tried to fix in a pattern to match the noises I had heard so many times when the bridge opened. Like the *whumps* of humping boxcars. Moans of pain deep in iron throats. Sounds of anger. Sounds of the dead rising out of the troubled earth. Steel sounds coming from the darkness of Pittsburgh or Bethlehem. Light and dark, persistent enemies to the death of one or the other, continued to fight above me and at the far ends of the bridge. Their silence was grim and eerie. Some of the geared wheels were, I swore without hesitation, as big as houses. Ugly toothed things that had to fit one another at some opportune time, *or else*! Ugly toothed mandibles that could mush things so hard between them nothing would be left but skin or traces of skin. But bodiless. They threatened with their ugly massiveness.

Below me the water seemed blacker. A soft scum road on the surface the way debris makes itself known. Oil slicks, catching early evening lights, traced their brilliant ways across the lapping undulations of tidal change. Greens and blues charged out first, taking command. At any moment, I thought, Grendel could be on the way up from the depths. A kick or a punch would buy me enough time.

What was not penetrating my senses, however, was the dim whistle trying to cross the air. It seemed far away, probably from the traffic. It came again, a high burble of a sound. Saliva was mixed with it, a cop in blue, his hand up and palm out. A car stopping. A Reo or Graham or Pierce Arrow strangely at idle.

What you want to hear you often hear.

But if an earthquake is ever to come beneath me, I will know its first shudder. I will know its tell-tale shudder. For suddenly it came through the skin of all that massed iron. It came through all those crazy angles and all those bulky joints. It came up through the soles of my feet and through the grip of my hands on steel, the first threat of movement.

I froze in place. Catwalk-bound. Stricken. Alone. A screech I had not heard before said metal was parting. I thought the rivet heads would pop off like Bee-Bees. I'd be shot! A groan my Grandfather could have owned came right along beside the screech. And I didn't believe my feet. I didn't believe my hands. I didn't believe my eyes, as the first solid shrug of all Mother Earth went passing beneath me. A wheel, laboriously, was nudged from its sleep. *CHUNG!* Another responded, *CHUNG!* Their aching tones came in unison, their teeth chugging against one another. Another shrug.

Another cry. The whistle again, only louder, demanding attention, harsh as chains rattling against my ears.

Grendel wasn't coming! It was just iron and steel at movement. The catwalk I was on began to swing. The wheels turned on themselves. They bit. They chewed, one cog at a time, one tooth at a time. They ground away. Silence leaped off to find a safer place. I'd be better off on the ice with No. 2 after me, into the corner, behind the net, diving for the bench. Would I ever see him again? Would I ever get to move back down Chelsea Street and get home again? The wheels turned noisily, the unseen throats of them disgorging awful noises. I thought of Peter Barry who lived directly over me in the block. Would he enjoy my fear now? I'd punch the smile off his face.

A picture of Eddie slamming a Canadian against the boards leaped into my head. I even heard the smash of it, saw the boards bend, hold, bend. He was what it was all about. I loved his anger and his hard play. A sea gull leaped from an unseen roost. Its wings slapped at the air. *Free as a bird* hit me. If the whole Garden moved, especially all that conglomeration of stuff in the high iron fields, wouldn't it sound just like this. The Warren Avenue bridge swinging open and me, seven, seven forever, never to be eight, me, stock still, caught on the middle of a catwalk moving out over the water, and the wheels, the houses of wheels, bearing ferociously down on me.

It was time to pay the piper.

I'd heard my father say those words and never fully understood.

Now I knew.

To say my heart was in my throat was accurate. I didn't like the feeling, but the wheels were huge, malevolent, hungry. To move would be an error. The catwalk was still here and it had obviously moved a thousand times. So I stayed frozen, my hands still gripped by the rail. The iron monster inched in its swing, it groaned, it *CHUNG'D* and *CHUNG'D*. It slipped sideways, the whole earth of it! Courage and smarts, I heard myself convince myself, means standing still. So I made that perilous under-arc journey out over the water. I promised that I'd skip the game and skip No. 2 if only I'd be able to get back to City Square. I settled on City Square rather than home. I knew, like I had always known, I had taken too many chances. I didn't deserve much more than City Square. Anyway, that was a short run to Bunker Hill Ave. Almost no further than the Boston Garden if you want to look at it that way.

A boat passed, a man on deck waved to me. He turned away as if I had been there every trip for him, a regular in his regular seat. The boat angled and channeled away. The groans of the bridge started anew, started on their comeback, and I moved slowly back to where I had been. I had been swept away in slow motion. I was swept back, time having no real rivals. And too so came the hard tack, the survivor's ruse, the return of confidence saying a mere storm had been weathered.

So City Square came and went. Sailors passed by in their parade, bell bottoms slapping their semaphores. Their noise and laughter rode over the hard surfaces, touching stone and steel and all things iron. And all things iron rang with their noise and laughter. Nothing had apparently changed. Nothing at all.

When I walked back over the bridge, once more self reliant, my nose and chin were out where they belonged. My eyes were wide open. The water was darker. The oil slicks had disappeared. The silence had resumed its stay.

No. 2 suddenly loomed on the horizon as if he had been shot down Causeway Street. He paused, tempted me, skated off into the unsettling darkness where all this began.

I could hear the puck drop at the face-off.

The Bill Collector

It was to be an eventful day, that hot August
Saturday in 1936 in Saugus, Massachusetts. Furniture
was coming. The front room of our third floor
apartment was dance hall bare, as my mother had said
many times, and it had been that way for months, a raw
corridor in itself. Every so often I'd catch her standing
at its door or in the middle of that *pound of silence* (her
favorite reference to it), looking as if one of her
children were missing. Tall, strong across shoulder,
dark haired and dark eyed, lovely white complexion she
said was a toast to Roscommon's clear air, where her
father was born. She was not one for using many
gestures to express herself. Only if you stared hard,
would you see a firmness tighten on her jaw, set her
lips; mind made up, deed to be done.

She was impervious to a host of things that
bogged down or disrupted less a soul, especially in
those difficult times. My father worked only partial
hours in a factory, coming home tired and his feet
hurting, three children always reaching for mostly what
wasn't there. My mother reacted indignantly and
impetuously to her own high-heeled steps across the
bare floor. That too-silent room, that *useless cubicle*,
was full of echoes of all kinds, needing only to be
triggered. And it was her heel clicks coming most alive
of all, each one unique, a message being sent one letter
at a time.

She would stop part way across that passage on
her way to peer out the front window, look over her
shoulder, and set her chin. A singular muscle would
tense beneath the skin of her jaw. One would think she
was being followed and had vowed to lose herself in
silence. My tall, lovely, warm, obstinate mother was
usually without gestures, featured in a black and white
movie, suddenly silent without her footsteps.

40

Late at night there had been arguments about furniture, oh arguments indeed, *the very need of it in the first place, an extravagance*, its less than full time utility, *we don't live in a barn.* I heard about the almost inexhaustible supply of hand-made doilies my Grandmother had crocheted for what seemed a hundred years gathering only the dust of history in old hat boxes. She rarely raised her voice. The smooth and rhythmic engine of her purring came through the other five rooms as if she were keeping her speed steadily at five miles an hour. To a word she was *intractable*. After much argument and setting stands a four-star general would have been proud of, and subsequent searches across a wide boundary of opportunities, she had found one Simon Westman. He was a man who was willing to arrange delivery of five pieces upon the promise of $2.15 being placed in his hands each Saturday morning thereafter, until *paid off* could be noted in his little black book.

So Simon came that hot August Saturday morning in 1936. And Simon spoke, loud enough for the neighborhood to get acquainted with the business tenor of his harsh voice. He was a crier reaching up and past his own tier, laddering himself no less, and forever the salesman.

"Up with it, boys," he said, "to the third floor, and don't hurt a curl of its luxury!"

Upward he pointed, Hannibal at the foot of the Alps, ready for the snowy terrors and what lay beyond. Then, hands on his hips, head wagging like the lead bitch at a dog show, his voice went magisterial, dictatorial, more European than other possibilities. Vestiges of Carthage and Waterloo were locked into it. He shaped himself up for our neighborhood gawkers, a grand host of window hanger-outers, lace curtain parters with faces held back. Deep in their souls they envied my mother's delivery. Their silence was akin to applause, almost luxurious in those harsh Thirties hanging over us. They had been there in such grip forever, every last one of them, and were still trapped in that time and in that mind set.

Simon had stepped out of his dark green Graham, pulled up tightly behind the canvas-covered truck, all 5' 4" of him. He wore a wide-brimmed felt hat, stiff collar, dark suit appearing to have faint orange stripes still in residence. His goggle- or pop-eyed stare almost hurt me. Pain sat on his puffy red cheeks as though six decades earlier an exuberant midwife had squeezed it permanently into place.

Stepping down from the running board, holding tightly to a door handle of the dark Graham for support, he could have been a valet exiting a Pullman belonging to the Czar. Or he could have been the Czar himself.

His compatriots were a diverse pair, oddest imaginable book ends in freighting. One, the larger of the two, was a bloated giant. He'd be, I thought, the mucker as anyone would have said, a miner, a lifter, a hunkin' stevie from the docks of Charlestown. His back was thick enough for toting an oaken ice box. He would most likely be voiceless, a mute acceptor of direction, of order, a pure piece worker whose every dollar earned, you could bet, would be quaffed off before nightfall.

The other was a coin of the obverse side, company clerk-ish (as in military). Small, thin, clean shaven, given to hand pointing, head nodding, minor grunts, he was a peacock of the first order. A bowler sat his head cocked at an angle, a precipitous angle, a daring angle. A scrawny green feather was etched to it as wayward and worn as an afterthought. His grin would come back to me years later as Barry Fitzgerald plotted his moves in *The Quiet Man*, his lips smacking at taste, at connivance.

The hunkie lifted, the clerk pointed, Simon watched, his arms folded across his chest. The puffy new sofa, two large red-and-blue easy chairs, a coffee table and an end table made their way up three flights to our bare dance hall. My mother, an absolute magician who could put a supper meal on the table from an empty larder, produced a dark red rug from her bedroom closet. None of us had seen it before, and it was Asian for sure. The age old, elegant and delicate doilies came out of their long darkness.

Her room shone; she shone; and Simon parted company with the dire challenge, "I'll be back next Saturday morning for the first payment."

Nodding at his crew, he said, "That's it, boys. Off we go."

The puffy eyes, the orange-striped suit, the corporal-ish man went out the door and down the stairs.

For the best part of a year Simon came on Saturday mornings, the Graham his advance calling card as it rolled into the Square below us. My mother would sigh almost inaudibly, set her chin in her way, and reach into an oatmeal box where she kept her change. Never once did she pay Simon his $2.15 with anything but coin, never a bill changing hands. If there was a message to her accounting, it never found Simon, never fazed him, and the creditable entry would be posted in his little book, which we all dreamed about reading someday. For a while I might even have been obsessed with whatever its contents revealed; it was almost an adversary.

Simon was a challenge, though, and took noting. He never sweat, never cursed a late entry, never came up the three flights without pausing a half dozen times on the stairs and lower levels. He'd smile at my mother, look in at the front room, nod his appreciation, accept her coin, make the entry in his little book. All the while his gray-white eyeballs protruded out of their sockets. They'd have made drill sergeants uncomfortable.

Once, in a cold and extremely raw January, he did not appear for three weeks and I suggested that he might have died and our payments would be done. My mother shook her head lightly. I wasn't sure if she were saying, "It's not in our luck", or "Don't bring pain on anybody." But, eventually, there was the Graham and Simon and the pauses on the stairs of his mountain climbing and the coin exchange and the book entry, as if nothing ever in life was going to change.

Simon, thus, was a certainty in our life, a piece of clock work. And the year moved on in its way, languid, hot and then cool, dry and then wet, seasons unfolding and fulfilling their prophecies and predictions. Time tumbled all around me (my pants one day going from knickers to *long* in one sweet afternoon I'll remember forever), and Simon came and Simon said and Simon went. Then, miraculously, a shift came, slowly, surely, in the way I looked at him, how I felt about him.

Most likely that may be traced to what my mother said one day when I stood quickly at the kitchen window at the sight of the Graham driving into the square. It was like a ship hitting our small island, coming to take our stores away. Perhaps dislike or distaste or discomfort rode freely on my face.

"Be careful how you remember Simon." Her voice was low, carrying no inflection, no tone to be deciphered. She was, acutely, a judge at warning, at guidance.

I began to look at him in different lights, eventually as a survivor. He was a little man who kept at his practice, who plied his way and his wares, who climbed slowly to face my mother each Saturday, not an easy task in itself, without many failures. He was a man who did not sweat, who was never wrinkled, who kept his car immaculate, who never looked at his watch.

The time came when I did not notice his eyes, forgot their awful prominence, did not pay them any mind. He survived because he was constant, and I began to appreciate that. Survival, and much of its lessons, had been thrown at my feet a few years earlier, before we had moved from cluttered Charlestown. Home there was at the very beginning of Bunker Hill Avenue adjacent to Chelsea Street and the Navy Yard where my father spent his last days in the Marine Corps.

Simon and I then had something in common, and my mother had linked the two of us. It was like accepting, grudgingly, the new kid in class who really wasn't a bad kid after all. And that moment of revelation and acceptance passed as quick as a shot. One day there's Simon, and the next Saturday there's a lanky, bony, thin-faced, tightly-suited replacement. He held Simon's book in one hand and the other hand out for his $2.15 plus $.10 for any late payment in the future. My mother lifted her eyebrow, the left one, the most expressive one, at that dictum. Simon had died of a heart attack and here was his nephew taking over his rounds.

Into my young life serious change had been incorporated.

Two weeks later it happened. After pounding on our apartment door, making all kinds of noises down in his throat as though he were gargling with acid, the long, lanky, tight-suited collector of sorts introduced his foot between the door and the stout jamb. My mother had told him she had no money for him that day.

He yelled, without any trace of accent, "I know you've got money. Simon said you always paid him and you're going to pay me. I'm not coming around this hole for nothing, you can bet on that! This whole place smells to high heaven, here and every apartment in this whole stretch of blocks! Now give me my money!"

On the front porch, looking down over the

peaceful square, no help anywhere in sight, my survival training kicked into high gear. I began to tug feverishly at each and every baluster of the porch railing looking for a loose weapon. My hands were stiff and hard and pulsing with righteousness. No baluster came free at such tugging. My mother had begun screaming for him to leave, obviously pushing desperately at the other side of the door, holding the fort high on the third floor. I took one more look down to the street before I knew I'd have to catapult weaponless onto his back in the next few seconds.

Suddenly, below me at street level, squat as a beetle, black canvas top beginning to shred but still showing remnants of its original luster, came a car. Against the curb bumped my uncle Owen's long-hooded Packard, and my father stepping out of it.

"Dad!" I yelled, putting panic in my voice with my most calculated manner, setting off the alarm of alarms, "Some guy's got his foot in the door and mom's crying."

You know what irony is, don't you, full-fledged irony? Well, I saw it unfold right before my eyes, irony and the lesson of sweetest justice. Lanky's foot was still in the door and my mother was still pushing on the other side. He heard the roars of a lion three floors below him and those fearful and heavy feet on the stairs, and the pounding and the roaring ascending as if from the pit of hell itself. And he *can't* get his foot out from that improvident vise because my strong, broad-shouldered and home-protecting mother holds firm to her station.

Oh, he struggled then, did Lanky. He shoved on the door, kicked with his other foot, banged the oak footer, tossed his head this way and that like a stallion under harness. His shoulders shook and convulsed and the threads of his suit threatened to burst, and his throat finally cleared of all debris.

"Let go, damn you, you absolute bitch you! Let go!" The lion is closer, the sounds are hell themselves and suddenly, in a movie, in a close-up film, there's this madman rising from the bowels of the earth and a final roar exits from the heart of Vesuvius.

"Let go, Helen!" yelled my father, his hands reaching steeled and awful as talons, his eyes full of what I'd never seen once in my life. A wild energy pulsed about him more terrible than electricity. Like a snap, quick as thought, down three flights of stairs went Lanky, pummeled every step of the way. He bounced pillar to post to baluster to the final newel on the ground floor. His bone and flesh touched every tread, a ball, a toy, a stick kicked on a wayward walk.

The cop on the beat rushed over and stepped aside as my father ushered Lanky to his car. Propping him behind the wheel, he put his finger under his nose and said, low and mean, more of Vesuvius rising again, "Don't come back!" He turned the ignition key, slammed the heel of his hand on the floor starter tucked against the seat, and pointed out of town.

Lanky never came back, and several years ago, when my mother was within a day of her death, she placed in my hands my father's metal box whose contents I had never seen. In it I found his Marine Corps discharge creased together in gray-yellow folds. There was a Corps commendation in the neatest script you can imagine, two Nicaraguan Service Medals circa Chesty Puller, and a faded post card from Captain James Devereaux (later at Wake Island). The card simply said, "Jim, do you remember the night Atlanta got treed?" There was a note from the first grade teacher in Charlestown, Miss Finn, begging my mother that we not move away until she had taught all the Sheehans. Lastly, it too fading away, was Simon Westman's little book, Lanky's loss no doubt, with nine blank spaces yet to be marked for coin.

Falling-down Jack, A Study

Early evening light, what was left of it, spilled near Jack Winters in his one lone room in the big house. The house, once flaunting and imposing in its stance, now lay cluttered like an old shed forgotten in a back lot. Debris was its main décor. He had a reputation as the town drunk, a ne'er-do-well from the first day, an inveterate crank. But there had been an instant and subtle attraction between me and the old codger. It was an attraction without early explanation.

At the moment substantial shadows played around him. A host of them were ready to take him in some rude and final manner. And no shadow around him ever bore much compassion, not to the alert of eye. It seemed, from my vantage at one of his windows, the north one, that light was seeking him out—and grasping, once it had him, something still warm in October's dying days. It was as if embers of anything were important; particles of light, pieces of moving air, slight jerking of his left knee as he knelt before the cotton-sheathed bed. In the middle of the bed catching parts of light, the latent day, was an empty bottle. It threw back similar silver and gold on the loose, the way precious coins flatter themselves.

All of this came up to me in its quick shot as one supplicating god kneeling before another supplicating god. I saw light-seeking, light-giving emanations grander than I could imagine. At the same time it was powerfully sad, so sad it could choke you, a crushing taking place.

The crèche scene, an unknown metaphor to me then, was working its way in the back of my mind. It drew distal parts together. It made alignments long before legions of metaphors would don their spurs and ride rampant on me.

On that October evening I was seven years old. Three of my years had been spent watching the old man in the old gray house on the next corner. I'd done this from whatever vantage I could find. There had been, early in the scheme of things, the front porch or the front steps of our house. In turn there came the edge of the lawn, widening out to the roadside, which was early adventure's abrupt perimeter. Then came a familiar trip to the corner in my fifth year where the dark green sentinel of the mail box was located. Finally, the long, cold-hot, sometimes-green, sometimes-white path to school. All of this was my social laboratory. And Jack Winters was a unique specimen or subject for that laboratory.

Falling-down Jack we called him, *barnacled* if I can say it, red-faced, slightly bearded. And all silence once the whiskey's stubborn and lengthy acquisition had passed its purchase. But he was somehow warm to me, pulling at me, a magnet I did not know was forever in place. This draw made me slink around in the near darkness on countless nights to watch Falling-down Jack. I always went alone and never with Richie or Wally or even my brother. He might have been the only one to understand if I had been caught at the glass watching him in the one room of his house that still had windows in it. Even then it was my young desire to see *his clock works, his interminable ticking*, what made a man like him *go*.

Oh, we had knocked out our share of the other window panes, six-over-six in that old Colonial pattern most of the other houses had. All of us were from Central Street and the lane and the cul-de-sac. But the one room of his stupor and his sleep was off limits. Though none of us ever said so. Even then I thought an element of fairness existed. It was a sense of fair play so honorable in its small passage and so acute it would never be trespassed upon. Drunks too had inviolable rights, prone or upright. My small world, our small world, could make its own share of profound statements.

The world is. I am here.

I'm long past seventy now. Some of his attributes, indeed some of his mean appearances and characteristics (remembered only by me, I swear) are mine. Now I am red-faced, the wide and round face both heather and hawthorn have leaned on. The taste is built into my throat as if a dry flume waits impatiently for its sides to be wetted. The small and memorable bubble of joy is at the roof of mouth when the first swallow rises over that tongued arch and flows coolness and heat and companionship down that tortured passage. Too, I have my silences. Some of them are like the long times he spent in that single room, a cell in sunlight or darkness. It's like the hour just before dawn when a single bird's cry, the first one looping out of still darkness, finds you ready and waiting for what's on the line for the day.

I can tell you it's been near seventy years' contemplation of that Scotsman who came one day to his just-dead sister Claire's house. The two main doors he closed off with the permanent clutch of six-inch spikes driven with a vengeance I measured all the way from my front steps. Then he drew down the curtains on all windows of the other seven rooms, as if shame were being hidden from view. That first evening he drank away, to its oblivion, as much a signal to the neighborhood as one could imagine. On the following days and weeks and months he collected a fair menagerie of likewise friends. Eventually, as if clearing the stages of his life, he passed them off on the world and began occasional retreats into the small redan of his room.

Some people in the neighborhood thought him a balled fist waiting to be thrown, so few of them came into punching range.

"He'd as soon as rap you as look at you," I heard the mailman say to old Kosko one day.

It's uncanny now, years later, how the light re-appears, the light that was in his room the night he knelt before his empty god. The bottle was empty except for light answering some other light, though there was no coming from or going to. It was mythical then, is mythical now. The grasping and touching of light is one I've never been sure of. The meekest of light fell on the bed. Its cotton sheathes with the *Xs* of flour bag contents were thin and pale as two-cent postage stamps I once paid attention to. Prisms, wherever they end up, whatever their inversion, have a way of channeling light.

That fractured illumination fell about his head, pointed out each devilish scar's waddle. Shadows cast across skin were more broken up than the lunar surface. If I tried to squander some of that light I'd not be able to put it aside. Now it is an aura in its entirety and must have been designed for such countenance in the very beginning, long before Falling-down Jack came our way. It was there before imagination began its long walk with me. It was there before a few hard years of my young life were gathered, as it were, in one hand and dealt this great desire to study another person. And all that to my parents' utter consternation.

"You keep your fool self away from Jack Winters' house or he'll steal off with you some night."

My mother had been the first to say anything, smiling at me a half tone, her head barely shaking in the lightest act of disgust she could muster. That moment passed. The threat passed from her mind. The occasion moved into the meager parcels of history she would only stir up at gala family events when *telling all* seemed to lighten family chains. When sharing was positive bonding. To her, as to many people of Saugus, Jack Winters was really no more than an oddity in our lives, in our neighborhood. Safety in her mind was the fact there were no rapes, no kidnappings, no child molesting, and no breaking and entering in the nighttime. At least not in our part of Saugus. We were back up from the river. The sea-borne river's tide never touched us, or the horrors of the world. Small gardens and lawns and grassy fields spelled silence and a quiet guardianship between houses. Our Saugus, to her, was inviolate; children, its chief commodities, were never bothered.

My father had a different mindset, as you might guess.

"What weighs on one end must be balanced on the other."

I can remember him saying that marriages, good ones, absorbed all of that demand. He also said, "You can look all you want, young man. At the way he limps, at the ugly set of his mouth most days of the week. At the misery that flows about him sure as you're breathing. But don't ever step across the threshold of that house."

He didn't wag his finger, but looked me straight in the eye. Commanding was that look.

As it was, his signal working, he had paused then, assuring me that an announcement was coming. I can remember it as clearly as if he'd just walked in from the other room.

In the most serious voice I had ever heard, even in admonition, he said, "Somehow we both realize he looks like the Grandfather you never saw past your first year. I freely admit the mystery of that recollection. I think I know the great draw that's been put on you and not on others." Those others he didn't have to name. "If there's a piece of that light left in your brain, a shadow

52

of that old face, a grimace or a grin or one wild look from the monster John Barleycorn he carried as his own baggage, I can understand. If you've found something in the air that sets him apart from everybody else hereabouts, I can understand. He's odd, we know. But he's hurt no one. Not even in his bad dreams when he's being chased or little folk sit in his shadows cool as embers left over from a *bad night*."

In that serious vein he had blessed my small campaign. Later I suspected he had traveled somewhat the same road. Perhaps he sought answers along the way, questioning as much as anybody his own recollection of occasional horrors.

How many times I have struggled to bring back the first sight of Jack Winters, I cannot tell you. He was coming toward me while I was hiding from my pals in the bushes along the edge of the canal. Come along he did, as loud and as vibrant as any man I'd seen on that rude path or anywhere else. His voice rang out as brilliantly pure as a tenor on stage. And just as unintelligible to me, words and rushes of sound whose meanings I could not begin to guess. He gave off long woeful cries that struck like nails in soft places (cries whose pain I can still bring back on my clearest days). Also, sudden beauties of notes any stage would shake with, soaring notes that followed those awful nails into my ears. They came high rising, majesties of another level, echoes as firm now as then in their grip. Then came low guttural demands as if a beast of awed proportions shared his skin.

"DOMINAE!" he screamed or yelled or sang. An echo for all times. "DOMINAE!" That's what it sounded like. It implored. It begged. It sounded god-like, ancient, though I knew no Latin or Greek.

I was captured! At first by the sound. Then by brazen details rushing into my eyes, details that fixed themselves into permanent niches of my mind. He had thick gray hair and the smallest face, nearly purple and crazed with lumps and scars. His eyes were as red as a cardinal bird I'd seen that very morning. His small chin-point beard was as dirty as the town dump. His khaki shirt was tight at the collar. A striped suit coat comfortable as bedclothes sat on his shoulders, the kind Rip Van Winkle slept in. I swore his boots had climbed distant mountains or other azure. At his sides his hands, huge hands, powerful hands, worked at squeezing the sense out of air. One thumb, the left one, lay splayed twice as wide as it ought to be. A blacksmith must have tended it with a hot hammer. And that fateful aroma came at me, on a sheet of air at first, and then purely by its voluptuousness. It triggered volume, ripe fruit at the core, sweet and pear-like and syrupy. Bright crimson cherries carried in the mix, nectarines or limes like beggars hiding just around the corner. Green and yellow melons seemed tossed in at random. Finally, as if to top it all off, an edge of peach cut through all the mix to throw its signature out front.

Immediately I thought of the contrast—he should smell as foul as he looked. I should be sucking my gut back down my throat through which it ought to be passing at any moment in abrupt stages. But the air about him was fruit-sweet. Perhaps it was too thick and too syrupy, but fruit-sweet. Then my mind, triggered again by a message on the air, plunged for recognition. To this moment of this clear day I am aware of how minor mechanics within me were appointed and discharged in a quick plunge into my short history. They scratched for identity, scratched for recall, scratched for a face or a body or a name. It was one I didn't know at first but would know for the striking. It was left back in the entrails of thought, maybe an identity squandered in a dim corridor. I could have screamed because I knew it was there, behind a corner, just inside some thin cover of gray matter's secrets. My mind held it back from me, teasing me, trying me out.

"DOMINAE!" he screamed or begged or sang again just as he passed by my cover of brush hide-and-seeking me from my brother and friends. The fruit came stronger than it would ever again in any encounter. And almost unholy was the cry. But dared not to be. An imploration it might have been, an expulsion, a plea and a curse in one breath, able to rough itself into leaf and limb all around us. An act in itself.

"DOMINAE!" At least, that's what I thought he yelled, though I've surely put some effort over the years into the spelling of that cry. I've never known what it was, what passed from his lips, his mouth, his throat. Most certainly, from his soul. Probably it was the most honest sound I have ever heard in all my life. I never heard it again, though, no matter how many times I crouched by his window or heard him coming down the canal path from town or wherever he had been. There had been but that unearthly cry up into leaves and limbs and the far-off blue or darkening sky, a soul rising. "DOMINAE!"

Even within the fruited air at full tilt, and the dense brush at my eyes, my heart shook its hammer inside my flattened chest. I could not help but pull more parts of him together, the full identity. If he were a time puzzle, I had but minutes to gather the millennium. Rough as junk was he, drum-like and thick, pushing exorbitantly at the one button of his jacket. I thought of barrel staves girding just under cover. Like stout oak, holding in, stiff, rigid, volume-grasping, formed not by the outer but by the inner.

Instinctively, within the fruited atmosphere and the body electric and the royalty of his voice, came something I already knew. Though it was under cover, or disguised, or coming at me from an odd tangent, I knew. That knowledge spilled itself at my feet, pooled, then flowed up into me. Warmly it came, slow-rising, taking care not to frighten me, as if reins tethered its climb. It was temptation and reach, it was touch and acceptance. I held my breath, and the millennium passed. While that breath was held, while it coiled its harsh wonder in my chest, it allowed itself to be separated for recognition some near seventy years later. If it's just now doing its final dance, strong urges and requirements had fallen into place then.

Days later, still spelled and caught up in the newness and its necessities, I began to take notes on the Scotsman, The Town Drunk, The Dread Baritone. Sheaves of information were scratched and scrawled at any moment of sight, drawers of notes the years gave growth to. I knew when Jack Winters left the house, every time out. How long he'd be gone. What he wore in all weather. Could predict the reappearance of a khaki shirt or a purple wool sweater that must have had a thousand lives. I cranked up admiration for the sheep from which it had been scored. And pegged to the hour Friday night's return down the canal path.

In one quick decision, and much concentration, I had become *expert* at something. The relationship was intractable.

More than once in those tender years, in that blood-seeking quest, that absolute need for patriarchal warmth and acceptance, I stood between Jack Winters and his mortality. All four or so feet of me did it. Once I called my father on a very sharp November evening, night coming heartily on from Montreal and the Maritimes. When I had ventured up the path, Jack was late coming down. I found him cold and fetal and near bare of breath, under a bush whose blanket he must have sought. My father called three neighbors, burly ones at that, and they carried him to his room. They wrapped him, dropped him on his bed, cranked on the man-killer kerosene stove sitting in the middle of the room like an Easter Island stone infant.

On my first visit, of course, I reacted to the room. He had no books but a Bible shimmed under a lamp on a small table. A dozen empty bottles (green and brown and crystal) were scattered like candlepins and blazoned with rainbows of wax. A blue insignia metal can without a cover that crackers belonged in sat in a corner. There was an icebox with its oaken door hanging by little more than one untidy hinge so you could see the gray rind on its oxidized corrugated inner surface. A whole wall surface showed where pain and loneliness wore themselves into its pale yellow expanse camouflaged with black and OD green, like Army canvas hiding targets. Beneath my shoes the floor felt more of yard and less of house, with sounds in mutual support of that argument. But there was no stench, not a whiff of it. One look said we ought to be assailed at any moment by such threat. Our trespass did not seem approved despite the mission done. We had infiltrated another man's domain. The exit was quick.

I dwelt a long time on the room that came away with me, and made its way into my notes, before the sun had risen over Saugus. Sketches of its boundaries and its contents rose on paper tucked in the back side of my notebook, the then *current* one, Number Three of my travels with Jack Winters. None of the burly lifters saw the godhead abed, only the faded flour legend on the thin sheet, veneer of another use, another occupation. More than once, I've already told you, I'd seen an empty bottle embedded there, crèche of all the crèches, a passion play acted out and I was the known audience, the lone pursuer.

Frankly, I don't think any of the men, including my father, saw much in or of the room, visible parts that tell so little, invisible parts that tell so much. Such information could practically spill all over you like unwanted company. But it had escaped all of them, my father too, who kept his eyes on my alertness. There was exhibited a need to be out of there. To not be contaminated by whatever had held this place together as long as it had. Strengths are not easily recognized.

The second time I stepped out in front for his mortality was one Halloween Night cold as a drawn dagger. Star-lit, it was, an evening star almost shouting at us it hung so low on the horizon. Airy cool signs came with the messages of our mouths, when the gathered clan of us neighborhood toughs dared speak of burning down Jack Winters' house. My brother was all for it, seeing an end perhaps of the attention paid to my attention, my mission. His voice did not quiver once, cool as judge without a trial. But his feet moved, little shifts on the coarse gravel, not a dance, mind you, but talking, a giveaway penchant I'd noticed too many times to ignore.

"They'd hum about it all winter," he said, "everyone would. It's a dump anyway. We all know that. Know about him all the way over to Wakefield, they do, our most famous citizen."

He snickered to mark his stance and shifted his feet a little more, more punctuation.

"He'd only have to go someplace else. Over there, or maybe the place he came from. Right now he won't be back for more than an hour and it'd be a glorious bonfire by then."

That was a pointed revelation, to say the least.

He came off as spokesman, and looked at me sort of indirectly, matching his feet in a way. Even under the cover of the cold night and the shivering shadows and the silence mostly about our strategy encampment, we both knew that he had looked at my notes. He had come away with some knowledge. I loved him and hated him at the known declaration. I was determined, though the youngest of the lot, that

58

they'd burn his house down over my dead body. Light of the evening star fell through the leaves at our heads, fell on countenances, shone from the eyes of all of them looking hard at me. I was the first and only obstacle to young pyromania.

"He's just a drunk, and you know it!" Wally advanced with a sudden burst of courage. I saw the star leap again in his eyes, heard the plea specializing itself in his voice. "It'd be the best fire ever. Everybody would be glad the house is gone. My mother talks about it all the time. How it must stink like socks or old drawers. How it'll catch fire some night from his *own* hand, falling down drunk and smoking and the man-killer sucking up the air all night long and the stupid candles dancing in the dark. Says he's always light as a clerk's lunch hour."

He'd never said so much at one time in all the time I'd known him, in all the time he'd been the closest friend of my brother's. But he was as tricky sometimes as the bakery driver swapping day-olds. I caught a bit of pride in his voice, some dare. He'd toss the match for sure. I sensed also the recording of his words, which he must have dragged right out of his mother's kitchen. He played it for us in our thin cover, under air sheer at the touch, under a star's reaching.

When I stood off the log, as much dais as any I'd known, I thought they would rise and mass against me. The only thing I was sure about was they'd leap at any viable alternative. I was ready to tell the whole world if they proceeded, that much I knew. And if it came down to the last minute of saving the house, I'd run inside it. That would panic my brother no end, them too, so I threw another bone for their gnawing:

"I know where there's fifty feet of chain. We could wrap it around a couple of his fence poles, such as they are, and the gate too and then hook it on the bumper of the 8:20 bus when it leaves for the Center."

I mimicked the jerking motion of the old Hart-Line Bus as it would pull away from the corner. I made it mulish, Mack-ish, the clutch in spasms. Gears scratching for holds. Windows shaking light off every surface. The muffler an abomination of the transport industry. I mimicked well, and tossed in sound effects for their ears, for my argument.

The picture played too much for them, the noise and commotion promising heady delight to cap off Halloween. They could talk about it in secret for months to come; for years to come, as it proved to be.

The bus left, the chain taut behind it, the links sure on post and beam and stave. The rending and riotous clatter was like empty drums in the wind as the bus bounced up the street,. I did not know that Jack Winters lay sick in the cold house. He had left earlier, but had returned, and we had not seen him. *I* had not seen him. The calamity brought him weakly to his door. He coughed and gagged on his own self. He wrapped stout arms about his gut as if holding some treasure within. His collapse, the sudden silence, the fear quickly riding on the dagger air, brought the burly neighbors again. They lifted him, bedded him, and lit the man-killer stove again. But we stayed our distance. The wrenching echoes of wood and steel were sharp yet in our hearing, pointing fingers at us, making claims against us. We noble toughs, believing the dread promise of the neighborhood about kicking a man when he was down, felt the threat. This was a man I thought warm as an old acquaintance generating trust, like a soft leather wallet you've pawed for years.

Jack came back from both those bouts. He bounced like the ball in the singalongs at the theater (*Camptown Races, Doo Dah Doo*). Healthy he came and kicking out of those depths as I thought few men could. There was no pity about him,that was evident. There was no wallowing in his own mire, no asking for help, no hand out for any spillage. He was just a gunny sack full of mash and potatoes and some raw ingredients it took me a long time to put names on. He was a tough man born to a tough path and damned sure he was staying on it.

Oh, there were other episodes that pulled us together, though I never once spoke with him. And baseball came and football and a girl just up the street one day who sat on a log with her skirt riding who knows where. There was Notebook No. 10 and Notebook No. 11, and eventually a drifting of my years.

Then, as sudden as not, I was in high school and the house on the corner stood yet in its blocky and stubborn way. Jack Winters went back and forth, shrunk a little, drank a lot, saying not two words to anybody. And one day, as I left my house to go to the game of the year, October clear as a rung bell around me, I saw him walking toward the canal path. His half-graced limp was still in place, arms out of step down his thighs as if he were hearing another music. I looked away for a moment when I heard the band music at the stadium. When I looked back, he was gone. I think my ears heard another ringing. My chest pawed for breath. Something was happening in the crisp air. I could feel it.

I never saw Jack Winters again. Nobody did. Gone, like a quick cloud. Gone, as if he'd never been. Gone, only to exist in my notebooks. Three of the books turned up a while back. My brother found them in his garage, tucked in an old bureau my parents had given him. Sixty some years and he read them for the first time just before returning them.

"I never knew he was like Grandfather to you," he said. "I'd never have thought that in a hundred years, but you and dad did, right from the start. The way he smelled and the way he walked with that little limp, and the stubborn ring he carried in his mind. Never came on me once."

He was, I knew, scratching for differences, the founding of relationships, the minor reasons for found differences.

I didn't tell him I still think of Jack Winters practically all year long. Often it's for hours at a stretch, or days: where he went when he went off, what took him off, and what kept him. When October's little knife begins its twist, when the evening star comes out to speak on the low horizon, I think of him. Always. I say to myself that if I hadn't kept him he would not be. If I had let him go he would not have been. Had he not been *there* there would have been no pain kneeling before his small godhead in that cell of a room. There would not have been the man-killer sucking up air, or the camouflage hiding him at times from his own self. There would not have been a minor light source pulling rainbows out of waxed bottles. Or a small god looking in a window at his own nativity.

Orion's Belt

All things in that year of 1936 (as well as other years in that prohibitive stretch of history), when I was eight, were temperate and moderate to say the least. Signs of that firm modesty lay everywhere one would look. For me it was meal time as much as anything else that gave off signs of the times. My stomach for much of every day had a language all its own and all our meals were fixed more by economics of the period than by the design of any cook.

If I could have been embarrassed then by being hungry and noisy in one fell swoop, I would have been. And with some justice or reason to it. But I wasn't, for it was not in the make-up that had been hatched for me. Hunger was an unknown though persistent sound, sub-vocal, more an ache in the gut than anything else. What I've only come to know recently as peristalsis was its somewhat literal accompaniment, a sort of down-to-earth, slightly-less-than-volcanic expression of a natural order in its calamitous state. Meals were strict copies of bland predecessors. Oatmeal was served in the morning, sometimes so thick and heavy it could be slabbed. Sometimes it was thin as the gruel you might only find a description of in the Brothers Grimm. One could say it was prepared in a thatched cottage or in a dank castle kitchen and given to the prisoners. Anything left over was given to my fiery Aunt Kay with which she tried to coax eggs out of a handful of oftentimes declining ducks. Tomato soup and oyster crackers passed for lunch when we came home from school at noon time (with the doubly deep baritone Singing Sam marking the time on the radio). Supper, long before the term became popular in the current magazine world, was always "pot luck" to my most magical mother and "catch of the day" to my stoic father.

As it turned out, we four girls and two boys were always hungry. State of the art my father came to call it later in the comfortable years. But we were as healthy as young piglets, though without the fat portion. We were thin, we were quick of feet, hand and mind, and we never wanted what we never had. We didn't crave lobster thermidor or roasted chicken or an eye of the round and heaps of fried mushrooms on the side. That menu turned our mouths to watery caves, but one more decent mouthful of what we just had finished would often have done the trick.

And the clothes we wore were ordinarily as drab as the drabbest part of the year. That was the stretch between the October fire and the first swirl of snow. For then the corduroy was thin and shiny in relevant spots. Denim was shiny too where it was most needed. Wool often stretched itself out to its ultimate usage. Cotton always came perilously near ready for Goldberg's junk wagon after one more wearing and one more wash and the ten thousandth time on the porch line. All of it appeared circuitously in the first place with another kind of a price tag on it for "those poor, poor children who live on the third floor of the block." That was the bunch of us, the Sheehan kids.

Such as how it came to be on a wild October Saturday in that fomenting year. A new wind rode at a frenzy, and leaves were well on their down-wind journeys. Evening limbs had become their spidery selves. The Canadian latitudes began laying down on us their most serious threats. And Orion Stepinsward's belt, fashionably buckled on gold-brown leather, which still had a sheen to it, was holding up my pants. They were the gray corduroy ones that no longer made any sound between the knees because those minute corrugations had long since disappeared.

Mind you, I was not wearing Orion's shirt or jacket, not his pants, not his underpants, but his belt!

Orion, schoolmate and classmate of mine, was soon to depart for the private school scene. Fauntleroy he was even before Fauntleroy was thought of in my mind. Actor Freddie Bartholomew brought him home to stay as a real persona shortly thereafter. Orion was the only son of the Gargantuan George—bank director, mill owner, store owner, holder of the first pew in church. The last word in town, he was, and ultimately God Awful Protector of All Public Lands the Rabble Might Abuse.

To say that Orion and I didn't see eye to eye was easy. He was a snot of a kid from the word go. Wrapped he came in ermine, silver-spooned, trying to speak the King's English so that we would know the difference. We Colonials, that is, whose grandparents or parents had been escaped prisoners from their own island. He was handsome, though; a lot more handsome than I was with my freckles and unruly red hair and teeth seemingly too big for my own mouth. I often thought my ears were too big too. None of my family ever brought that up, though Patricia, once pointing at them, had obviously considered it in one of her moments. Of his good looks, you'd know the type right off the mark, having seen lots of them in the movies. Dark and thick and wavy hair was chief with him, and a high forehead, above deep gray-blue eyes, nice nose, a mouth just short of pursed. His chin was cut from some noble lord most recently out of armor. Normal ears, the kind that are mostly flat to the head and somehow not noticeable at all, were his. His fair skin was absolutely without a sign of blemish. The long dark lashes, I think, made sisters Patricia or Mary look at him more than once. To my everlasting dismay. A Norman, a Saxon, a Britisher he was, rolled into the noble and everlasting One.

For the three years I had known him he was harmless, never saying much against me or mine. He stayed on the neutral edge, which I never once thought existed except for the faint of heart. He skipped recess every now and then. By arrangement with the teacher, it seemed, when we played Total War so that he would not be involved, not get hurt, not get dirty. I would have to say, however, in his defense, that he was an artful observer of all activities on and off the school grounds. If he talked about me early in the game it was only to my face. There, he had earned some respect from me. Plenty of my own kind had often shot off their mouths, like absurd asides, without thinking of what kind of debris would come out with the charge.

As I said, it was October, the day was cool, the wind was whistling. My dark worn felt-like jacket with a wide flat collar was tucked inside my pants and belt line. Where the jacket had come from, I had no idea. My mother, a few weeks earlier, had gone into her room, just before I was to leave only sweatered for school, and came out with it in her hands. She was tall and beautiful, with dark hair and great blue eyes that could tell tales without beginnings or ends. Warm as bricks behind the stove she was. She did not look like other mothers, did not talk like them, gave little explanation and demanded less. "This is for you," she said, without any more qualification. She didn't carry on about source—whatever was *was*. The jacket was not new, but was clean and fit me like a glove. I could feel its wrap as secure as the kitchen stove.

I bundled myself, buttoned, cocoonish, feeling tight and secure as a drum. Suddenly I pulled down my pants and stuck the jacket down inside my pants. I felt thoroughly braced. My mother had walked back into her room and came out with a belt. "Wear this."

The belt had a splendid brass buckle that looked like sets of horns head to head. It was made of finely tooled leather, though a design I could not identify with any culture or creed. At my waist, cinched, jacket enclosed, it felt snazzy. It was elegant and adventurous at one and the same time, and had a girth grip that called at me. My arms and chest even seemed bigger. I did not question the source of such good feelings, or any part of that good feeling. Just to feel so rock-ribbed, strong, invincible on any playground and in any schoolyard, was tonic enough to me. I hugged my mother. I can still feel the touch of her hand at the back of my head, as if she had said I understand everything you feel. The touch is airy, it is feathery, it is full of small charges of neutrons or other electrical energy that carry a message just as surely and as quickly as does any of today's media.

That touch said a lot of things. It said I love you. Be brave. Your time is coming. Things will get better. There will come a time when you will not be hungry. I got this belt and this jacket for you to wear. I love you. Don't ask questions so that your sisters won't ask questions. I depend on you so much at times like this. Always remember how this hand of mine feels on the back of your head and what I am telling you now without having to say it. Love me back the same way. Always love me back the same way and no matter what, I'll know it. You can depend on that.

Orion's belt, then, on that cool Saturday, was doing its job, and no wind or cool air could seek its quick way down inside my belt line. It was cinched tight, perhaps an extra hole slipped through the buckle. We were at the side of the school, hanging on the iron fire escape. The gang of us; Donnie Gearty, Billie Maxon, Vito Rossi, Beau LeBlanc, Dermott MacReady, Endell Shah, Orion Stepinsward, and me. We were a regular League of Nations kind of gathering. Orion had a new football. He wanted us to play and he would referee. If we didn't, he was going to take his ball home; another message in a line of messages he had broadcast. Donnie and Endell could not have cared less, both of them sort of waxy and white and firm as clover. Vito and Beau and Billie could have spit. Someone's teeth were grinding, and at least two of them looked at me as if to say let's jump him and take his ball!

I said, "I could take your ball away from you, Orion, and you could run home crying. Do you want me to do that?" I'm sure I framed the whole statement with my chest thrust out and the jacket tucked tightly into my belt line. Charles Atlas himself inside jacket inside belt inside a busting frame. The warm dark collar, almost felt-like, was thick and firm against the back of my neck, part of the ramrod affect it had on me. It even touched into my hands that had become fists approaching the hardness of rocks. The feather of my mother's hand touched again, touched on that hardness that was me and getting harder.

When he looked at me he had this funny sort of look in his eyes that I had not seen before. I had read a lot of his expressions, you can bet, and knew something different was going to come out of him.

"Sure, you could take my ball, and then, surprise of surprises, you'd have my ball and my belt." He managed a real serious smile that tore its way right down inside me. "That's my belt you're wearing. Might as well take my ball, too. All my leather, all yours."

"You're a liar!" I screamed. "My mother got this belt for me."

"She got it from a box of stuff my father left over to Reiser's Bank. Hand-me-downs he called them. For the poor. For the destitute. For the needy. My mother and Juliet, our maid, scraped them out of my room. Now you have my belt. It might be my jacket, too, but I can't tell the way you're wearing it."

I ripped the jacket up out of my pants. "Is this your jacket?" I demanded to know, its full waist now exposed. Donnie and some of the others stared at me. Vito's eyes, though, had filled with fire, a black fire I

68

supposed was also in my eyes. I don't know what really hit me then, but I was suddenly marking my friends, my enemies, setting people off to this side or that side. There were no fence riders as far as I was concerned. Not in this life anyway. Vito, I knew, was right in my corner. He was feeling just the way I felt, this awful sense of exposure, of being stripped of some of my respect, of some of my stature. I didn't like how I felt and could see the same reaction in Vito's eyes. And Beau had it too, that sudden heat you might have to count upon sometime, rising from the deepest part of the body, coming up out of all the roots. Their jaws were tight, locked hard and fast.

"It's not my jacket, but it's still my belt," said Orion.

In his haughtiest manner, with a face that has taken me a long time to forget, his eyes screwed up under that wide forehead. They were slit so that he couldn't possibly take in all of me. His mouth was in a pussy purse, his chin pointing at me like his big-shit father would do. Then he flipped the ball at me. What disdain!

My fist landed high on his head as he ducked. I heard my pants split someplace aft. He ran off crying. My drawers were showing. Vito slammed one fist into his other open hand. Beau faked a punch, a little jerk of his fist saying, Oh, boy, you just showed him! The others didn't seem to count any more. They stood there like sacks of flour or sacks of oatmeal, their mouths open, their eyes blue and neutral and no kind of flame anyplace in them where you'd want a fire. I walked off toward home with my white drawers punctuating my backside. I had to talk to my mother.

So much was rushing at me as I walked home. There'd be noise from Orion's father that my father would have to contend with. There'd be raised voices, a few threats tossed on the air, and a hands-off agreement finally cemented in place. The heat under my collar was still raging in a quiet way. The unspoken words my mother had offered when the belt and the jacket were given to me tried to find clearer meaning in my head. If I really was such a disappointment after her careful approach, how could I face her? But I needed to know. I wanted explanations.

The walk home was a major adventure in my mind because so many messages were coming directly at me. And so many images. Foremost of all of them was my mother, and the blue-eyed and dark-haired solemnity that she bore with her, and which had crossed somehow between us. It was not so much a ritual but a feeling that such a crossing had been entirely necessary. And it was only possible between the two of us. Nobody else could share that. She was harbor and haven, as steady as steady could be, and that import was in some manner at bequest. She had gifted me and it was up to me to use it. And here I was, hot under the collar, ragged at breath, a bit of blood on my knuckle. And Orion Stepinsward's belt still cinched about my waist. I felt the misery of failure swamp me as I climbed the three flights of stairs to our apartment. Still in recall is the weight of that feeling, a hollow sense of imperfection that crawled all over me. I kicked the risers practically all the way up. Unknown to me at the time, such action cut a clear message to her that I was coming along and bringing some kind of problem with me.

She stood at the top of the third landing, in a light blue dress that caught at her eyes, a dark blue belt gathered at her waist that made her taller than she was. One foot she set lightly on the landing edge so that her frame was slightly cocked at an angle. It gave her an aura of an impatient mystic. There stood my giant of a mother. Her arms were not folded across her chest as one might think. Her hands were clasped in front of her as if in minor prayer, a quick request for the good Lord's assistance.

"You've not forgotten what we talked about?" she asked. It was immediately clear to me that she had picked her words carefully. She had not said, You didn't forget what I told you, did you? That was not her style at all. She wouldn't lay it all across your shoulders at one time. The messages and the revelations were still coming at me. And here was this great dispenser of sagacity and behavioral attitudes. Somehow she had known that I was due at her doorstep with another package of trouble. Amazement transcended her. You have to know some other things about my mother, and about me, I'd guess, at the same time.

Here I was at eight years of age ascending the stairs and seeing her on the landing and I finding myself measuring my own mother. What she was and how she looked came straight at me. Her skin was as white and without blemishes as any imaginable. You might see the like of it once in a blue moon. Or every once in a while on something, like a brooch maybe, made of pearl or something from some island someplace. Not a mark on her. She wore no color on cheeks or lips, no red, no pink, and never got colored by embarrassment in any kind of situation, no matter what was done or what was said. She didn't poke at her hair all the time like some woman do, fixing what didn't need to be fixed. You never saw her with her hands on her hips as if she was getting ready to remind you of something she'd said beforehand about something you didn't do. There was none of that for her. Reasons were around for all kinds of things. Both the good and the bad. Control was the ultimate of graces in her mind. She didn't preach it, she did it, so that we could see what it was all about. Frailty might be part of the human child, but it was not to be accepted without some cause or some explanation.

On the landing above me, tall, white like a birch after rain, her eyes as good as any kindly sky in summer, I saw in her my own immediate failing. She was what I wasn't and the world of difference leaped up inside me.

"I did it again, Mom. Orion said this was his belt and maybe his jacket and I punched him. He ran home crying. He said it in front of all the kids and I just had to hit him. He made me so mad I couldn't help it."

"That's not the truest statement you've ever made, is it?" If there was one thing you could count on, more than what I've already said about her, it was that she'd always give you the first chance to explain a deed or a misdeed. My father was not like that at all. There'd be a problem and a strap or a whipping, neither of them too heavy or too careless to be sure, but punishment of itself, and mere explanations would come along afterward from either side. I felt like leaping upon her and being drawn in. But she would let me know that there was a small bridge to be crossed before such twining could take place. One of her difficult-to-imagine but obviously true adages was that growing up is letting go. I knew at that moment I was at the very edge of a new life. It was difficult to acknowledge the break. But brother James had made it and I'd be expected to make the same break. An ominous sense of loss came over me on the stairs, at her feet. I looked up at her, feeling eight but feeling much older. I loved her with my whole heart, feeling terrible again that I had let her down. I waited for some note of calmness and acceptance that all would be right in my life, that she would not show disappointment in me.

Then, in the merest second, with the utmost illumination one can imagine, all of life began to change before my very eyes. I can tell you now that color changed and thought changed and imagery

changed and decades changed and history changed—
and love changed, right down to the last penny of it.
Love became a real thing, not a rose-smelling
satisfaction, not a self-indulgent ache. In one instant it
became, at another and most infinite level, a command
of life. There above me, birch tall and white as I said,
the light suddenly left her eyes as if it was drawn in, as
if a vacuum was drawing on her outer parts. Her right
hand leaped to her left breast. Her left hand reached out
to touch me, to speak, to talk to me, to tell me what it
was at that mere moment. She seemed to implode,
going back in to herself, all her parts drawn inward like
a reclamation of sorts, a claim being made. Her mouth
opened, yet her cheeks were sucked in on themselves as
if she was going to utter one Oh, one long and drawn
out Oh, one Oh to last me a whole lifetime, which
indeed it has. An Oh I am bound to carry all the days of
my life. I felt the nails of her left hand raked my cheek.
Then that hand joined her other hand. They clasped
over her breast tighter than prayer, more serious than
prayer, fists of bone yet the skin still so white, so much
better than pearl.

On my cheek I could feel the remnant of pain
and the onset of blood being freed. It flowed down my
face. My mother had cut me! But something greater
was wrong. There was a knife of thought gouging at me
and digging up disbelief. It dug deeper. She imploded
and I exploded as a wild, wild agony cut loose itself.
Her eyes had gone back into that past only she knew.
She was not sharing, that I knew. Her hands clenched
themselves more strongly and more possessively, some
treasure being squeezed up in them, some artifact with
one handle left for grasping.

Then, slowly, a soft look surfaced on her face,
almost an apology on that beautiful whiteness now only
finding a new color tinting it. Perhaps she had a minor
heart attack that took years to complete. I was at that

moment, I thought, her universal child, her one contact with this life. To this day I know that she tried desperately to hold within herself the minute pain she felt. Mortality raked me. At that instant I knew that one day she would leave me like this. And it was locked in place forever. My tastes changed. My colors changed. My imagery changed. My thought changed. All the elements of my history changed. My love, perhaps, had moved into a clarity and might never come again. In that revelatory moment she had touched me, had drawn my blood, had cast my life anew. The belt had done this.

And Orion Stepinsward would pay for it!

I'd spend my life getting even with him, though there came the realization of association; Orion the Hunted and Orion the Hunter!

I wondered what else was growing in me. The small hatred grew in me, but it was not alone. I had to temper it. It was her doing. Something else started with it, kept that hatred company. The idea of mortality hung in tightly. I could not move it away. So I made a partnership. I would plant a tree for her at the cemetery, though it would prove to be more than fifty years before she died. It would be like a continual prayer. It would be my altar. It would be my thank you.

Even as I thought of planting it down beside the river, at the cemetery, mad October crawled away from me. The sky was hard and steely blue, a few clouds as set and as trim and as cold as diamonds, the ground threatening to close itself off. I was able to think of my father and brother and sisters. I hoped it would be a century before we would gather by the tree I'd plant. Yet the ominous pairing welled up inside me. Threats seemed to hang in the air for an unknown reason. And on the cool air I almost caught some of her ultimate words, but a little zephyr of wind carried them off. I looked around old Riverside Cemetery and saw immediately that the winds and snow of November and on would eventually blow across my mother's tree like runaway trains across the prairie. There was not a bit of shelter, no hummocks, no trees, no walls, just a flat expanse with sparse dominoes of gray stones sticking up in their quick play at geometry. A bit of tolerance came on me then, her hand touching again, no doubt exacting promises. I promised I'd care for her tree before I'd do anything about Orion Stepinsward. I'd get him, but there had to be the tree before that anger. I'd know the anchor of that vow forever.

So the next April, Orion still eating away at me a whole winter's worth, I went to the edge of the Iron Works pit down behind our house. I came away with a young maple sapling about as thick as my thumb. Its roots were long and searching already, like a kid at play, or like an old dowser at work, either telling me that messages abounded. Just about dark I planted it in a far corner of the cemetery. I guided it well into the ground, sopped it wet, but someone there or thereabouts had it in for me or trees or shade, because I had to do it five times.

The fourth time the little tree was sawed into a dozen pieces. A weird message to say the least. The pieces were piled neatly on the ground. So I left my message tied on the fifth one with an elastic band: *Who takes down my mother's tree one more time will have his balls cut off by my uncle Nicolai.* I said uncle Nicolai, even though he was not my uncle, because he was the meanest looking man I had ever seen in my life. He worked in the package store and had a dark beard and one eye as red as a sore and a white scar that cut well into his upper lip. These marks gave him the fiercest look. He was devilish looking, right out of the Saturday afternoon movies. Whoever had been cutting down the trees must have known Nicolai, for that fifth tree took good root and the small limbs and leaves began to grow, and a needle of shadow began its life at my mother's tree. If it continued its well being, I believed, she would keep the pace.

Out of love and duty and a desire to see it grow as tall as possible, and wide as a dozen umbrellas for shade, I watered it every day. Sometimes I heard laughter from way off, or now and then a snicker of disdain from perhaps behind a stone or from someone secreted from me, but kept at my task. It took a lot of time and a lot of trips and a lot of water. Every once in a while, of course, the ground trembled a bit under my sneakered or bared feet. Or a small wind would slide itself across a limb of the tree or across the edge of a leaf, or would slip up beside a piece of granite as if it had been held back for surprise. And my mother's voice would always be in it. Always that loveliest of sounds, always that sweetest of voices. It was difficult to hear a simple sigh because she did not use sighs to communicate. She did not let you guess, did not try to threaten you by throat clearings, by phlegm letting sounds move through it. She always used words, not sounds, plain and beautiful words, simple words, songs of words. There were times when I had heard them in the hallway at night, a statement she'd make, or a piece of a song she'd sing, things hanging out for me to remember, the lips softly pushing them at me. Be alert. Hear this.

Struggling to hear, cocking my head in my best alert, I waited some evenings by the tree for her words to repeat themselves, for comprehension, for direction, for example. I was afraid to let her know I feared failure again. That apparent attack of hers frightened me every waking moment.

Unbeknownst to me, though, things were already done and cemented; it was in my act. All that summer it was in my act, in my deed. It was in my watering. The watering purged me and August fled with its dread heat, its overhead punishment of sun, its

76

nighttime depressions of claustrophobic pounding. Orion Stepinsward thusly had skipped away from my first attention.

And one particularly hot night in the last week of August, I slipped quietly and quickly from the house to water the tree. All the others slept. The heat was as thick as the darkness around me. Time slapped itself out across the merciful heavens.

I lay under the tree looking up into the galaxies of stars flung throughout its limbs. Orion I recognized against that flat darkness and in that mix of limbs, and saw his arms at bow and his belt line cinched. It hit me solidly again, the difference; Orion the Hunter, Orion the Hunted, mere symbols. Suddenly I knew how far away Orion was out there and Orion was down here and how close my mother always was, how she talked in the leaves, what her unending messages said, even when she cut my cheek that mad October.

The Day Titanic Drowned

We were sitting on empty nail kegs next to his icehouse on the edge of Lily Pond in Saugus, Doc Sawyer and me. We were talking about everything and nothing in particular. It was his way of communicating. He wore a gray felt hat, shirt collar buttoned but with no tie, Mackinaw open so I could see red suspenders clasped at his paunch. Doc always had time to talk to kids, dropping lore and legend in his wake.

"Where you're sitting right now, son, is the geographical middle of our town. It's right under your feet, or," and he chuckled, "under your butt." I felt special, being ten years old, on the inside where real data was concerned.

He was full of tidbits like that. "Bazooka Bobby Burns scored the first touchdown on that field when it was dedicated this past fall," he said. Pointing across Appleton Street to Stackpole Field, re-dedicated in 1938, he added, "and young Jackie Harrington scored the second one. You watch that young one now." He could make declarations, too.

It was Saturday. It was cold again, as it had been for a good spell, and the ice cutting would begin today, the temperature holding below freezing for more than a week. On the pond the ice was over fourteen inches thick, thick enough to hold the small army of men soon to be on it. Morning light fell gray yet vivid across the face of the pond. It raced off toward the island in the middle and the Turnpike beyond. It was a long skate from one end of the pond to the other. Some skating days it paid to bring lunch.

Crows were sending brittle messages to each other out across the frozen surface, over the cliff on Cliff Road, into the woods. Now and then I could hear the tires on a truck as it ran north to Maine or Canada on the Turnpike. Sounds ran over the pond as though they came through a funnel. Old Doc turned as he heard hoof beats on the pavement of Summer Street running alongside Stackpole Field. Like a drummer playing games, I thought.

The biggest horse I had ever seen in my ten years came down the street. Mitch Crocker was guiding him with a set of long reins, not snapping them but laying them easy on that great back. That horse was so big it even made Doc stand up and take off his hat. He shook his head, light bouncing off his glasses, and said, "Where'd you come on him, Mitch? Win him in a game?"

Horses in those days always awed me, fearsome things, huge as boulders, with great teeth and hooves like catcher's mitts. Horses hauled milk wagons, and honey wagons, and now in winter the clumsy snow plows behind them, dragging on their muscles, calling on their hearts. This one with Mitch Crocker was a tower of an animal, dark chestnut in color. His teeth were yellow and enormous and now and then he'd pull his lips back to show them to you. Steam pulsed from his mouth like any other great engine of a thing.

"What's his name?" Doc said, laying a hand on the rippled neck, rubbing that fur coat smoothly, easily, talking another way, something closeted in his voice.

"I call him Titanic," Mitch said, "though I don't expect him to answer none. He don't happen to answer to any name unless he downright feels like it. So names don't make any difference and one's as good's another."

"For the ship?" Doc said. The horse's eyes were a mix of lime green and yellow, and deep, as if he were reading my mind. I figured he had already read Mitch's mind. I looked away from those eyes.

"As well as any I could pick on, specially for size," Mitch said. "It'll do until another comes along. This boy can take care of all your hauling today, Doc."

He patted Titanic on his broad chest. "Drag all the floes into place, get them up on to the ramp so's they can be cranked up and stored. Yes, sir, do it all."

For a few hours that Saturday I watched the strange army of itinerant ice cutters saw and chink up the ice of Lily Pond. I saw Titanic with long chains hitched to his leather gear easily haul the huge cakes of ice to the slabbing point. From there they'd be carried up the chain-driven ramp to where they'd get buried under shavings and saw-dust. Easily and steadily he worked, the steam puffing in great clouds from his mouth and circling around his head like halos. Now and then, as if to reaffirm who was really in charge, he'd throw off a head-shaking command and bring attention to himself.

Never a sound came from his throat.

Throughout the morning old Doc Sawyer kept nodding his head, admiring that animal as if he'd never seen his like before. Noon crawled toward us, still cold, still steamy about that great beast. Then the heart leap came and a fearful noise, a renting, a crashing. It was just before lunch when Titanic went down. I heard a yell, a scream, the unforgettable thundering noise as though a crack was going to sprint the length of the pond. Titanic was in the water. In the deepest part of the pond. His legs thrashed at the ice, breaking off huge chunks. The noise was like an enormous ice machine at work, like an icebreaker in frozen Boston Harbor I'd seen before.

Under my feet the ice shook.

The day stood still for me.

I'd never before seen a huge creature like him frightened. His eyes said just that. They were like baseballs. Yellow-green baseballs, all wet and frosty, with tunnels behind them and all kinds of talk in them. He made sounds, too, desperate sounds down in his lungs, deeply bellowed sounds inside that huge canister of a chest. They came blurting out of his mouth along with the torrent of steam. Could have been grenades going off beneath the water.

Everybody leaped to grab chains and ropes, to pull that thrashing and ponderous beast out onto the surface of the pond. But the ice kept breaking under his hooves. And he tired and sank two or three times and came back up thrashing and kicking more, and the steam rising off his great back. The chains snarled and came caught up in ropes, and in his legs I suppose. You could see the lines of them somehow get shorter and shorter. There was no slack in them at all. None of the men could steer or drag that ship of a horse onto the top of the ice.

Mitch Crocker, just before Titanic went down for the last time, dropped a length of chain from his bare hands. He blew into his cupped hands and tried to rub them. He was wet all over, dark stains growing across his clothes. His thick fur hat bobbed in the water. Then a last bubble came circling around it where Titanic's lungs had let go for the final time.

Doc Sawyer put his arm around Mitch's shoulders.

"That was some animal, Mitch. I'm really sorry for your loss."

I remember thinking it was like standing in line at the funeral parlor. Everybody was sad, their heads down, striking for one correct word, a passable word. Cold and quiet were twin elements around us. In the water all the bubbles had gone.

Then, about five minutes later, itinerant ice cutters in odd clothes and knee-high leather boots and kids and on-lookers still standing quietly on the ice, it happened. About ten or twelve feet of chain, yet laying out on top of the ice as though remnants of a disaster, just slipped off the edge link by link and went down out of sight. Perhaps one last lunge by that great horse.

When all the noise was made about the movie of the same name in these recent years, I thought about the other Titanic going down. I remembered how quiet it was afterward, how cold it was, the last hunk of chain, getting dragged off the ice, still making a connection.

Fred Rippon's Mushroom House

"What the good Jesus!" Pete Tura yelled and disappeared. He said it again, his voice muffled, his mouth most likely closed by horse manure. With its whole nine yards, the bottom of the collection box hanging from the second floor of the Hood's Milk Company horse barn in West Lynn had let go. It took my pal with it.

I last saw one arm, not waving goodbye, probably trying to keep the pitchfork from doing him damage. Possibly he had tried to throw it behind him. That innocent weapon of deadly tines was not in sight. I peered down into the mixture of black clutter and hay still settling down with a metronomic slowness you could count.

In my throat came this heart of mine, bursting, threatening, making echoes of its own, surrealistic at best. Sounds of soft thumping rose up. I thought of giant corduroys rubbing each other or horsehide and emery at toil. At once a bodily bang, a whoosh of air, came back with a smell I can recall yet, but no scream at first. Again I looked down at the pile, like a miniature pyramid of horseshit, in the bed of the truck, an old Chevy stake body. Oh, fair, fair oh Pete, the new Egyptian, entombed. Then he sounded out, he was down there, grunting, cursing in a closed mouth emphasis his surprise, his anxiety, his pissed-off frame of mind. Would he tell some girl tonight, I wondered, where he had been today? I saw the handle of the pitchfork extending from the pointed pile, motionless, obviously not having gored my pal. Pistol Pete, safe but cruddy.

Dark-eyed, pimple-faced but still a ladies' man to hear him tell it, Pete was facing Navy service in a few months. He had driven the truck from Fred Rippon's Mushroom House on the edge of Lily Pond in Saugus for the weekly collection of horse manure from a scattered half dozen horse barns. Whiting's, McLean's, Hood's, The Creamery, all lined our route for the morning. The afternoon ride would take us to a long, narrow fence-lined field in West Peabody. There a pile of manure, now fifty yards long, five feet high, ten feet wide, waited new deposit.

It was 1943, the war on in newsreels at the State Theater and in onionskin letters from brothers out there where it was happening. Milk was still being delivered by horse-drawn wagon. And mushrooms were dependent upon the humus horse remnants and stall hay for successful spawning of the button type that Fred Rippon raised in the old icehouse. Once the mushroom house was Monteith's Icehouse. That's where ice off Lily Pond, at the tale end of winter, would stand thirty feet high in cut blocks amid a mix of insulating sawdust. Now a steam boiler, a-huffing and a-puffing, kept the temperature at 120 degrees Fahrenheit during mushroom crop growth. These days, they tell me, the whole process of raising mushrooms is computer-controlled, down to the critically required degree of heat and per cent of humidity.

The bottom box-wide doors of the contraption had been unpinned and dropped open. Usually the week's collection, from its own plunge at wet gravity, dropped without hesitation to the truck bed aligned under it. Stake sides of the truck were made taller by the insertion of high boarding. This morning the box load hadn't dropped. We tamped at the stubborn mass, jabbed it, forked it, and levered it with pitchforks angled against the edge of floor. We were grunts at grunt labor, straining muscles, trying not to breathe too deeply, but working in unison. Mule-stubborn, the horse manure would not find release. Perhaps it clutched unknown edges or was frozen against the sides of the metal box. The box was eight feet wide, eight feet deep, eight feet high, and angled steel held the box below and grasped it from above. During the week the barn sweepers cleaned the stalls and dropped wheelbarrows of manure into the box. Contracted for free, we took the detritus, a weekly chore for some select Saugus boys wanting cash on the barrelhead for a day's work. Generally it came on Saturday of a school week. The pleasant rides from one barn to the next had a routine. We told stories, drank cold Coca Cola or Royal Crown or Moxie from bottles. We filled in the passage by waving to girls, whistling, and singing. Waiting on us was some stinking hard work that left its residue odor upon the person.

Coming into Saugus Center one or more voices could be heard. They'd come from the steps of the Rathole Pool Hall or the front of the Slop Shop Diner or the doorway of McCarrier's Package Store. Sometimes they came in unison, always at a higher than ordinary octave.

"Hey, guys," they'd yell, "there go the shit kickers!" And with that yell there was lots of hand waving and pointing us out to general citizenry.

Pete, unfazed generally, now and then would yell out his window, "Go play with yourself, pal. I got *cash* in *my* pants!"

In the dead of winter he had initially taken me to the field in West Peabody, up the Newburyport Turnpike, westerly on Lake Street. Perhaps the day was at 25 degrees, though the Saturday sun was bright as a bottle top in the sky. I was thirteen, the newest hire. Rippling with young muscles ready for trying on hard labor, I yearned for coin in my pockets. Of the pile of manure there had been stories. It would steam no matter the temperature when worked on. You could strip to the waist in mid-winter toiling in the middle of it. Steam poured from it like an engine off the Saugus Linden Branch. Not as black as that cloud but as impure in odor and fetid thickness that rippled in the nose strong as a summer outhouse.

Pete was no harbinger of fairy tales.

"There are times, will be times, Tom, when you'll bust your ass working, but the pay is good. You can jingle your pockets at night. Even take my kid sister to the movies like you did the night we sicced the dog on you and he chased you all the way home. Shit, we laughed all night at that."

Pete roared with laughter as he drove the old Chevy truck up the Newburyport Turnpike.

I had never been there before, and Pete had said it flung itself, that pile, down the length of a field. It was as much as 150 feet long, he said. "Could be somewhat longer, spread its blackness ten to twelve feet wide, and loom four to five feet high at a glance. And black as Hades," he said. "Black as Hades."

It had a dark crust frozen over the length of it in winter. Some days it had to be chopped open, broken apart, with axes or sledges. Loose, it would be tossed into a spreader machine and fed other vermin- or pest-chasing materials, such as peroxide.

"Some pests, like flies, can ruin a whole crop," he told me, holding the wheel with one hand, sitting back like a teacher in class.

As he often did, he paused and looked me in the eye, and I knew that was a signal for one of his worldly observations.

"You don't have to know all that, but it takes a special will to work on it." Pause again. "I shit you none," he guffawed, "and it makes demands!"

And he could laugh at it all in that special way he had, possibly the art of suddenly putting unimportant things aside. Then, after a long moment of silence, he reflected more on the pile. It was as if he had spent time on its introduction, weighing all the possibilities, measuring portent or promise.

Then he said, "All that heat being held in just for us, just for that mid-winter steam bath. It seems like it's always waiting for us."

He said "us" collectively, and with some warmth. I liked that association and I suspected he was thinking about soon leaving it all behind. Many of our pals, neighborhood guys, slightly older, heroes before donning a uniform, were leaving us. In a hazy kind of celebration we'd learn ourselves only a few years later, Korea becoming a new word in our lexicon, we saw them off. There was a whole gang of us, mostly from the nearby neighborhoods. Some of us off the farms that still greened part of the town, and off both sides of the river shoe-lacing through our end of Saugus. We desperately wanted a few bucks in our pockets, or to bring it home to parents, the lessons of the Depression still etched on our souls.

Oh, the names. Stan and Kenny and Lonnie and Donald Green, of which Stan had his own mushroom house later on. Smiling Everett "Dingle" (last name lost forever but who could laugh from one end of the day to the other). Pete and Lennie and Charlie and Joe Tura who lived over against the edge of Vinegar Hill and who had a sister named Mildred. Don Ryder, who became a pretty fair boxer I fought with once and who was in Korea with me later on and was wounded and walked with a limp. (After his discharge, while working in Alaska, he saw poet friend Dan'l Shanahan addressing a letter to me and asked, "Is that Tom Sheehan from Saugus?") Charlie McMillan from the edge of the pond. Ussed Hashem from across the river opposite the First Iron Works of America and who was universally liked and had a great smile of white teeth in a dark face. Reliable George Cronin, who went in the Navy with Ussed and his own brother Larry and they had lost their cousin Joe Berrett in Burma. Berrett was a young, bruising giant of a kid I'll remember forever, with great wrists and who could throw a football about the length of Stackpole Field. Everett Jiggsy Woods and Wally Woods, whose brother Dick had a power boat on the pond. He also had a blue, propeller-driven iceboat that went like hell across the pond after telling skaters to clear the ice. Their future brother-in-law Alfred Trahan who married their sister Tessie. Charlie Lawrence with whom I had a long bout in the ring set up in Don Ryder's garage. A kid named Manuel also off the edge of the pond. He had dark eyes and a nice serious face and one day just disappeared out of my life like some of the others did, including tall and likable Bobby Lightizer. Bobby stepped out his front door one morning when I was walking the mile to school to tell me there was no school because it was 17 degrees below zero and hustled back inside.

They are all memorable, but of all the memories, I can see them most vividly at the pile of manure at Lake Street in West Peabody. Summer would be down on the top of us, or winter coming up out of the pile, the steam bathing us stripped to the waist and red as tissue paper. Or we'd be shoveling it into the back of one of Rippon's trucks or stomping it out of one of the milk company's huge collection boxes on the second floor of huge barns. Some days we carried into the mushroom house hundreds and hundreds of baskets of manure. The *substrate* I learned later on it was properly called, that the elite button mushrooms were to grow in. That and a top inch of sterilized loam we also hustled into place. Vermin and disease could raise hell with a mushroom crop. A crop could die. That happened too.

Life and hope and loss went on all around us, even as we spent our energies. We were thirteen- and fourteen- year old bodies coming of age. Coming with inordinate demands being made on us. Coming with the flow of grown-up mysteries. Coming with hair in the crotch and strange misty mornings that somehow started to rule our lives, or put credence into them.

One of those days the telegram from the War Department about Joe Berrett came. Fire Chief George Drew, in perhaps a draw of the cards, had ended up with the awful assignment of walking up front walks all around town to tell parents their sons had been wounded or killed in action against the enemy. How he must had dreaded those trips, yet he wore his white hat with the shiny black visor, and a single medal on his chest, and gold buttons down the front of his jacket. Joe's was one of those telegrams that sent a silence down a street of Saugus until the whispers gathered to a small storm in Saugus Center.

My early casualties, along with Joe Berrett, never let go. Not ever.

Yet mushrooms and horse shit continued to play a role for us. We'd have stripped the mushroom house in our work, or one section of the house, of all the mushroom beds. We would break down the beds built earlier, seven-beds high and each one about four feet wide. The planks and boards would be taken outside the house, cleaned, steamed and sterilized before being taken back into the house, and piled up for the next bed construction. For the new crop we'd set the first bed, then fill it with the warm compost, then set the second bed and fill it up, until we reached the top one.

The process consisted of preparing the manure or substrate compost in the beds We added spawn (you might call it seed) to it with a sterilized loam over the top of the manure about an inch thick. It had to be taken care of then for a number of weeks under the most suitable environmental conditions, until the mushroom crop was ready for harvest. The growing period often took eight or more weeks. The critical cultivation was completely independent of weather or seasonal changes. Temperature and humidity had to be carefully controlled for ultimate growth and reaping.

Our growing medium or compost was, as I've said, milk wagon horse manure. It did not come off the streets the way some gardeners in those days would walk out with a bucket and shovel to scoop up the droppings for small gardens. Weekly we cycled it out of the barns and added it to the pile, until the compost was ripe. Mushrooms do not contain chlorophyll and do not need sunlight for their nutrients. Their nutrients come from the organic matter in the compost, in this case the richness of treated horse manure. And they do not grow from seeds, but from microscopic spores, which are fungi, grown from mature mushrooms. After a matter of a couple of weeks, the spawn shows it has grown throughout the treated manure and looks like a thinly-veined network of white lace, called mycelium. It is actually the roots of the coming mushrooms. The beds, now covered by this veining, are topped with a layer of sterilized or pasteurized soil or loam which acts as a reservoir for moisture. The mycelium grows up through this last layer and forms white pins, which grow sometimes twice their size in 24 hours. They grow until the button mushrooms are ready for the knife, and the neat five-pound basket, and the market.

The walls of the mushroom house, the old Monteith Icehouse, of course, were nearly two feet thick. They were filled with an almost orange sawdust, providing the best known insulation for the time. It always makes me think of two closely related things; Sawyer's Icehouse at the other end of Lily Pond, where I worked one and only one winter, and my return from Korea where I had gone in my turn at departure.

But those days were our own glory days at Rippon's Mushroom House. We worked hard, sweated, were part of a force, the group effort, and had cash put into our hands at the end of the day. Part of that force moved off and away from us at regular intervals, bound for army fatigues or sailor blue or marine or flyer's gear.

And younger replacements came as we moved manure from the milk wagon barns to the field for the compost pile and mixing of peroxide to kill vermin and pests. Finally, after many turnings and aeration, we trucked it to the mushroom house where we filled and hauled and carried hundreds and hundreds of baskets of it inside.

In summer weather, the day of labor behind us, we'd often go fully clothed into Lily Pond off the remnants of the ice ramps. That's where ice floes once were hustled into the building when it was an old icehouse. There'd be hollering and noise and snapping of wet clothes in an attempt to rid them of the day's odors. Eventually we moved back into sopping dungarees and sneakers for the walk home.

Now and then we'd catch sight of a girl or two peeking at us from behind bushes and we'd vie to get their names. Some of us might have paid for that information. But we paraded like soldiers afterward, a day's work done. Our spirits ran high, and we marched joined, confederated, clubbed by our choice at labor. The shit kickers at payday, dropping coin onto the kitchen table. We pitched in while our older brothers were out there in all that noise we only heard in the newsreels of the State Theater. Or when a silence on one street would suddenly thunder down into the center of town. That happened after the fire chief got out of his car in front of some friend's house.

In June of 1952, after a year in Korea, I came home and was separated from the Army. The next month, at ten o'clock on the night before the Fourth of July, the mushroom house caught fire. Flames roared through the sides and came up through the roof as all that wall-packed sawdust exploded like canon shot.

When the roof imploded a huge ball of fire and smoke shot into the sky. Gutters and roof tops in Lynnhurst more than half a mile away caught fire. Alarms and sirens sounded everywhere. I sat on the peak of my parents' home watching the flames carry away lots of memories that have just started to come back. And I wonder about Bobby Lightizer and Manuel and Donny Ryder and where they are and what they are doing, and some of those other warm and memorable shit kickers who have passed on but are here remembered, for this moment at least.

Assault on Mount Carmel

It's just how I remember it on VJ Day. It was night, the war was over, the Pacific was quiet, and my brother soon on his way home. I was thumbing home from the next town with my cousin Warren in his Army uniform. Nobody gave us a ride, which pissed me off no end, him having run across Europe with Patton and that armored lance into Germany. All the way from Bastogne.

And the card game was still going on over on Mount Carmel Road, as it had been for the years of the war and many before that.

Mount Carmel Road was a quiet dead end street in the north section of Saugus, a little more than a half century ago. In the middle of the night when the noise in the Far East was over and the radios blared out the news, all the lights went on in all the houses on that blind street. Except where the card game was being played. Many of the neighbors were solidly indignant about the turn of events that VJ Night. Two Mount Carmel boys were among those who would not be coming back from the mad Pacific, which most of us had only seen in Saturday newsreels at the theater. The family living in that house now is unaware of its past. Tenants and landlords hardly leave scribed notations of a dwelling, thinking all things will ferment, dissipate, and eventually pass on. Fifty years or more of recall usually get dulled, terribly pockmarked, or fade into the twilight the way one ages. Dimming of the eyes proceeds, trouble arrives at the knees, a slow turn at mortality ensues. But I remember that night.

For nearly fifteen years at the gray house at the end of the road the big weekly poker game had been going on. All during the war it had been conducted behind thick black curtains that let out no light.

"They'll be no beacon trail markers from this game to the Navy Yard," a few miles distant, said Mountain Ben Capri. Mountain Ben, once an expert trapper and fishing guide, owned the house. He ran the game, and his wife, the Blackfoot named Dread Child Lovey, made sandwiches on occasion, poured drinks, and picked up loose change. That loose change would have paid some mortgages, for the stakes in the game were sometimes momentous. That was according to some neighbors on that dark cul-de-sac and other parties around town. A few people in town remembered when Mother Shannon had a shady place of business in the same abode, most of them elderly men. A few elderly wives or widows remembered Mother Shannon, too.

The only outsider allowed inside that coveted and dark setting was young and pesky Frankie Pike, high school football hero of some renown. They told me Frankie tried to sit in one night, but didn't have enough money so he asked to simply look on. In time, because of good humor and energy, Frankie became the company runner. He'd get special orders from the half dozen classy restaurants out on the turnpike. Or he'd hit the package store for beer, wine and hard stuff when necessary (ordinarily through the back door), or collared the best cigars in town. Often he directed unwanted players away from the game site. It was an occupation of sorts.

After a few games Frankie saw all the opportunities around him. With no flies on him from what I could see, he cut a deal with Smokey Carlton of Smokey's Diner. They would get a supply of bags, wrappers and boxes from the big restaurants and provide their own *specials*, as if the biggies had done the service. Smokey was glad to oblige, even though some of the town's big spenders and known tough guys took part in the game.

"They're all playing with somebody else's money anyway," Smokey would say if caught up for a reason.

Frankie, to up the kitty, even went to work at Gargan's Texan Hilltop Restaurant for two days. That was time enough to stash a supply of purloined imprinted bags and napkins out in the woods. I'd have to say that flies stayed off Frankie like he'd been sprayed with killer bug juice.

But Frankie and Smokey made a good deal, and they fooled the players with substitute foodstuffs. They prepared it right in the back of the small chintzy diner rather than buy it at one of the popular restaurants.

I heard Frankie giving Smokey the lowdown.

"I bring so much booze in there, Smokey," Frankie said, "that they're half drunk half the time and well drunk into the other half. That old lobster boater Cal Landers wants Hilltop sandwiches all the time. Now yours are as good as theirs are, only Cal don't know it seeing the Hilltop wrappers all the time. Some nights, I swear, they can't tell Grade A from swill. And I see DC Lovey scooping a bit of change every now and then, too. She puts the wet tray with booze and stuff right on the pot or on top of someone's stash and lets that old green paper stick to the bottom. There ain't no pesky bugs setting on that old mountain man either. Not the way he goes through coat pockets when no one's looking. Moves easy for a big man. Hate to have him tracking me down. I've seen him go outside and go through some of the cars more than a few times. Smooth he does it, like a ghost in the night, like maybe he heard special information during the game."

So the game went on, and in one quick night the war was over, that special August night. The whole town celebrated. Lights flashed on and off. A few stored up firecrackers or bottle rockets were set off. A lot of horns and sirens cut loose from long silences… except the house on Mount Carmel. Nobody went in and pulled a shade back. Nobody came out on the porch to see what was going on. The game was the thing. Only the game.

Warren and I heard about it that same night, tired from the long walk, still angry.

And it didn't sit well with a lot of people. I was all ears later on.

"Tell me, Frankie," Clint Wardley the undertaker said one night around the cracker barrel in the back of the package store, "what the hell makes you think they're such sacred cows in there?" Clint was always in a starched collar, locked into his trade. "They all come my way sooner or later," he often said. Nobody knew if Clint's words were promise or threat.

"I'll say this for those boyos," handsome Frankie Pike replied, "they're not afraid of anybody or anything 'cepting the game not getting its place of a Friday night. In the storm a couple of years ago that shut down the power for nearly a week, they had Mountain get Coleman lanterns and fire them all up. Mountain knows about those camp lamps and them little wicks he calls mantles. Like butterfly wings almost. Had three or four of them going he did, almost boiling the room away. Way I hear it, they talk about the game all week long. Who did what last game. Who can make the big fake and pull it off. Who's getting shit luck with his cards and when it began. I think they have a pool on when it runs out, each having some kind of turn at a losing streak. They heard the war was over and that was it. They wasn't in it and wasn't getting away from it."

Frankie's sense of timing was as good as an actor. His eyes collected and measured the audience.

"Jake Crews said he ain't celebrating people getting killed or not killed. His daddy came home from the Great Stink in France back in '18 all gassed up and not much of a father from then on. Said his old man never got laid again, even though the old lady was a laundry bag. Life just became a big sourball for him. Jake ought to know, him wearing the scars of it all, the only boy in that big house with that bad ass bastard. 'Cept for the game, he's been a loner his whole life. I'll tell you this," Frankie added, bringing football right back into the balance, putting it all in his own perspective, "I'd be comfortable with him across the huddle from me in a big game. He has that fire in his eye you don't always get, if you know what I mean." Frankie got them nodding as though they had the inside privy on certain players that "didn't bring it with them all the time the way Frankie did."

Frankie liked to sit in the back of McGarrihan's Package Store, around the wood stove puffing on a winter day. A dozen pair of boots were hoisted on the rim of the big iron stove. They all held forth with the other gabbers. They were the psuedo-historians, gossips, ward-heelers and petty politicians looking for the grip on someone, for rich gossip or a shared bottle they didn't have to pay for. Frankie shone there because of his football exploits, being, as many of them would say, "the best damn money player to come down the pike since Harmony Hiltz worked his magic at the stadium in the early Thirties, and then went up-country and played for Dartmouth College."

The players in the game were a cut from another life, the way it's told. Few of them had regular jobs yet always had a "piece" of some small operation. A jacket's inner pocket was an office. For most of them money spilled out of their pockets like an algae growing down inside with the lint. None of them carried money in a wallet. Rather they doled it out of thick clusters kept in the inner breast pocket of a jacket or in a shirt pocket under a sweater.

"They buy their chips with a wad of bills, ever last one of them, taking it out of an iron clip." Frankie said "iron" as if it were "eye-ron," bringing the boys deeper into the fold, getting real up-country homey with them. It was true old Yankee stuff he could get at when he had a mind to. Frankie had timing, if you know what I mean.

"How much money you think been showed in that room, Frankie, best lot?"

Andy Tolliver was a member of the school committee who never went to college, never could spell curriculum, but had a magic for trading off "one for you and one for me" when things got tight. He would feel undressed if he were caught without a bow tie. For twenty-six years he had been on the school committee. Andy, they all knew, could get anything in the system, from the mix of teachers, for those who wanted it bad enough. Including himself. Frankie had seen Andy pick up the new history teacher as she walked home late at night. Had seen it a four or five times, once waiting for two hours by her house before Andy dropped her off, just to see how things went. Now Andy wanted to know how much money was in that room at one time.

"Well," said Frankie, probably thinking Andy was at least twice as old as the new teacher and having a sudden admiration for him, curriculum or no curriculum, "one night, and this is the truth because I was able to count it out, there was over twelve thousand dollars in that room. Course," he added, the sparkle in his eyes, "some of that was loose change." The laughter was pleasant and a few of the listeners elbowed the guy beside them.

Andy's eyes lit up. "Twelve thousand dollars! My, God, that's almost the budget on raises for the next two-three years."

"Hell," Frankie said, "one night Mountain came back in from sniffing through the cars and leaned over Jud Duvall and whispered in his ear. They say Mountain told him someone had been fooling around his car. He has that Pierce Arrow with the big lights up on the fenders. So Jud went out and came back in with his sweater wrapped around something and kept it under his chair and Mountain was real nervous. I heard later Mountain had come across a stash of twenty-five thousand bucks and was scared to death of touching it. But he had to tell Jud some way. He didn't want to be pegged for grabbing it. Mountain knows Jud would have him dropped in the river for less."

But of all the guys who talked shop and whatever around the stove, it was Wolf Stearns who kept alive the VJ Night ignorance of the game players,. Every chance he could he'd go back to that dark and bright night. I'd seen Wolf's eyes light up more than once when the subject was opened, eyes light up and his lips get tight. One of the boys not coming back was Wolf's cousin, Edwin Talbot. Edwin was a Marine fighter pilot lost in the Solomon Seas on the day of his eleventh kill.

"Guess whose birthday is next Wednesday, guys? You couldn't guess in a hundred years, now could you? It's Eddie Talbot's birthday. The kid would be twenty-five years old next Wednesday. Do you think those dinks at the game give a shit? Not in a hundred years. They played all through the war and when it came stand up time they stayed behind the damn curtains. Never even came out on the porch to see what was going on, never mind saluting someone for a change."

Now *his* eyes made movies and darkened as if he were measuring an infinitesimal edge, like a wave of heat off the stovetop or another space unaccounted for. Now and then he dropped cautious tidbits like,

"Somebody ought to teach them a lesson or two. 'S'all I got to say about it."

Then Wolf would look again at a point in space none of the others hoped to find. Wolf had been around a lot and never left much trail about where he was or what he was after. He had scars here and there, on his cheeks, one on his wrist as if it had been ripped by barb wire. Perhaps on his back the way he scowled so much of the time, bitter angry, the world to be pissed on occasionally.

A few other men seemed to side up with Wolf but never got too vocal about it. Under the layers it was apparent that a means of revenge was swilling in the thicker cloth. Probably would come dark and mean, and naturally would have the backing of the whole of Saugus, loving its heroes to the death.

When it happened it was clean and quick. God, I wished I was there. So did cousin Warren. It was just after midnight. Mountain getting sleepy in one corner. Dread Child Lovey about done with her work and smoking a cigar. Frankie Pike's errands long over and ready to go home. The door burst open and four masked gunsmiths stood aiming their sawed-off shotguns at the players. Mountain rose from his seat and one of the gunsmiths hit him with a crow bar. Mountain smacked the floor like a pallet of concrete blocks. Dread Child Lovey continued to smoke her cigar, ignoring all the men in the room, never batting an eyelash.

Jud Duval, pivoting idly in his chair, said, "If I were you guys, I'd...." He said no more as the barrel of a shotgun was stuck in his mouth.

"There'll be no talking but us," said one of the masked men. "Rake it up, Three," he said, pointing to the players. "Empty their pockets, their money belts, their wallets. Clean out their jackets. Look under the chairs, too."

The leader heard Mountain groan and nodded to another gunsmith. "Hit him, Two." The man popped Mountain on the head again with the crow bar. Dread Child Lovey kept on smoking. Jud said that he noted the men were all in sweat suits and sneakers. The sweepdown was complete in every sense. Every coin, every bit of currency in the room including the entire cash drawer kept by Mountain and Dread Child Lovey, was scooped up. All of it was placed in a black bag that looked like a doctor's bag.

Frankie, fidgeting, started to move, looking to get to a door, but was jabbed in the backside by one of the gun wielders.

"Uh, uh, kid, we need you. You're gonna be a bit of security for us. Hostage stuff. You're gonna earn your keep this night, hero."

The guy turned to the card players and said, "One bad word outta any you guys, we knock off the kid. We're taking him with us. Don't nobody move around or scream until the big guy wakes up, and I'd be real gentle about that. That's gonna be one pissed-off big gent."

One of the gunsmiths opened a door to a small pantry and motioned all the players and Dread Child Lovey into the soon-crowded space. The door was slammed behind them and a couple of spikes were hammered into the door and the jamb. Silence came. Darkness set about everything, falling like clouds on top of Mountain who was out of it for almost another hour. Later it was said a couple of the players copped a few feels of Dread Child Lovey. She never batted an eyelash then or said a word in that small crowded room. Mountain was really upset when he finally woke up and freed the players and his wife from the pantry, because he found her underpants on the floor.

Mountain was like old Mountain, ranting and raving and carrying on like a wounded bear. Every one of the players he marked with a terrible eye, cowing them right out of his house as if a curse had been placed on them.

Two days later the police gave up the search for kidnapped Frankie Pike when he walked back into town. A couple of angry marks sat on his face, but he was healthy as ever otherwise. Mountain never had another game at his house. The players, after a break of a few weeks, found a new place to play, in the back of Tal Rumson's boathouse.

And Frankie Pike walked with a jingle and a tingle in his pockets and was never out of coin for the whole next year. But nobody did anything about it. They figured the players had finally paid their real dues for not standing to when they should have, that VJ Night so long ago, the night my cousin and I couldn't get a ride.

Parkie, Tanker, Tiger of Tobruk

Hardly with a hop, skip and a jump did Frank Parkinson come home from Tobruk, Egypt, North Africa, madness, World War II in general. A lot of pit stops were made along the way where delicate-handed surgeons and associates did their very best to get him back into working order. From practically every vantage thereafter we never saw, facially or bodily, any scar, bunching of flesh, major or minor skin disturbance. There was no permanent redness, no welts as part of his features, no thin and faintly visible testaments to a doctor's faulty hand or to the enemy's angry fragmentation. For sure, it was as if he were the ultimate and perfect patient, the great recovery, the risen Lazarus.

But he was different, it was easy to see, by a whole long shot.

Parkie. Tanker. Tiger of Tobruk.

It was the end of some trying times for my friend. One lazy afternoon we sat looking over the sun looking over Lily Pond, and I noted some things about him for the first time. A redness glared on the pond's face as bright as an ache. This was the pond face we had skated on for almost twenty years. Here we had whipped the long hand-held whip line of us and our friends screaming and wind-blown toward the frosted shore on countless coffee and cider evenings. That afternoon I realized Parkie had come home to die.

The September sun was on for a short stay. We had bagged a dozen bottles of beer and laid them easily down in the pond, watching a flotilla of pickerel poking slowly about when the sediment settled. Their shadowy thinness pointed, like inert submarines or torpedoes, at the bags.

Our differences were obvious, though we did not speak of them. The sands of North Africa had clutched at him and almost taken him. Off a mountain in Korea I had come with my feet nearly frozen. Under skin they often felt like graceless pieces of marble, thinking they might have been blown off the same quarry where unknown sculptors had once farmed torsos.

I had kept no souvenirs, especially none of Korea and its craggy mountains, and had seen nothing of his memento scenery. But once I saw a pair of tanker goggles hanging like an outsize Rosary on the post of his bed at Dutch Siciliano's garage. That's where he roomed on the second floor, in three small rooms, dusty and cluttered and strongly odored. You could smell oil and grease from below. You'd swear along with them you could smell acid-like cosmoline and spent gunpowder. It was like the residue of a convoy's passing still hanging in the air, telling of itself at the nostrils with sharp reminders, rising right through the floorboards.

Most of us left our wars behind us. As much as we could. But with Parkie it was different...pieces of it hung on as if they were on for the long ride. I don't mean that he was a flag waver or mufti hero, now that he was out of uniform. But the whole war kept coming back to him in ways he had no control over. There are people to whom such things befall. They don't choose them, that's for sure, but it's as if they somehow get appointed for all the attendant crap life gets filled with.

And Parkie had no control over the visitations.

I don't know how many times we had been sitting in the Angels' Club, hanging out, the big booms long down the tubes, when someone from Parkie's old outfit would show up out of the blue. It was like Lamont Cranston appearing from the shadows. There'd be a guy standing at the door looking in and we'd all notice him, and then his eyes and Parkie's eyes'd lock. Recognition was instant; reaction was slower, as if neither one believed what he was seeing. There would be a quiet acceptance of the other's presence. They'd draw their heads together and have a beer in a corner. Parkie, as sort of an announcement, would speak to no one in particular and the whole room in general, "This guy was with me in North Africa."

He never gave a name. All of them were odd lots, all of them. They were thin like Parkie, drawn in the face, little shoulders and long arms, nervous, itchy, wearing that same darkness in the eyes. A sum of darkness you'd think was too much for one man to carry. They would hang on for days at a time, holing up some place, sometimes at Parkie's and sometimes elsewhere. They'd drink up a storm, carouse, and one morning the stranger would be gone and never seen again. Some guys said a ritual had taken place. A solemn ritual. Apparitions almost from the slippery darkness! Dark-eyed. The nameless out of North Africa and whatever other place they had been to and come from. Noble wanderers, it seemed, but nameless, rankless, placeless, itinerants.

Parkie never got a card or a letter from any one of them. Never a phone call. Nothing. He never mentioned them after they were gone. That, to me, was notice he knew they would never be back. It was like a date had been kept, a vow paid off. It wasn't at all like "We'll meet at Trafalgar Square after the war, or Times Square, or under the clock at The Ritz." Not at all. The sadness of it hit me solidly, frontally. I had had some good buddies, guy's I'd be tickled to death to see again if they walked in just like his pals did, and I knew that I'd never see them again. Things were like that, cut and dried like adobe, a place and a job in the world and you couldn't cry about it. Part of the fine-tuned fatalism that grows in your bones, becomes part of you, core deep, gut deep.

The sun's redness shivered under the breeze. Pickerel nosed at the bags. The beer cooled. Parkie sipped at a bottle, his eyes dark and locked on the pond, seeing something I hadn't seen, I guess. The long hatchet-like face, the full-blown Indian complexion he owed great allegiance to, made his dark visage darker than it might have been. With parted lips his teeth showed long and off-white or slightly yellowed, real incisors in a deep-red gum line. On a smooth gray rock he sat with his heels jammed up under his butt, the redness still locked in his eyes. Like some long-gone Chief, I thought, locked in meditation of the spirits.

For a long while he was distant, who knows where, in what guise and in what act, out of touch. This really wasn't that unusual with him before, and surely wasn't now, since his return. Actually it was a little eerie, this sudden transport, but a lot of things had become eerie with Parkie around. He didn't like being indoors for too long a stretch. He craved fresh air and walked a lot, and must have worn his own path around the pond. It went through the alders, then through the clump of birch that some nights looked like ghosts at attention. It coursed down along the edge where all the kids fished for kibby and sunfish, then over the knoll at the end of the pond. There you'd go out of sight for maybe five minutes of a walk, and then it went down along the near shore and came up to the Angels' where we hung out.

Most of the guys said when you couldn't locate Parkie, you knew where to find him.

He talked to me from his crouch, the bottle in his hand catching the sun, his eyes as dark as ever in their deep contrast.

"Remember that Kirby kid, Ellen Kirby. When we pulled her out of the channel on Christmas vacation in her snowsuit and she kept skating around for a couple of hours, afraid to go home? We saved her for nothing, it seems, but for another try at it. I heard she drowned in a lake in Maine January of the year I went away. Like she never learned anything at all."

Parkie hadn't taken his eyes off the pond. Stillness still trying to take hold of him. He sipped and sipped and finally drank off the bottle and reached into the water for another. The pickerel force moved away as quickly as minnows.

Their quickness seemed to make fun of our inertia. If there was a clock handy, I knew its hands would be moving, the ticking going on, but I seriously wouldn't bet on it. We seemed to be holding our collected breath. The sun froze itself on the water's face, the slightest breath of wind held itself off. There was no ticking, no bells, no alarms, no sudden disturbances in the air, no more war, and no passage of time. For a moment at least we hung at breathlessness and eternity. We were, as Parkie had said on more than one occasion, "Down-in deep counting the bones in ourselves, trying to get literate."

"We just got her ready to die at another time." The church key opener in his hand pried at the bottle cap as slow as a crowbar and permitted a slight "pop." He palmed the cap in his hand and shook it like half a dice set and skipped it across the redness. The deliberate things he did came off as code transmissions. I had spent hours trying to read what kind of message was being carried along by them. They did not clamor for attention, but if you were only barely alert you knew something was cooking in him.

"You might not believe it," I said, "but I thought of her when I was in Korea and swore my ass was ice. I remember how she skated around after we pulled her out with that gray-green snowsuit on and the old pilot's cap on her head. She had the flaps down over her ears and the goggles against her eyes and the ice was like a clear, fine lacquer all over her clothes. I thought she was going to freeze standing up right on the pond."

Parkie said, "I used to think about the pond a lot when I was in the desert. At Tobruk. At Al Shar-Efan. At The Sod Oasis. At all the dry holes along the way. But it was always summer and fishing and swimming and going bare ass off the rock at midnight or two or three in the morning on some hot-ass August night. Those nights we couldn't sleep and sneaked out of the house. Remember how Gracie slipped into the pond that night and slipped out of her bathing suit and hung it up on a spike on the raft? Remember how she told us she was going to teach us everything we'd ever need to know?"

His head nodded two or three times, accenting its own movement, making a grand pronouncement. The recall was just as tender and just as complete as that long-ago compelling night. He sipped at the bottle again, and tried to look through its amber passage, dark eyes meeting dark obstacles of more than one sort. As much a fortuneteller he looked, peeking into life.

All across the pond a stillness made itself known, a stillness as pure as any I've known. I don't know what he saw in the amber fluid, but it couldn't have been anything he hadn't seen before.

I just got the feeling it was nothing different.

When I called him Frank he looked at me squarely. His thick black brows lifted like chunks of punctuation, his mouth formed an Oh of more punctuation, both of us suddenly serious. It had always been that way with us, the reliance on the more proper name to pull a halt to what was about us, or explain what was about us. He drank off a heavy draught of beer, his Adam's apple flopping on his thin neck. The picture of a turkey wattle came uneasily to mind, making me feel slightly ridiculous, and slightly embarrassed. Frank was an announcement of sorts, a declaration that a change, no matter subtle or not, was being introduced into our conversation. It was not as serious as Francis but it was serious enough.

His comrades from North Africa, as always, had intrigued me. On a number of instances I had searched in imagination's land for stories that might lie there waiting to get plowed up. Nothing I had turned over had come anywhere close to reality, or the terrors I had known in my own stead. No rubble. No chaff. No field residue.

Perhaps Parkie had seen something in that last bottle, something swimming about in the amber liquid, or something just on the other side of it. He turned to me and said, "I think you want to know about my friends who visit, my friends from North Africa, from my tank outfit. I never told you their names because their names are not important. Where they come from or where they are going is not important either. That information would mean nothing to you."

For the moment the silence was accepted by both of us.

Across the stretch of water the sun was making its last retreat of the day. A quick grasp of reflection hung for a bare second on the face of the pond. It leaped off somewhere as if shot, past the worm-curled roots, a minute but energized flash darting into the trees. Then it was gone, absolutely gone. None of it yet curled round a branch or root. And no evidence of it lay about… except for the life it had given sustenance to, had maintained at all levels. It was like the shutter of a camera had opened and closed at its own speed.

Parkie acknowledged that disappearance with a slight nod of his head. An additional twist was there. It was obvious he saw the darkness coming on even before it gathered itself to call on us. I thought another kind of clock ticked for him, a clock of a far different dimension. He was still chipping away at what had been his old self. That came home clean as a desert bone; but where he was taking it all was as much mystery as ever.

The beer, though, was making sly headway, the beer and stillness, and the companionship we had shared over the years. The mystery of the sun's quick disappearance played with what we knew of the horizon, the thin edge of warmth it left behind. And it played with all those strange comrades of his. They had stood in the doorway of the Angel's Club, framed as they were by the nowhere they had come from, almost purposeless in their missions. They too had been of dark visage. They too were lank and thin and narrow in the shoulder. They too were scored by that same pit of infinity locked deeply in their eyes. They were not haggard, but they were deep. I knew twin brothers who were not as close to their own core the same way these men were. These men had obviously leaned their souls entirely on some common element in their lives. I did not find it as intense even with reconnected battle brothers who had lain in the same hole with me while the Chinese used old German 76'ers. Not even when the shells screamed and slammed overhead and all around us, the shrapnel routed in the awful trajectories.

The flotilla of pickerel nosed against the bags of beer. Parkie's Adam's apple bobbed on his thin neck. He began slowly, all that long reserve suddenly beginning to fall away.

"We were behind German lines, but had no idea how we got there. We ran out of gas in a low crater and threw some canvas against the sides of the three tanks that had been left after our last battle. If we could keep out of sight, sort of camouflaged, we might have a chance. It got cold that night. We had little food, little water, little ammo, and no gas. It was best, we thought, to wait out our chances. If we didn't know where we were, perhaps the Jerries wouldn't know either. Sixteen

110

of us were there. We had lost a lot of tanks, had our
butts kicked."

He wasn't dramatizing anything, you could tell.
It was coming as straight as he could make it. Whatever
was coming, though, had to be pretty wild, or
exorbitant, or eerie or, indeed, inhuman. The last option
came home pretty cold to me. The hair on the back of
my neck told me so.

"We woke up in the false dawn and they were
all around us. Fish in the bottom of the tank is what we
were. No two ways about it. Plain, all-out fish lying
there, as flat as those pickerel. They took us without a
shot being fired. Took us like babies in the pram."

"All day they questioned us. One guy was an SS
guy. A real mean son of a bitch if you ever met one.
Once I spit at him and he jammed me with a rifle barrel
I swear six inches deep. Ten times he must have kicked
me in the guts. Ten times! I couldn't get to his throat,
I'd've taken him with me. They stripped our tanks,
what was left in them. That night they pushed us into
our tanks. I saw the flash of a torch through one of the
gun holes. You could hear a generator working nearby.
Something was crackling and blistering on the hull or
the turret top. Blue light jumped every which way
through the gun holes. It was getting hot. Then I
realized the sounds and smells and weird lights were
welding rods being burned. The sons of bitches were
welding us inside our own tanks. A hell of a lot of
arguing and screaming was going on outside us. The
light went flashing on and off, like a strobe light, if you
know what I mean. Blue and white. Blue and white. Off
and on. Off and on. But no real terror yet. Not until we
heard the roar of a huge diesel engine. And the sound of
it getting louder. And then came scraping and brushing
against the sides of our tanks. Sand began to seep
through the gun holes and peep sights. The sons of
bitches were burying us in our own tanks! All I could

see was that rotten SS bastard smiling down at us. I saw his little mustache and his pale green eyes and his red nose and a smile the devil must have created. And his shining crow-black boots."

I couldn't talk. I couldn't ask him a question. A stunned sensation swept clean through me. First, disbelief, a surging block of disbelief, as if my veins had frozen in place. The dark pit in his eyes could be read; the darkness inside the tank, the utter, inhuman darkness that had become part of Parkie and part of his comrades. The imagined sense of it hit me slowly. It crept within me. I knew a sudden likeness to that feeling. It was peering over the edge of a high place. The ground would rush up to meet me and then fall away. The long descent, the torturous fall, would become part of me...in the veins, in the mind. A shiver ran through every part of my body. And then hate welled in me, stark, naked, unadorned hate, hate of the vilest kind.

Parkie put his hand on my knee. His grip was hard.

"I never wanted to tell you, none of you. We all had our thing. You had yours. I had mine. I'm so sorry your feet are screwed up. I wish nothing had happened to you. But a lot of guys've had worse."

"What happened?" I said, letting his hand carry most of his message, letting my own small miseries fall away as if they did not exist. Not by comparison anyway. My feet had iced up practically in my sleep. I knew the ignoble difference.

"The sand was almost over all the tank, and the noise inside the tank started. Screaming and cursing and crying. Cries like you never heard in your life. Godawful cries. I know I never heard anything like them. And coming out of guys I'd known a long time, tough guys, valiant guys, guys with balls who had gone on the line for me. I heard some of them call for their

112

mothers. There was screaming, and then whimpering and then screaming again. And curses! My God, curses that would raise the friggin' dead. The most unholy of curses. Everything dead and unholy and illegitimate raised from wherever they were being brought against the Germans and that little SS bastard. He was castrated and ripped and damned and denounced to the fires of hell. You have not heard profanity and terror and utter and absolute hatred all in one voice at the same time. The volume was turned way up. It filled the tank. It filled that makeshift and permanent vault. And it filled our useless and agonized banging barehanded against the hull of the tank. Knuckles and fists and back-handers against the steel. And the outside noise drowning all of it out."

I was still reeling, kept shaking my head, kept feeling the old glacier-like ice in my veins. And the heat of hatred coexisted with that ice. I was a mass of contradictions. Parkie kept squeezing my knee. The pickerel kept nosing the bags, hung up in their own world of silence. Silence extended itself to the whole of Earth. The quiet out there, the final and eventual quiet out there, after the war, was all around us.

"Suddenly," he continued, "there was nothing. The sand stopped its brushing and grating against the steel of the tank. Then the diesel noise grew louder, as if it was coming right through us. And powerful thrusts came banging at the tank. I didn't know what it was. And then we were being shoved and shaken, the whole structure. And I heard curses from outside and a lot of German on the air, and we seemed to be moving away from our hole in the ground. Whatever it was was pushing at us. And then it went away and we heard the same banging and grinding and grunting of the engine nearby. Then the blue and white light again as a torch burned around us and the tank heated up, and lots of screaming but all of it German. And there were more engine noises and more banging and smashing of big bodies of steel. Finally the turret was opened and we were hauled out and canteens shoved in our faces and the other tanks were being opened up and guys scrambling out, some of them still crying and screaming and cursing everything around them."

He reached for the last bottle in one of the bags. The bag began to drift slowly away in wavy pieces. The pickerel had gone. The bottle cap snapped off in his hand. I thought of the tank's turret top being snapped open, the rush of clean air filling his lungs, a new light in his eyes.

"Then I saw him," Parkie said. "The minute I saw him I knew who he was. General Rommel. He was looking at us. He looked me right in the eye, straight and true and bone-steady and no shit at all in it. I didn't think he was breathing, he was so still. But I read him right off the bat. The whole being of that man was right in his eyes. He shook his head and uttered a cry I can't repeat. Then he took a pistol from another guy, maybe his driver, a skinny itchy little guy, and just shot that miserable SS son of a bitch right between the eyes as he stood in front of him. Shot him like he was the high executioner himself; no deliberation, no second thought, no pause in his movement. Bang! One shot heard round the world if you really think about it. He screamed something in German as if it were at the whole German army itself, each and every man of it. Perhaps it was lifted to whatever God he might have believed in because it was so loud, so unearthly. Then he just walked off toward a personnel carrier, not looking at us anymore or the SS guy on the ground, a nice-sized hole in his forehead."

He drained off the last bottle. He mouthed the taste of it for a while and wet his lips a few times. I thought he was remembering the dry sands, the heat, the embarrassed German general walking away on the desert. Or this parched earth being an ultimate graveyard for so many men, for so many dreams.

"They gave us water and food, the Germans did. One of them brought up one of our own jeeps. It was beat to hell, but it was working. One German major, keeping his head down, his eyes on the sand, not looking at us, pointed off across the sand. We started out, the sixteen of us, some walking, some riding, some still crying or whimpering. Some still cursing. The next day we met some Brits. They brought us to their headquarters company. We were returned to our outfit. Some guys, of course, didn't get to go back on line, but were sent home as head cases. Can't blame them for that. I kept thinking about General Rommel, kept seeing his eyes in my mind. I can see the Germans now, the look on their faces, the shame that was in them. It was absolute, that shame, and he knew we knew. It was something he couldn't talk about, I bet. If he could have talked to us, we might have been taken to one of their prison camps. But he knew he couldn't do that to us. Make amends is what he had to do. He had to give us another chance. Just like we gave Ellen Kirby another chance at drowning."

In his short flight he had circled all the way back to the Kirby circumstance and all that played with it.

Frankie Parkinson, tanker, survivor of Tobruk and other places in the northern horrors of Africa, who walked away from death in the sand on more than one occasion. Parkie, who might be called Rommel's last known foe, who rolled over three cars on U.S. Route 1 and waged six major and distinct bouts with John Barleycorn thereafter in his time. He was a man who got to know the insidious trek of cancer in his slight frame. I loved him more than any comrade that had shared a hole with me. He hurt practically every day of his life after his return from Africa, and hung on for twenty-five more torturous and tumultuous and mind-driven years. They found him one night at the far end of the pond when nobody knew where he was for two days. A handful of damp earth was squeezed into one fist, and the metal crypt, perhaps, was long gone, just as perhaps were the days of Africa.

Wingsy

Long and lanky and always of a dark eye, ever adept at study of any kind, Wingsy held a broad maple leaf aloft. His fine fingers at the end of one long thin arm held the leaf against an angle of penetrating August sunlight. To a young friend he pointed out the webbing of shadowed filaments. As he pointed out the leafy veins, he spoke in an instructive manner, yet indirectly, as if for the moment he had but half interest. This was somewhat unlike him. *Interest* was something he had a facility of generating, no matter the subject.

From my vantage I watched, perched on the fence rail above the dry culvert across from the State Theater. The Lone Ranger serial was coming for the fifteenth and final time that summer of 1938. It was New England quiet, America quiet, practically all of Europe finally beginning to scratch itself awake. I felt a small surge of uneasiness pass through a span of intelligence within me. It almost assumed matter in its surge, like dough cranked up with yeast. I'd recall it a number of times over the years, looking at it differently at times, as if something had been partially decoded. Almost handed to me in its bare essence, but not quite. Wingsy was never easy to handle, and he talked a lot but only to a few close friends:

If you really want to know, I suppose I'll have to explain it all to you, but you have to pay attention all the time. Don't dare relax! Don't turn your head away for the least second! You get nothing free if you don't want to know about it. Nobody else will care what you find inside a leaf or on a mountaintop for all that matter. And they'll poke fun at you if you stick at it, but they'll never know what you know, not in a thousand years, because they are not open to it. I'll tell you about a leaf and all its parts.I'll tell you about magic and photosynthesis and a hundred other things you just haven't got the hang of yet. You'll begin to realize there's a whole other world around us that you haven't seen yet, not a whisker of it, and they'll never trespass upon it. And don't ever pretend that it's NOT important to you. Don't ever quit on it, no matter what they do to try to upset you and not learn what they can't learn.

I watched him giving his version of a miracle to a much shorter friend with thick glasses, a thick bush of red hair and a sweater too heavy for the day. But it certainly was heavy enough to speak of a mother's overdressing hand.

Nature's miracles, no matter the size or the impact, had no better advocate than Hugh (Wingsy) Menzies. He was the promise that staid and trite biology teachers, caught between mediocrity and the languid, waited for. He was the new chance they dreamed about. The teachers needed a protégé to thrust between their chlorophyll and Bunsen burners, to post as armor against every passerby or commentator on the scene.

Wingsy, taller than average, average weight, but with an eye twisted on interest, was a stick-out in any crowd. He was so in any classroom, in any gang of kids hanging on a corner or sitting under a park pavilion with the rain lolling around as company. His name came from the size and span of his ears. We had exclaimed about them ("membranous" and not too kindly if you must know the truth) from the first day in school. They were enormous ears that also showed a webbing of veins under the scrutiny of sunlight that plied its ways beneath his pale skin. His ears conjured up images of wind and sail, or, more likely, a hawk on an upper and mysterious trail of passing air. We'd have called him *Teddy Thermal* if we could have thought of it.

Thin, dark-haired, forehead jutting up as a scarp into that dark hair, he had a long nose the target of every winter season. His eyes seemed at once cool and penetrating in their grayness. Wingsy came off all in one shot as studious, quiet, lots of reserve in his backpack, and especially clumsy. (All right, we called him oafish, if you must know). He didn't join us in any of our hell raisin' games that had ball, bat or basket. All that time gasping for air was hardly worth the energy put into it. There were graces one didn't have to attain because they didn't amount to much in the end anyhow. If you must know, we didn't treat Wingsy the same way we treated ourselves. He was target and scapegoat of much that we did and didn't do. He was an outlet.

We found ourselves awed both by his interests and his aloofness, a sort of distance he managed any time it was required. Detaching himself from us and our stand in the world, he put us in our places. Stare right on through you he could like an engineer aiming his train down the merging tracks coming to the far juncture. The distant merger of lines was out there, and there simply was no other target. It was armor and protection we had no clue about.

You can kid me all you want, poke fun for all that matter, even call me names whose roots you couldn't even begin to trace. Or throw me to the best of the wolves in and around you. But it would never hold me back, not from what I'm reaching for. You couldn't begin to believe what triggers me, what lingers in me, what crooks its small finger at me every living hour, every breath in me! You run across this field of grass in your timeless games and you never have even the slightest idea that this grass span gives off enough oxygen to keep ten people alive for a whole day! Ten

119

people, mind you, who might otherwise be left airless. Ten people! Five sets of your parents, doting all day on each of you. Or all the Flaverty's in one fell swoop on their knees begging for air that might begin on Stackpole Field. Or Shirley Majors and nine of her handmaid classmates. Now wouldn't THAT make a difference in your lives!

Once, at the edge of Lily Pond, I saw Wingsy poring over the structure of a cat-o-nine tails. Standing in his hand as brown as a cigar or a rocket left over from the Fourth, its face and tail burned with harsh expression. He must have pushed himself through the edge of the swampy area to get it. His pants were covered with slime and muck and he held the blunt creature like it was a prize relic retrieved from a medieval site. Dark and missile-looking, the cat-o-nine did not look out of place in his hands. Rather, it came off as a laboratory piece at common perusal. As he showed it to a friend of the same age, Kendall Tucker, he spoke so that I could not hear, a mumbo-jumbo I was convinced was poking some kind of fun at me.

He won't bother us, not when he's alone, not when the others aren't here to join his cause. He'll just sit there on that log, not knowing it houses a snake's family, because he's leery of THIS.

He held the cat-o-nine aloft again, higher, against the sun.

He thinks I'm telling you all about this, what it's for, how it came, that I know all about it. But it's next on the list to find out about. Right now it's just armor against him, against his ignorance, against his know-it-all attitude. He really thinks I know EVERYTHING, and I'm going to keep him thinking that way, keeping things

*in place. In class once I was telling the teacher, Miss
Voss, about an internal combustion engine, the kind his
own uncle works on. I could see in his eyes he wished
he knew what I knew and could talk to his uncle about it.
You could see he would have busted a gut to be able to
talk about pistons and cams and magnetos. But I think
those other guys would beat the hell out of him if he got
too much like me, like us. We know better, don't we?
How we can fill the mind up and there's still room for
the whole universe in there, all the names of stars old
and new and planets yet to come, and satellites we
haven't heard about yet. For a lot of our time we'll be
on the edge in one way, but on the other side we'll be
deep in knowing.*

I should have challenged him the way he looked
back at me a couple of times, but it would not be a fair
fight. He stood in the sunlight like a spare limb torn
prematurely from one of the alders lining the shore of
the pond. He looked bland and sort of neuter, as if
nothing important was ever going to happen around him.
A bare breeze trickled in his hair. Appeared colorless he
did even in the sunlight. But I should have known better.
Odds and chances always work against supposition.

As I turned away and walked through the brush,
bristles caught hold of me as if something was trying to
keep me in place. Something not speakable. I carried
the stark picture of him in my mind. Not ten feet into
that mat of underbrush, I heard Kendall Tucker cry for
help. They were half-hearted yaps at first, as at games,
and then a full-throated terrified scream.

I tore back through the brush. I expected to see
Wingsy beating on little Kendall, the long thin arms
raised over him and coming down on him with
tempered blows. But Wingsy was erect and still at the
edge of the swampy part of the pond. And Kendall
Tucker was standing up to his waist in water and muck,

struggling to get back to shore. Wingsy stood frozen in place, staring at his friend, or through him, or rapt at some other enterprise I couldn't reach.

"It's quicksand, Wingsy!" Kendall screamed. "Help me! Help me!" The more he struggled, the less he seemed to move, appearing as if his feet indeed were locked in the terrifying grip of quicksand.

"Wingsy! Wingsy!" he pleaded, not knowing there was no quicksand any place around us.

I raced toward them, however, the struggling and terrified Kendall Tucker and Hugh Menzies standing as if he had been frozen in place. A long thick branch, long since dead, had hung itself almost upright in a thicket of brush. I grabbed at it as I ran by. At once a thorn of the bush and a long knife-like sliver of the limb ran themselves as a pair into the wrist of my right arm, announcing sharply on nerve ends. Out over the six or seven feet of water and muck I dropped the branch in front of Kendall. I yelled to him to grab it. I pulled him to shore, not without some struggle on my own part, the pain shooting in my arm from the coarse incisions. Hugh Menzies did not move a muscle. Not one finger did he lift to help me. And when Kendall was safe ashore, drenched, sobbing, staring at Wingsy as if he hated him forever, the apt and studious companion remained trance-like in his place. His eyes were dull, glassed over. His mouth was stuck open, his hands, the long hands and the long fingers, remained stationary at his side. He hadn't even flinched.

I screamed at him. "What the hell's wrong with you, Wingsy?"

Kendall had fallen in a clump at my feet and was bawling his eyes out, shaking like a dog just out of water. That's when I first saw something else in Wingsy that maybe nobody else had seen. What it was I couldn't put a name on. It beat about him with a scent I could almost smell or a magnetic field flowing off an awed core and was working its way all around him.

I grabbed his arm and was surprised how hard that thin arm felt. It was vise-gripped, heavy of tendons, locked as tight as a clock spring at the first tick.

"What's wrong, Wingsy? Why didn't you help him? He could have drowned!"

Words spit a torrent from my mouth. His arm remained stiff, long and angular and stiff. His mouth stayed ajar. The glassy stare of his eyes was still in place, searching for something, or having found it, found it as detestable as it must have been.

For the first time I noticed the skin on his face. It clung like veneer to the skeletal structure, stretching onto every inch of bone, taking on a near-satin finish in the frantic clutch. A small knob showed on one side of his jaw like a pea alone in a shell. It pulled tautly at the corners of his eyes after the fashion of mannequins. The earliest hint of hair, a down on his upper lip, caught on sunlight, and showed a golden curl curled over on itself. Almost angelic, but not! Then, in a brace of time where we measure things, coming at us or moving away, messages carried. They tipped our lives out of the very ordinary. And I was suddenly aware that darkness and light were at concert. Wingsy stood for a moment in a deep shadow against the sunlight, or the sunlight itself fell about his long thin frame as though peeled and spared for this dark, omnipresent image. It was a terrific shot I received, blue-belted, ion-charged, letting all the old pap and cream of wheat go its neutral way, all the soft crap of mediocrity.

Then I smelled the sweat, or whatever exuded from him, a rough odor I had not encountered before. A new identity, a new recognition, a new state of affairs, started up. High it came, almost crystal on the air but not quite up to that clarity. More than image in being was a message demanding to be decoded, to be read, if the capability was within me to do so. What did leap out at me was that he appeared dark, cool, enigmatic, and all that at once. Yet the sun continued about him wildly in its heat waves. The shimmering taking place made the puzzle much darker in spite of itself. He was an awed boy in an awed atmosphere, a peer but not a peer, or seemed not to be so.

I don't know how many times later on I thought about that day. Following me like a bad dream not letting go, it stayed through the rest of the year. A sudden flurry of any kind of dark activity, any image, would bring it back full force. It slipped into mornings and evenings with equal force, not particular in its approach. Bounced it did from a leaf falling across the sky or a cat-o-nine ready to take off like a July rocket. Or its shadow leaned in a copse, almost saying his name, and with it whatever insights I thought I had about Wingsy. A lot of times I thought about it but never a clear revelation penetrated the bunch.

Oh, the year moved on. I saw Wingsy a lot, close at times but mostly from a distance, the stick of him, the lean shadow. He was a slim sword against an evening sunset. His hair was black and wind-tossed, eyes sunken with Atlantic gray, and his nose grasping for what caricature loomed doubly within it. Sometimes he was radiant with the sun around him and a leaf in his hand aloft to its grasp. Always he wore a gray nondescript jacket with big pockets whose contents one would die to learn about. I'd be in the line for a theater ticket (a huge dime in those days), sucking away on a sherbet cup, fingering two cents worth of candy and lint in my pocket. And there'd be Wingsy down the Linden Branch railroad tracks putting slugs on the silver rails before the Lynn-Boston slicker came pounding through. Or he'd be off on the edge of Riverside Cemetery beside the stream and the parallel tracks where cat-o-nines stood ten feet tall. Him and them both throwing the longest shadows, spears to the last of them, nature's armory standing at attention. I'd see him and think about that day at the pond and shivers would run right on through me, two fingers right in the open socket. And I never knew what it was. Except that it was eerie, like something boded, formulated, and waiting to happen. Jarred, perhaps, but ready to be freed.

It was slightly less than a year later when a fire broke out in the Odd Fellows Hall in the square. Great columns of black smoke rose as though two fires burned. I could smell the asphalt shingles burning way down past the park. When I rushed into the square, the fire was clawing its way through that grand old building taking huge chunks at a time. The red bricks of that four-storied hall were in the oven for the last time. Fire engines were everywhere in the square and were from at least a half-dozen towns. Clumsily, like tethered beetles, firemen ran about in their great boots and black and yellow slickers and warrior hats. Yelling to each other they pointed out places in the fire, their arms and hands full of exclamation. A great rushing noise seemed to dwarf all of us, like a rushing up out of a maelstrom, a gushing. A last breath from a fallen giant.

And there, at the edge of the crowd, as though not only not at a fire, but also not in a crowd either, was Wingsy. Straight and stiff as a cat-o-nine tail he stood. He cast no shadow at high noon, but his eyes contained that same dulled look, that trance look I had seen almost a year earlier. It was not the mien of an arsonist, I knew. There was no excitement in those Atlantic gray orbs, no bubbles at trouble. He was outside of himself for the time being, the old detachment. If it hadn't been for the thick tar-burning smell driven across the air, a huge tongue of it hanging over our heads like licorice, I bet I could have smelled the same old pond smell on him. The same old odor perhaps only Kendall had known besides me. Only we two people in the whole world getting some kind of sign and never knowing just what it was.

A policeman urged us back from the fire, pushing roughly when he had to. He yelled that the walls were probably going to come down. His voice was thick with age and anxiety, winded, his eyes more of the arsonist than anyone's. A long mustache fell sadly at both ends. Most of us moved back sort of quickly, touching each other gently, unionized and getting self-support and awareness. All the time we eyed the flames at their enormous task. It was only Wingsy who didn't move, unresponsive, becoming the stiff puzzle again. He did not move even when he was shoved and threatened by the policeman.

"Move on, lad! Back it up there! Move it or I'll pop you one on the side of the head!"

Inside me the telltale surge suddenly shot its wad, true voltage, known voltage, a mad thrust from inertia's bed. Wingsy was stunned or in a stupor and stood alone in the face of the policeman. And nothing the policeman said moved Wingsy. Finally he had to be lifted forcibly off the ground and carried plank-like back to the barrier line. His hair fell wick-like over the gray jacket with the big pockets, an unlit candle waiting on more darkness. He never said a word, never uttered a cry. When he was stood on his feet behind the barrier he continued to stand stock still, not moving at all. In that seeming haziness I felt that only I had seen another dimension. Again, I thought, I was privy to darkness.

One day the seventh grade geography teacher, Miss Kellock, was talking just outside the teacher's room. A tell-tale trail of cigarette smoke, a thin sheet, flowed from the door standing ajar. My ears were pinned to her words.

"He's not apathetic! Not in any way. Knows more than any child I've ever had, or absorbs more. It's just *that way* he has, covering up or hiding something. I don't mean it's sinful or anything like that, but it *is different* and definitely *at odds* with everything else around him. Sometimes I just swear he knows a lot more than he's letting us know."

I could tell that she wished she was back behind that door and puffing on her cigarette again. Her hands sort of washed themselves without any water, no books or papers to grasp, her long nails and thin white fingers finally crossed each other in punctuation.

"There's just him, no brothers or sisters, and the parents quite a bit older than the rest, almost elderly. He's a conductor on the B&M, but looks as if he could be retired, gray and slow, a thin face like the boy's, no ready aptitude for anything special that I know of. She's only slightly younger looking. Stares away a lot in conversation, but not nervous at all in her manner. She's as limp as a laundry bag. Brought him in once when he was truant. No big deal, as it was, but making her own statement. He could miss a week of school, a whole term for that matter, and still be ahead of everybody else and I think she knows it full well."

"So?" asked her almost-confidante, both of them oblivious of me, not the best student by a long shot, not the best listener, at least not to their minds.

"Well, all secrets are dangerous or valuable. If you could, you'd take your pick of how they're going to hit you. That's just what this all seems to be—he knows something we're not privy to, and will never be. He's keeping it from us at all costs, dangerous or valuable or whatever label's put on it. You might think I'm ludicrous or too far-fetched. If you could see him locked away from me in class, I think you'd come round to my way of thinking. He's just so special as a student most of the time, while this other *thing* just seems so pronounced! So disrupting! Oh, only a few times I'll admit, but striking at that."

We never knew how to take Miss Kellock, not really. She wore the same blue dress most of the year, anyway. That would sure get you wondering. She stood there against the corridor wall like I didn't exist at all. Hearing what she had to say about no one else but Wingsy puzzled me all the more. I was caught between the two tides. Wingsy on the one side and them on the other. Secrets and puzzles. The darkness about him and the stretching, pleasant, warm, slightly electric, secretive languor I'd noticed infiltrating me whenever I thought of teachers behind that barricade. The smoke still curled from the partly shut door. I had a thousand and one images of the teachers in their slips and thigh-grasping panties and how they'd lounge carefree on a couch or a big soft chair. I imagined them smoking long cigarettes, their legs hanging lasciviously over the arm of the sofa, their eyes full of soft hell. Daytime soft.

Her legs were exquisitely long and shapely. She stood on one stiff leg with the calf making a grand pronouncement because of her high heel and propped the other leg tightly at an angle against the skirt of her dress. I could see the line of her underpants against the other thigh, like the edge of a drapery in a dim room. For a moment she was vivid, her skin exceptionally white and cheeks high and animated and rouged as if they had just been squeezed. And she talked about a pupil, a peer! Not very often you'd get a teacher talking like Miss Kellock did. They didn't do that, honor wouldn't let them it said, yet she had voiced some of what had come at me. A teacher had ear-marked a bit of the mystery of a pupil, made public what was mine. Quickly I put her behind that door and sat her all legs and lack of mystery in place, all but to serve her right, to put her in a more proper attitude.

It was finally more than Wingsy Menzies made the air electric.

All those episodes about him merged at some point in time, so that he became a stark character in my life's story. Eventually he became a shadow at the periphery. At some point I stopped poking fun at him, stopped finding odd ways of looking at him in untrue measurement. A few times I called him Hugh or Hughie on the way past his front steps, but never in a crowd. On the edge of crowds he whispered, and loomed on dim horizons as a slim shadow against the slicing sunset. He passed through the same periods I went through. Breathing earth air was our only common ground.

Into and out of high school we passed and never once bumped fully into each other. Different strokes for different folks, as they say. Finally he went over that horizon, on a day I can't remember, on to his own destiny. I know that he finished high school a year after me. I went off to the war in Korea in 1950, came back in 1952 and started college.

One cold day in January of 1966, I was going to pick up a car pooler on the way to work. I saw a garland of flowers tied onto a metal pole at the intersection of four streets in the far end of town. The flowers appeared fresh and colorful and looked no way out of context on the pole. The reds and whites and faint purples of them were as much at home as you could imagine. On top of the pole sat a gray, heavy cast iron sign in which were forged the words in thick black letters, PFC HUGH MENZIES SQUARE.

The electricity stung me again! I had passed that sign a hundred or more times and had never once seen that bold legend. I never knew he had died. I never knew he was in Korea. And I wondered who had hung the flowers. Who had reached high on tiptoes and knotted a small piece of twine about a cold metal pole on the side of the road. Who had hung a heart out. I went looking.

At Riverside Cemetery, in the Veterans Section, at the meeting of four internal roads and under the most stately of elm trees, I found the final word. A bronze plate marker lie in the very first row; PFC HUGH MENZIES PH 179th INFANTRY KOREA JUNE 1929 MAR 1952. The gravesite was separated by another grave from that of Eddie McCarthy who had died in Korea in April of 1951. Eddie had been a tough little fighter, a boxer of some renown. I did not know that he too had fallen in Korea. I had seen him fight a number of times. His long-time girlfriend had been a neighbor of mine. I gasped at the earth air again.

For many months I found myself visiting there, standing in the shade of the elms, little limbs of shadows coming across my face, my eyes. The wind and sweet airs tried to get up enough gumption to have voices of their own. Much of the time was spent in searching the back of my mind for pieces of Hugh that I had forgotten. But I could not get away from calling him Wingsy, or forget my laughing so many times at something I found odd about him. Nor could I get away from the presence of something dark and boding that had existed as much as he had.

His parents were gone. There were no other known relatives. No brother or sister or old aunt off in the hinterlands. Kendall Tucker and others of his friends had departed town or dropped completely from sight. Nothing. Except someone who had hung a bouquet of flowers on a cold metal pole on a cold gray day of January.

Nobody I questioned knew the least detail of his death. He had simply passed through my life. I had laughed at him in my own ludicrous way and he died where Eddie McCarthy died, where I could have died. The haunt was in place, full-fledged, leaping all over me at any time of the day. Whole episodes about him came back to me; the day at the pond, the day at the fire, other days which I had never thought about a second time. I was, I thought, sharing some kind of hell that really had come about over fifty years ago, a darkness that I might have put aside but never got rid of.

One day at the dentist's office a veteran's magazine fell open as I thumbed through a pile of magazines. A column requesting information caught my eye. Readers were asking for back-up proof of disabilities, histories on certain military units, seeking mementos and souvenirs of the oddest kind. Some requested last known addresses of comrades from the dim past. Beside me I envisioned Hugh Menzies standing dark and vague but as tall as ever. The thin evidence of shadow fell across my whole life, never having departed.

My letter, addressed to the column, said: *WANTED, FOR A MEMORIAL ARTICLE, INFORMATION ON THE FINAL SACRIFICE OF PFC HUGH MENZIES, 179th INFANTRY, WHO FELL IN KOREA ON 25 MARCH 1952.*

More than two years passed after the request was printed. I had given up hope of ever receiving any information from that quarter, but not going without Hugh's constant company. I never went without visiting in decent or tolerable weather both his and Eddie's final resting places. The elms were still in place, their shadows sometimes leafy but always of limbs passing down over my visits, almost temperance of a sort. One day I found a plain manila envelope in my mail.

I knew Hugh. I was with him the day he died. This letter, for the longest time, was not going to be written. I saw the magazine the day it came out and I guess there hasn't been a day since he died that I haven't thought about him. We were in Basic together, both of us with a little more reserve than all the others, and drawn together. He had a serious presence to him and I was still scarred by a lot of my young life. We were the odd buddies, if you want to know, but we liked

131

each other's company. Perhaps, as I've said, we were driven together. I am not sure. A couple of times, on weekend leaves from camp in Colorado, we visited my parents' small ranch in Utah. They liked Hugh, even though my father thought he had a too serious side to him. But he knew so much about everything that he just captivated them in spite of my father's reservations. I mean ranching and cactus and desert life and land erosion and coyote habits. He told river histories and wild horse stories filled with great stallions, stories that could take over a kitchen in bare minutes. And, of course, we spent a lot of time together traveling back and forth. You catch things that really aren't thrown at you in such situation. Those are the near secrets and hopes and the dreams that come out of the void of all of us. You learn to temper your own likes and dislikes when something different comes along. Hugh was different. But the biggest thing of all was that from the very beginning he knew, to the very day, almost to the hour, when he was going to die. He told me on the way back to camp from one of our visits to see my folks. He was positive of it. Spoke of it a number of times. He said it was going to be in March of the next year, late in the month, late in the day, on a hillside strewn with hell. He said he had known it for most of his life, that it was one of the things he found on the way to wherever he was going and was neither hurt nor discouraged by it.

Once, in a very grave conversation on the way over to Korea by ship, he even said, "It might be up to me to make it happen. But I will be a hero when it happens." He never added to that, or took any of it back. I just knew he was counting down the days the way he had of looking at leaves or insects or a piece of shale from a riverbed, as if committing all their parts to memory for the hereafter. And that darkness hung over me too. I have to admit there were times when I did not want to be caught standing near him, or filling up the

132

*same foxhole with him when the shells were coming in.
Those things kind of passed off in their way, like UFO's
I suppose, there but not there. I never wanted for
anything when he was around; his money, his goods,
even at times his ammunition. Once, by an evening fire
in a reserve area, he hugged me and it was the warmest
feeling I ever had in my whole life. It drove that old
darkness away for a while. The pressure from his arm
was never far from my shoulders, the sweet wrap of it.
And one day, in the valley of Saepori, when things were
as hot as they ever got, Hugh came down out of his hole
and pulled me back up the hill. Blood was spilling
wildly out of my thigh from a hot piece of shrapnel. He
put me down inside the hole and said he had to go get
Buckner. He smiled at me as he slid over the edge, and
said, "This is the time, Sherman." The sun was low on
the rugged horizon, ready to pass away behind the
mountains. I knew it was getting cooler. Minutes later,
hell still being raised all around us, he dropped
Buckner into the hole and fell down himself at my feet,
all according to scripture. I must have passed out. I
woke up in the hospital. Hugh was dead. Buckner was
dead. Now the shadow passes from me. I feel it leaving.
I've carried it so long, I must pass it on. Excuse my
quick departure.*

His comrade, Sherman Gilbreth

Hugh Menzies always knew a hell of a lot more
than I did. Now I measure it daily.

The Coalman

When the bounteous and splendidly round
Kamilla Liskart died her husband dove into a clumsy
silence. With his wife five years dead, and his son
suddenly off to World War II out in the vast Pacific
noise, he changed. Our coalman Milan Carl Liskart
began plowing through his days as if he were
unconscious or barely breathing. Coal delivery became,
as if it were, his life.

A quiet man to begin with, he brought any and
all trappings with him into that studied silence. Nothing
but labor marked his days. He carried pain neither upon
his brow nor spread on his sleeve bold as insignia of
rank. Early mornings, his tonnage loaded and on the
road, he could have said to the rising sun he had beaten
out of bed, "Hello, angry dish! You here again late as
usual? What's in the pipeline today for me?"

The day's route and schedule with no degree of
effort must have formed and reformed continuously at
the back of his mind. There were times, as evidenced on
occasion, that he lost the whole plan of the day; but
hard work endured for him and proved itself endless.

Meanwhile, in his neighborhood, the old-timers
spoke of the couple that for long years had searched out
the mushrooms on the tall elm trees of Cliftondale
Square. Milan knocked the white knobs from their high
gardens with his long telescopic pole. Kamilla caught
them in the basket of her apron. The old ones, in hushed
whispers, told of the union, how they whistled and sang
at their Sunday work. God, they said, sat himself on a
high limb for the advance of their prayers. Sunday
evenings, they reflected, there were services of
mushrooms and red wine on the Liskarts's screened
porch. Now and then a low-sung song slipped from
those happy confines, or a sudden twist of laughter gay
as ribbons.

In one quick year, ending on a cold and dark October evening, lights steady and blazing in all rooms of their house, Kamilla's laughter and roundness and the sure net of her apron left him. Such a tragedy was not unknown to me. I had lost my beloved Grandfather John Igoe but months earlier. I looked at our coalman with a different eye from the day of her death, the lonely perception of sharing in command. There had come to me a sense of measurement, and a sense of contrast. It was more than the beginning of manhood, which had been announced at about that same time with physical changes and other valid pronouncements.

Thenceforward, dawn to dusk for sure, Milan smelled of coal, a thick, acidic rankness that identified him in the doorway. I noticed it even at a chance encounter on the walk or at the roadside. Kerosene, it seemed, rode him its liquid finery, or the crudest of oil with tinplate knowledge in it. Never was he as clean as leaded glass or pewter work or an amalgam solder, anything token of a craft or brought by keenness. Often I thought he must have slept at night in a mine. Right down where the air is thin and ferric and smothered with its quality of gas, or in some colliery counterpart. He smelled like the coal bins I know fifty years later as remnants of that time. Again, like the old lanterns railroad men used to stop traffic with and which I occasionally find these days useless in old barns. Or those round black-bomb lanterns that town workers set aside to mark off trenches for water pipes along the line of traffic. There comes, replete and terribly savory of nostalgia, the gray image of his dead-gray mackintosh standing like a sentinel on our front steps. He'd be but steps away plying basket atop basket to the coal bin in the cellar. Determined, rodent busy, he went at his work.

Coal, those calamitous and combative years, was $12-14 a ton, anthracite with red or blue spots that today's TV commercials would make merry music about, and knuckle hard. Soft coal was cheaper, but came dustier, burned faster, and needed more tending. Milan Carl Liskart, who lived on the edge of the great Rumney Marsh in the sight of the General Electric's huge Riverworks Plant and the Atlantic's edge, had one truck. It was a cumbersome Reo, seemingly of one speed forward and one sense of duty, and delivered the kind of coal the customer wanted. Milan and the Reo were a decided pair.

Sometimes at our house, just outside Saugus Center on the North Shore above Boston, we had to get the cheaper soft coal due to financial calls. My father, his own military tours done, was a guard at the General Electric Company. My mother was a sweeper there before and after meals and the wash done and hung on the line. My older brother Jim was off in the explosive Pacific, his onionskin letters passing like diamonds between us in the kitchen. The winter of 1944 scratched the pocketbook deeply. Our lives were scratched too. The scratches and scars were all around us. Now and then the blood oozed free or gushed loose. Incidents in Europe and North Africa and the southern Pacific islands of madness converged like instant phantoms on our street. Often they came in ghostly collision, a boy's face somehow rampant on the air. Now and then the morning came greeted with a mother's scream. A few of those days were so quiet we were afraid to breathe, afraid to set a bubble adrift.

I can see him now, Milan Liskart, arms huge as timbers, Atlas shoulders, and blue shirtsleeves gone black where they rolled on his forearms. Rugged big teeth, worthy of new apples or tough steak, gleamed whiter on his darker face. His forehead was broad as a brick above thick brows, and his black hair was sent straight back to his neck by comb or hand. Every day he carried coal in a basket down into dark coal bins. I'd swear he only smiled at the drop of the final basket, that minute reprieve. The last basket dumped in our cellar achieved but a slight nod. The evening sun would daily mark his return from labors, the Reo chugging at its gait down the street close to the marsh. Milan parked in the driveway of his small house sided by reeds and rushed to the mailbox to check on letters from his son. On some days there'd be a small eruption of jubilation. He'd delay his retreat, pour a glass of whiskey into a glass on his porch, sit into the soft evening in his old Morris chair and read for hours. We never knew what his son had written. The letters were, beside his wife Kamilla, the most prized and secretive thing Milan Liskart ever knew.

My Grandfather was one of the few men I had seen head to head with Milan. Obviously they had some agreements in life, some related memories, or some aspect of their existence they shared or had kinship with. It was my Grandfather who said Milan most likely had his share of peace while he drove the cumbersome Reo. That driving the monster was a palliative to his troubled silence, allowing him a rare respite in his labored days.

"No one knows what cooks in that man's mind, more than the black spirit of silence, while he runs through the town from dark to dark and being black himself."

It was on holidays or Sundays, when there was no mail delivery, he'd sit an hour or two in the White Eagle Café. The Eagle was a Polish weekend stronghold. Sipping on strong whiskey, sitting among other quiet old Polish friends, they all measured out the hours, the days, now and then a lifetime.

Which partially explains why Milan, on another Sunday afternoon, the winds from the north as robust as they had been all that season, came to the White Eagle and his friends later than usual on a Sunday. He said he'd had a soak for hours in the tub reading the latest letter. Then he had fallen asleep and the letter, free of his hand and consciousness, sank at length to the bottom of the tub. It was no longer legible. The image rocked his solid frame.

"By God, Milan," Pordgorski said, trying and failing to divert the shock, "but Kiska carried his eighty-two years one too many. Old bozo lived past one boy and one daughter. That's the hell of it, getting on like that, two going in a matter of months, like there's no sense in praying for else wise."

"The thing is we don't know what he knew," Milan might have said if he had anything to say, thinking about the man thinking about his dying. Some people said Milan's eyes, from that day on, were like marbles the kids played with on the school grounds.

Later at the White Eagle, cold spells leaping down from Montreal in waves, short days still getting longer for him, Milan first heard about the fire chief's new task in life. It was a Sunday afternoon, church was over as well as dinner. The old work warriors were tossing down some hard stuff, wind talking at the windows, with an occasional utterance at the door.

Milan was with Kowszolski and Pordgorski and Petras at the bar, as old Eagle said, "Say, Milan, hear yet about Chief Drew knocking on doors around town? Knocked on Sev Matrick's door he did and had the telegram in his hand saying young Sev was lost at sea from off his ship. I remember that little shit. Oh, what a one he was, sneaking around for a beer all the time with his tongue hanging out a yard long. Had a way with the girls, was a spitfire to say the least. Like the old man. Seems nobody in the town wanted the job of delivering those sad words, so Drew took it on. Be a man of his size take to do it, seeing he's been in two, three tough places already." He shook his head and added, "Probably that and then some."

Old Kowszolski put in his piece: "He brought Joey Tighe out of the warehouse in Malden, didn't he?

Word has it was one of the bad ones, bouncing through the walls and getting on top of them in the ceiling spaces before it blew. Chief sees Tighe's buddy come out alone, almost melted they say, and the chief goes in for Tighe. Has him over his shoulder when he comes out. Jeezus, he met the lion a couple of times that day, how he lost the hair on the back of his head, fire must have been right behind him crawling up his ass."

"Take a man like that to do it," Petras said, "carrying the pup out of the flames. But worse is, I think, knocking on a door like he does, holding death in his hands, kind of like the other way around." They were all looking in the bar mirror at themselves, measuring manhood one would figure. "We all know the measure of a man," Petras added, "and some don't add up like some do."

Later Eagle told my Grandfather about it. Much later when stuff had gone down. "Milan only listened when they talked about the chief walking up someone's walk, the telegram in his hand like an odd glove," Eagle said. "Never said a word, did he. The others had no boys out there, not like Milan, Adam off in that hard part of the world. Man has little to say, even under a few stiff ones, like he's someplace else not here in town."

Stories, of course, bounced around about him. When Taggart died and the wife and the kids were hard up he staked them to a winter of coal. Never said a word about it, but the word got around. Mel Timmons tried shaking him down for price break, and Milan said he'd stop his regular deliveries, him not making that much to begin with.

The coal man, it seemed, knew little of nor cared much for the passage of time, nor frivolities of meaningless intent. No sense of time passing proved invasive. Only the mail did that... it gave him age... it gave him matter...it gave him the avowed sense of maturity. And it gave him silence, like an after-chew, a gum-liner, a bubble in the cheek, the way some men seek solace in a chew.

Yet it was said his son Adam, Adam the football player "as tough as nails" they said, Adam the hockey player who skated with the wind, who wrote no soft letters but real letters. He wrote foxhole letters, letters of the last lament, letters that finally owed up to the pain he had known. Adam, who knew of death, had seen his mother shrink away and his father dive into silence. He had been there at the hospital when his father had seen the doctor walking down the hall toward them. The doctor's eyes were buried in his face, his hands limp and senseless at his side, useless signposts but telling the whole story.

So it was all in the making. All the stage was set, the character and characters in place, the sun coming down and a stiff wind coming right out of the Northeast and across the marsh reeds and dikes with no home of its own. A wild January was at its chill when Chief Drew stepped out of his old Packard coupe, the big black behemoth with the futuristic chrome grille and the hood as long as a canal. The chief started the walk up the long driveway to Milan Liskart's side door. The huge and cumbersome Reo sat off to the side of the driveway abutting the marsh, a monolithic and staid testament to its owner, the silent Milan Carl Liskart.

The chief looked nervous, though his white hat with black visor was perched in place with aplomb. Impeccably clean white gloves sat his hands, his uniform pressed into an ebon smoothness, his pants creased like an iron seam. The yellow-signal telegram was grasped in one hand. A neighbor, through a kitchen window, caught his breath seeing the yellow missive in the chief's hand. His own two sons were out there in that calamitous madness of the Pacific, whole chains of islands coming up daily in the newspaper headlines.

It was January of 1944... it was cold...things had popped up and off around the world with frightening and horrific reality. Millions of pounds of bombs had been dropped on Berlin early in the month, practically obliterating three aircraft plants. The Russians had a bit later crossed the Polish border. Monte Casino was attacked. In a surprise move our troops had made the invasion at Anzio, 60 miles behind enemy lines. And out there in that mad Pacific where my brother Jim was, Adam Liskart's outfit leaped ashore in the Marshall Islands/Kwajalein Islands, where my brother, it turned out, had ferried some of the Marines ashore. At that time word was passed around the world about Japanese atrocities heaved upon survivors in the Philippine Islands, the Death March from Corregidor and Bataan.

It must be assumed that Milan knew all this, that he would read of it, hear it on the radio, hear the gospel of it at the White Eagle... indeed some of the members had been in Europe after their emigration, during World War I. They had known the gas, the shells, the stench of death, the trenches of blood where all truth drowned in misery.

It all gathered for him in the neatly uniformed man walking up his driveway on a bitterly cold January evening, a yellow missive in his hand.

Milan leaned at the garage, came away with a deep, pear-shaped coal shovel in his hands. Over his head he waved it, that clumsy shovel, adroitly and menacingly at Chief Drew.

"Don't you goddamn come on my property, you son of a bitch!"

He roared, he raced at Chief Drew, the shovel still swinging wildly overhead. It was a voice the chief, even in his tough outings of meeting roaring fires, had not heard before. The chief decided not to deliver the telegram at that miraculous moment. The deadly, easily-wielded shovel loomed a sure weapon above the coalman's head, a weapon of sure destruction, thicker than fire and heavier, bearing the kind of pain fire might not have in its bowels.

Yellow light spilled from the Liskart house and from neighbors' houses. Two corner street lights glowed a soft war-time yellow. The early stars were open and lit. A crescent moon lay out over the marsh like a sliver of light, like a distant flame of a struck match. Remnant ice, sprawled over flat lawns and tangled in reeds from an earlier storm, caught a variety of light, yellow, near-silver, hushed golden, fading to a strange opaqueness. Glitter gathered and departed from the chief's vision, from the corners of his eyes. Peripheral glitter. Come and gone glitter that could have been yard markers. Once a track star in high school, he called upon the old drive and the old measures to hasten himself down the middle of the street. Called on adrenalin's rush he had known in more than a few fires with the lion, and felt the anguish and pain chasing him down the middle of Saugus Avenue skirting the marsh and the southern slopes of Baker Hill. He tried to remember the face of the boy he had seen rushing the football at Stackpole Field. He could not find that face. But he knew the face of the man chasing him. He knew the wide, brick-shaped brow, the cavernous eyes, the broad middle European nose, the ledge of chin, the darkness that there abided.

He prayed the coalman would not catch him. He did not.

A week later, the world still topsy-turvy, the Pacific war spreading like wildfire, Chief Drew, out of uniform, slipped into the White Eagle late on a Sunday afternoon. He sat on a bar stool nearest the door and ordered a glass of whiskey. From a group of men, from the midst of Kowszolski and Pordgorski and Petras and Eagle himself, Milan Carl Liskart excused himself.

He placed his drink on the bar and walked sad-faced, shamefaced, hand out to the fire chief who slid off his seat and stood at a kind of attention, his face lit with signal.

They are both gone now, long gone, Milan Carl Liskart and Chief Drew. And Adam Liskart has been at sea all these years, more than a half century's worth, floating there in memory forever. Every now and then I bring him back to Stackpole Field, the rushing fullback, the young bruiser so hard to tackle, so hard to bring down. I see him still driving forward with the ball, that great forearm shiver and lethal straight arm his ultimate weapons. And I see his father, the dark coalman, sitting off in a far corner, never fully understanding the game but noting the bravery and relentless motions of his son.

The Quiet, Empty
Bedrooms of Saugus

All of earth once growled and gnarled its way to
an instant conflagration, a calamitous roar. All its gears
began to shift in the near-middle of this last century,
and Saugus, Massachusetts, a small town just north of
Boston, started to empty its bedrooms. It emptied the
ones in the attic, in the space out over the garage, third
floor second door on the left. It emptied the bedrooms
facing on the pond or the cemetery or those looking
broadly down on the wide marshes or quickly down on
quiet Cliftondale Square. The bedrooms where boys
cruised into manhood, almost overnight at that.

Saugus did this, just as all of sleepy America
did, in the days beginning our most persistent glory.

She gave up her men, and soon her women.

Saugus and all of America sent from those
bedrooms, our sons, our fathers, our brothers, our
uncles, our nephews and cousins, the young and the
older, male and female. Saugus and all of America
stripped herself of her young blood, and sent her
youngsters off to war. Saugonians, in swift journeys,
many whose measure we will never know, found
themselves on the beaches of Guadalcanal and Iwo
Jima. On the shores and sands of North Africa. On the
lap of Europe on D-Day. In the heart of the Italian Alps
coming onto Mount Casino. And then they crossed the
Rhine at Remargen, bursting across France and
Germany with the Third Armored Division and other
units. Saugus blood soaked into those foreign soils. It
consecrated dim ground, hardpan and glacier-slugged
rock, Asian limestone and, at length, the final Pacific
sands.

Final...or so we thought.

The rooms continued to get emptied. Our sons and daughters spilled out of those personal confines into the mountains of Korea, into the horrors of Viet Nam, onto shores the world over. The guitars and fiddles and drums in their empty rooms went silent, gathered dust.

Their baseball cards went into shoeboxes into the attic, into the cellar, into the barn.

Their Indian cards.

Their Little Big Books.

Their pin collections and jackknifes and Merit Badges.

Their keepsakes became keepsakes.

Sometimes into history.

Oftentimes into a half century of lasting silence.

Some of them left us at the railroad station at Essex and Eustis Streets or at Depot Square in Saugus Center, as they started the journey to save Saugus, America, and the world. They congregated, they gabbed, they kissed girlfriends and shook hands as diversions came upon their partings. Mothers and fathers and brothers and sisters and neighbors came to say bon voyage, good luck, "Give 'em hell!"

The trains took away parts of Saugus. Parts of America. Arthur DeFranzo, his name and deeds to be carved forever in the stone of heroes, left early, left first, driven by what was happening in Europe.

Another young man asked his parents not to go to the railroad station, to say goodbye at home. Clutching his bag he walked down their driveway, down their street, down Main Street. The father, shaken by the request, hustled the mother out the side door, into the car, drove down side streets on the sly. They lovingly and proudly watched their son an extra ten minutes or so as he strode to the train station along with a few friends from high school.

They never saw him again.

Suddenly, half a world away, there's eager Sgt. Arthur DeFranzo lighting up Europe; his courage, his bravery, his devotion to God, family, town, country, becoming bench-marks forever. Saugonian, Saugus High boy, neighbor, young man with a vision. Hero for all time to come.

One of ours.

He fought, he died, he slept in France.

Now he sleeps here.

The Kasabuski brothers fought and died and slept in Italy, falling mere days apart in the torrid uphill battle in the Italian Alps, fighting the dreaded German army in a savage campaign. John and Walter Kasabuski were born and raised in Saugus, graduated from Saugus High. Each was president of the Ski Club, and they arranged, upon entering the service, to be assigned to Company E of the U. S. Army's 87th Regiment of the 10th Mountain Division. It was an elite mountain fighting troop, which excelled in winter operations. They served in the Kiska invasion when the Japanese brought the war closest to home, in Alaska's Aleutian Islands. In the spring of 1945 they were sent to northern Italy to help drive the Germans out of the Alps. John was fatally wounded by a grenade on April 15 and lived long enough for Walter, two years the elder, to get to his side. Twelve days later Sgt. Walter Kasabuski was killed by a sniper's bullet.

The hockey rink at the entrance to Breakheart Reservation is named in their honor.

The Veterans of Foreign Wars post is named for Sgt. Arthur DeFranzo, upon whom was bestowed the nation's highest decoration, the Medal of Honor.

They are remembered.

As are the handfuls of sons of other Saugonians who served: the five sons of Mr. and Mrs. Charles Ward of Lincoln Avenue—Robie, Kenneth, Seldon, Russell and Charles Jr., two Navy, three Army; the five

146

sons of Mr. and Mrs. Rene Field of Ballard Street—Robert, Jack, Rene Jr., Gordon and Richard, five Army; the five sailors from the home of Elgin Ludwig on Jackson Street—Samuel, John, James, Herbert, and Arthur MacDonald brought home by Sammy from a visit to Boys Town (Frankie served in Korea in the Army and later joined the Naval Reserve); six Vatchers— Walter, Warren, Helen, Gertrude, Harriet and Calvin; and the eight Buckless brothers from Baker Hill—Alexander, Willard, Gordon, Roy, Kenneth, George, Raymond, and Lloyd; seven Nagle brothers from Baker Hill. They are listed here as examples of our involvement, the list going on and on.

They who left the safety of their bedrooms, who lit up Europe, just as those who lit up the sands on hundreds of beaches in the Pacific, were Saugonians. They were Americans of the first order, of the great generation of Americans. Marine Platoon Sgt. Billy McCarthy, former high school cheerleader, fought at Bougainville and Guam before he was killed on Iwo Jima. "A natural leader," reports said of him. "Mac had one of the most vital personalities I've ever seen," wrote his first sergeant. "You didn't have to worry about the men's morale when he was around." Master Sgt. Thomas 'Pop ' Virnelli, flying veteran of two wars, was killed in France. Pvt. Harold Turner, an Army Medic, died on June 19, 1944, shortly after the invasion of Europe began. Saugus men declared Missing in Action in Europe in the same Combat Engineers outfit included T/5 Walter French of Sunnyside Ave., Sgt. Walter Wetmore, Main Street, Sgt. Irving Cameron, Central Street, Harry Woodland, Cottage Street and Harold Maribella, Western Avenue, though news came later that some had become prisoners of war, some to return home. Boyhood playmates and chums PFC. Vitold Glinski of Atherton Street and Marine Corporal

Alexander Chojnowski of Rhodes Street died within a month of each other, fighting on Pacific islands.

More empty rooms.

Many other Saugus families sent off two and three and four sons into the long war, and many sent their daughters to places all over the world.

It was the second war to end all wars.

As peace came out of Europe, out of the Pacific, we thought all that hell was over and done with.

Then, suddenly, overnight it seemed, youngsters Eddie McCarthy and Hughie Menzies were killed in Korea, in a new onslaught. They, who died a year apart in Korea, lie a grave apart at Riverside Cemetery. As does Frank Parkinson, who was left to die in the murderous sands of the Sahara and who rose up and now lies here. Like so many others of our young men, sooner or later, dying from this cause or that cause; Laurence Daniels, Fiore Sacco, the Ludwig brothers, Soupie Campbell, Richard Gabry, like some of our fathers and sons from different wars; the endless circle widening, the empty rooms gathering up more silence.

To walk through the Veterans' Section of Riverside Cemetery, to read the names on the flat stones, to remember the faces of those who bailed out of their bedrooms when the whole earth itself was in trouble, is more than a simple exercise in memory. Whether they left us then or later is no great divider; for they went in harm's way for all our good. See their names scribed on our war memorial, those who stood and were counted.

For those whose names pass too quickly, we call a pause. It is truth that cold stone brings them back alive in our midst. We remember their dreams, their faces, their ever-changing young voices as they romped into manhood in the hell of the whole universe. Boldly they went into the paths of bullets and bombs and grenades and torpedoes with the ultimate wrath of mankind seriously at odds with itself.

But they left marks, our young men; told and untold stories of heroism, of a Medal of Honor and countless Silver Stars and Bronze Stars and Flying Medals and Distinguished Service Crosses and valor and gallantry without end. They left battlefield promotions and unit decorations. The widening circle finally came to peace, that momentary silence out there where Billy centerfield left his arm in Kwajalein debris, and the brother I did not fully know until he came home and I saw his seabag decorated with his wife's picture and the map and the names Saipan, Iwo Jima, Kwajalein... the war.

Cold stones are warm with their names and their memories; Riverside plaques, the new memorial markers in the front of the old high school site, the eighteen names from World War I on the stone in the green of Cliftondale Square, the full-dressed soldier memorial to PFC Richard Devine in front of the Town Hall.

Now and then that old warmth rises from the still quiet bedrooms of the Saugus they left from, fitted with shadows.

The Hermit of Breakheart Woods

Over millions of years ago Breakheart Woods, between Saugus and Wakefield in Massachusetts, had been bookmarked by boulders and blow-offs and earthly cataclysm. To this day, somewhere in its innards from those first struggles of granite and earth fire, from violent fractures and upheavals to be known again only at the end of it all, was a cave. A cave as dark as a heart. A cave that once, I believed, pulsed with a heart. Now we were searching for that cave, in earnest.

Nobody I knew growing up had ever seen or visited the cave, but I knew it was there, I'd been told. The old man of the benches told me, the reclusive reader told me, this late and distant friend told me. Once he had said, as we sat on a Breakheart bench under the sun, books swapping owners, time spilling its nearly empty cup for us, that we were in a syzygy with his home, his place of rest. The word *syzygy* was perhaps salvaged from his reading. He twisted his stiff neck, eyes dark as hidden sin or pain, it seemed, as they rolled across my face, the breeze twisting his hair into a small errant banner. Over one slightly muscled shoulder he had looked with what appeared to be unerring accuracy into the depths of Breakheart Woods. I had no idea how far into the woods he looked. Or how far knowledge and familiarity took him, but I felt the astronomer's true line of that course. He and I and the cave were fatefully cast in a spatial line of supposed sight. He knew and I didn't, not as yet, that I was part of that syzygy.

Now I wondered, did that heavenly cave hold his sickly frame or house his corpse? Had it become, in turn, chamber, then crypt, for one man separated entirely from the rest of the world? Thinking of the old man at that moment, I thought of Charlie, my old pal Charlie. If he had been here, would have called it the

150

dead-gone grotto. Charlie, too, alliterative Charlie, my book merchant, had left me, sprinting into death the final leg man on a 400-meter relay. All-too-dead Charlie carried a dread disease as surely as a baton. He too would have been here for the search, looking for the old man of the benches, along with the rest of our friends. I had friends to count on.

Surprise, disbelief, query, all manner of reaction from my companions came to mind. I'd guess disbelief figured to be the headliner for my pals. But, October crowding us, its breath tinged by Montreal and points north, we were really into the search. I mean really into it, all five of us, with maps that laid out sections and quadrants for the search. We were spread our responsible ways to cover all depths of Breakheart Woods. Pal Jay even brought whistles along for all of us, which was par for him. I never would have thought of it, that's for sure.

My long-time pals, to a man, were convinced, finally, we were looking for the old man of the benches. I was convinced we were looking for his body.

At about 150 feet apart, we were spread out in a line. We were obligated to look under every rock of any size, into each solitary crevice, under distinct cliff faces. We looked behind every blow-down whose roots in the endless dance of earthly upheaval fanned the air. To deploy our own fan across each foot of Breakheart's ground was our goal.

It wasn't so much that the others believed me. I thought the old guy was dead in the woods, most likely entombed if I was to believe his words. But they trusted me, and we were the best of friends. *Enough said*, that's all it took. We each had secrets of youth none of us had divulged to this day. I asked them for help. They came the next morning, dressed warmly, October primping on us, lunches packed, Thermoses in a variety of slings and backpacks, hanging in as always. If I were the type

I'd have cried. We'd been classmates and teammates forty some years before and nobody else would have believed me anyway. Old men, at least older than we were, don't ordinarily crawl off like elephants to die, especially in Breakheart. The place was part of the Commonwealth's park system, squeezed in between Saugus and Wakefield, a bare twelve miles from downtown Boston. In summer it probably held more homeless people than we could contend with. Finding one man would be difficult.

All my pals but Charlie were here. It was a point with Charlie that still held true: We thought about him, always, when he wasn't around. Some people do not disappear, no matter what happens to them.

Jay Brazos didn't ask how I knew about the old man, but instead inquired if I had any leads. Had I seen the man coming and going in one dedicated route? If there were any time differentials we could surmise on, draw from? Any propensities I had observed? Jay once was a tackle, a good, rugged one, who many years ago turned accountant. Big thumbs he had, but good at figures, and loyal. He had as much energy as any man I'd ever met, but never wasted it. Shortcuts were part of his make-up, a bit of the contrast working in him, CPAs being detailers, meticulous from the word go.

Kurt Ogden was as good as gold, as he was in all things. He shrugged and smiled amiably and innocently, still. His grin said, *I'm here, lead me.* Being himself, he was, knowing he'd never be a leader, but wouldn't be last either. He was handsome in a way that said he should have been an organizer, a point man. He'd be grateful to his dying days we hadn't called him KO. That would have made some days tougher to handle.

Shjon Borraille arrived in denim and a puffy ski jacket that cost a bundle, boots that cost twice as much, a backpack he must have gone out last night to buy. Jon

B we'd called him since the fifth grade when he moved into town from the Maritimes. He looked as though he were bound for Yosemite or the Grand Canyon. In spite of his money, in spite of his gold and his stocks and his silver spoon, Jon B was steel down to the last fiber. He was a rich boy who was a blocking back way back when, a devastating blocker. In the depths of Breakheart,he would be the last man to quit the search. It wasn't that he had anything to prove, to us or to himself, but it was the way he was made. The genes, he'd often said, come when the fire's going, not when it's out. Itching to get his section done and then help out somewhere else, he'd beat the clock if he could.

Lastly, Dermott Hulrihan and I shared at least four pints of blood over the years. Once when he went through the windshield of his sister's car, and once when I almost sliced my arm off at the old icehouse. The crazily vibrating band saw still screeched in recall. We were best friends besides, at home in each other's house, with each other's family. When I said I needed help, he was at my side in ten minutes. This time, though, he didn't have to bring his electrical tool kit or his TV repair kit or his brake-fixing tools.

Right up front I decided that I'd have to tell them the whole story. Realizing it would have to grow and be formed as I told it, I built it up and brought them on. I needed all four of them. So I made the preliminaries known. I thought an old man was dead in Breakheart. If he wasn't dead, then he was most likely sick and socked away in some kind of rocky cave or shelter, which had been home to him for about two years. I'd met him at the benches of the reservation, sopping up the good rays. Now, he'd been out of sight for three days. But he and I had met daily for something like thirty-seven or thirty-eight days in a row, at the benches of the park. Evidently there was something amiss.

I told them everything, as clearly and as truly as I could. I did not let anything mask the feeling I had found in myself for a vagrant, for a street person, an old but quizzical man who had come out of nowhere into my life. The quadruple bypass I'd undergone two years before had also put me on the street. A walker and wanderer I had become trying to keep going the sole organ the aorta serves with distinction.

So, I said, every now and then in life you have these absolutely brilliant illuminations about another member of the species. If you're lucky, that is, and awake at the time. It can be the clarity of a person so explicit you feel you know them down to the bottom of their feet, what's between their toes. And instantaneous, in part. It doesn't happen very often, it's true, or not often enough, but when it does it grabs you right by the socks and shakes you up. It was that way with Charlie. We all know it. We know why he went so fast, toting what he thought was all that dread disease with him, keeping it for himself.

It seemed it was that way with *him*, the old man of the benches, nameless for the longest while. His face had come at me as I passed him by, sitting on a bench near the first pond of the reservation. There had been no obvious, unbalanced measure about him, like his face was so interesting and his clothes so decrepit, no opposites that had attracted me. An aura about him, I would say, being a more accurate explanation.

From a distance I had seen him before. Enough times to believe that he was homeless. That his nights were filled with uncertainty and conjecture. That he had no close ties to anybody around us, but that he was a survivor despite whatever rigors had beset him. In his wayward way there seemed to be a purpose emanating, a role to be fulfilled, a routine to be discharged. I couldn't put my finger on it. But something solid existed with him or in him or alongside him, a shadow

154

in a place I couldn't find though the sunlight angled in on him like a spotlight, old Sol at his best.

Neither smile nor scowl did he wear. His eyes came gray or pale blue behind dark-rimmed glasses breaking his face into quadrants. His hair came closer to white than gray, making it cleaner than one might think it would be. It was almost shoulder-length, an old Hippie, a hanger-on we could have seen and passed by a hundred times. Perhaps, I thought, he'd been graced by the tumultuous Sixties and still carried the torch. Perhaps, again, Kerouac at a standstill. Acknowledged outright they'd been slept in, the clothes he wore were not disgraceful in any measure. Though they were not neat, they were not dirty, at least not contemptuously dirty. Not back-alley dirty. Not dumpster dirty. From the beginning I could feel myself drawing a host of conclusions, making assumptions. Making excuses, I suppose, for what had attracted me, feeling myself an odd lot in the bargain.

The truth of the matter is that I had seen him around for the better part of two years, around much of the town, always in a slow and meandering walk. *Without appointment*, Charlie would have said. But I had never really noticed him. The real truth of the matter was, blatant as it might seem, I had not accepted him.

And one day in late August, at Breakheart, old Roman Sol slipping his fingers through the treetops, a breeze keeping those extremities company, we came to the same bench together. We looked into each other's eyes for the first time.

The illumination and clarity I'd experienced before leaped at me. Immediate attraction, there was. It was undeniable. I liked the way his white hair curled under his ears. The fisherman's ruddiness of his face so full of world exposure. The crow's feet lancing the skin

155

about his eyes. The intelligence sitting in those eyes reminded me of an old English professor at Boston College. Beacon Street John Norton was one of the warmest and sincerest men I had met in life. This old man's hands looked industrious despite the rest of his appearance. The dark cover and white pages of a book stuck up out of his once-yellow cardigan pocket. I put him at seventy-five years of age, perhaps a bit older.

Even before we spoke I had a flashback over forty years old. The recall jammed itself at me. Clarity coming with it, and a face from Winslow, Arizona. I was heading home from Yang Du and Mung Dung Ni and Inchon and Seoul and all the ugly pit stops in between. Winslow, Arizona was under rail, the train at rest, and the train captain saying we had a fifteen-minute layover. I had sprinted to a small cabstand. Four cabbies were lounging against their cabs. One face out of the four came at me, something immediate and accessible written on it past a smile, interest and compassion. An *I've been where you've been* kind of expression, a clarity of acceptance, showed.

"How close is the nearest shoe store?" I asked.

"What do you need, kid?" His smile worked brightly, his body was already leaning to an unannounced action, a sprinter at the gun line, a quick hand reaching for the cab door handle.

"I'll be five more days on this train and I need size 8 1/2 moccasins and I've only got fifteen minutes."

We ran two red lights after he flipped open his door for me, the horn blowing all the way. Just off the main drag we ran into a store. Four people were in the store, a man behind the counter, two women talking to him, a man in the far corner. The perfumes of new leather assailed me.

"Harry!" the cabby yelled. "Kid here is on his way home from Korea, Sonny's outfit, the 7th Division. He needs 8 1/2 moccasins and pronto!" Pointing back over his shoulder, he added, "I don't think the train will wait for him," his voice loaded with minute irony.

Harry, the clerk and owner I presume to this day, spun about even as the whistle of the train echoed threateningly across town, across the leathered interior of the store. The box of 8 1/2 moccasins was hurled at me. I reached for my wallet and the both of them said, in unison, "Forget it, kid."

We just made the train. The cabbie said his name was Earl Coombs, his godson and Harry's son was in the 17th Regiment of the 7th Division. For the next five days we swooped across America, laying by in Chicago and a few other points. I was the only one on the train of five hundred returnees not shod, required for the meal car, with heavy combat boots.

The illumination of the spirit of Earl Coombs had never left me, him and the 38th Parallel of Korea loping along together.

I said "Hello," as I sat on the same bench with the old man.

He nodded and replied, "I've seen you around a lot. You must live nearby. On an exercise regimen, probably cardiac I'd guess. I come here a lot myself. Sometimes I read." One fingertip touched the top of the book sticking out of his pocket. "Sometimes I watch the birds or the chipmunks. Now and then the people."

There was no mockery in his face, and none in any of his words.

Suddenly prevailing in me was the realization I should not ask any questions of him. I really don't know why that came upon me so quickly, except some of that clarity or illumination told me it was necessary. Of course, I wanted to ask him where he lived and what he read and a number of other questions sloshing their way through the mud in my mind. But we talked lightly about the weather and the birds and the industry of the squirrels and chipmunks. Little else was volunteered by him and less was asked by me, though I squirmed in my seat for information.

A dozen or so times we spoke in the following weeks. Once or twice he hailed me down, a yell or a wave from a distance if our paths appeared not to be crossing at the same juncture. Little was transferred between us except the quiet amenities of listening, paying attention to words and noting the appropriate time to speak. He was decently shaved most of the time. His clothes went through a small routine of change, though nothing apparently went out of use. Once I saw him pick something off the pavement of the ground and thought it to be a coin the way the sun angled from it. He pocketed the picked-up item. That's when I began dropping coins about the area. Not that I salted the place, mind you, but here and there let a quarter or a dime slip from my fingers. It made me feel good that I didn't have to make an offer or donation outright. And on many occasions it was his hand that picked up my offering. That was not one of my original ideas, I will admit. Years before I'd seen my Grandfather, the storyteller, the Yeats reader, the Roscommon Emigrant, dropping coins in my sure path. There was candy coin and book coin, now and then Hershey coin or *G-8 and His Battle Aces* coin. And there was a neighbor who, putting in terraced steps of cement in his hilly garden, liberally set coins in the wet cement. He spent his nights listening to us chip away at dimes and nickels with our little hammers and our little chisels, the glow of his cigarette signaling his porch watch. I have never forgotten his investment in the neighborhood.

September came, the days still warm, the nights getting off a bit on their own. I still had not prodded him with one question. Thoroughly likable he was, a man of few words, no self choruses, no dictates or tastes used to spread his good word, serious about his own place in the scheme of things. I noticed that the book ends changed colors a few times, so he was progressing, had resources, finished one and went on with another. My curiosity kicked me endlessly, but that illumination would come full circle, I knew.

I told him all about myself, about the guys, how we've hung in together all these years. About my surgery, how slow it was coming back, how good the walking was. I think he got to know the guys somewhat, each one of them. He knew about Charlie. One day he told me he was reading a French poet named Baudelaire, but not in French. Said he liked him a lot. But he didn't look too good that day, coughed and choked a bit and said he'd fight off everything that came at him, in place or out of place. I liked that in him. I liked it a lot. He reminded me of my buddies. They're like him, down deep, not backing off, saying their own thing in their own way. I guess that's what grabbed me the most—he was like my pals.. And there's nothing more important than that.

A couple of days later, a few coins lighter, I left a poet's book on the bench after he had walked off to wherever he goes. I went off and watched him come back and take the book. I could tell he was pleased, even from a distance. The next day I brought a big Italian sub sandwich cut in quarters. We had a picnic of sorts. He ate and coughed and recited some words he had put by for me. I was really touched by them. Nothing ludicrous or silly about any of it. He also reminded me of my Grandfather, who used to read Yeats to me on the summer porch with the moths floating around like linnets. I bet he wasn't ten years older than any of us, though he'd been chewed up by something in this life. I'd bet a whole great big chunk had been taken out of him. We never know, do we, what's coming down on top of us? How it's going to hit? Some of us are going to get hit in the mind or at the heart by a runaway train, like Charlie was, here one day and gone the next. Others by a slight touch so weak we'd never see it otherwise except it bothers the mindset we're in.

But we came together for thirty-seven or thirty-eight days in a row. I knew he was sick with something besides heartache and loneliness. He said he'd never go to a hospital he couldn't afford, and he'd never be put by in a pauper burial. Eventually he alluded to his nights and how he kept warm. "Mother Earth has a warm embrace if you nestle deep enough. Sleeping in a natural curve is a bodily enlightenment."

We spoke of poets he had read, his dislikes.

Once he said, talking of Sandburg, "Carl's not good, Carl's bad." His eyes were lit up.

I said I loved "Chicago" and "Grass."

"Believe what I said," he replied.

That was the first inclination I had that he was playing word games with me. The light almost sang in his eyes. I saw Beacon Street Professor John Norton all over again. I felt the air passing through an open window of Gasson Hall, May pushing itself through the linden trees, the last class of the year, his eyes giving out answers.

Dermott had leaped all over that. "You finally meet a kindred spirit, a poetry buff, unlike us poor slobs, and you disagree. You'll never change."

I knew he was saying that you have nothing if you don't have a tool in your hands, something to grasp, to lean on. He slapped me on the back and said, "But you've always had it your way and we've stood by, but not without a question of sanity!"

What the old gent was doing, I told them, was giving me his secrets, letting me in on things. He was telling me what I wanted to know all along and had never asked: where he spent his nights, how he lived, what kept him alive. He respected my respect of his privacy, that I wasn't a do-gooder digging in his back yard for all his bones.

Jay asked, "So what did you learn? I trust you just told us something that we missed and you found out, but it's past me. Way past! So give!"

"It wasn't just that," I said to them as they looked at me like the Buster Brown dog, all quizzical and suddenly disbelieving. "That was only one more thing in a line of information he had been feeding me and I had not caught on. He had been enjoying himself, playing at me and with me, oh-so-good-naturedly, though. I didn't know what he had done in life. He never said anything of his past, what had driven him out of the mainstream, no details. The only bit of distaste he had ever uttered was that he didn't care one bit for what he called kiss-ass opportunists. The immediate clarity, of course, was playing with me, and it suddenly came to light. He had told me what took him to the streets. I could feel it and see it."

"Yuh, and what else?" Jay demanded.

I roped them all in with my eyes, each one, one at a time. I laid it on them. I said, "He lives in a cave or underground or under a blow-down."

Jay and Dermott laughed like hell. Jay said, "Don't tell me you're giving us this Carlsbad shit! Saturday! October! A game at the field! Cut the crap, Tom! You've got to have more than this to drag us out here." His face reddened, his lips pursed in an old read.

I told them nothing was so clear to me in life. The old man was special. I needed their help.

There was a silence in the air, a silence all about my friends. I saw them, all at once, in so many postures and situations over the long years. I loved them dearly and needed them. I clutched for the closeness one more time, as if it didn't come this time it might go off for good. I reached for it with my soul. They looked at me the way they had looked at me on more than one occasion, I can say. The measure was made again, for at

161

length, in the midst of a moving silence, I think they saw something of what I had seen in the old man. Something Beacon Street John Norton tried to tell me one day in class when nobody else was listening. And I had heard.

They broke and walked off, setting themselves apart by 150 feet or so. We began to fan through Breakheart for an old man none of them had known, perhaps dead, perhaps buried. For four hours on an October Saturday, the sun glorious, the leaves catching coins of light as they took wing, the thinning shade cooler, we fanned ourselves through the woods of Breakheart. We hailed each other, checked out here or there a possibility, waved ourselves onward. We did hill and dale and cliff face and swung about and went over the small mountain of stone by the lake.

It happened after a lunch of sandwiches. The coffee was gone and the legs seemed to go the way of the spirits. Dermott, on my left, standing at the foot of a small cliff, hailed me and then the others. His cry was accompanied by Jay's whistle cutting through the thinning trees off to Dermott's left.

Dermott was shaking his head, and then he nodded to me as we all gathered at the cliff face. The light was in his eyes and I knew he had found something he had not expected to find, though he had been willing to try. Pointing to a small aperture at the base of the cliff, cut low into the stone and behind a small clump of brush, he handed me his flashlight.

"You check, Tom," he said, and looked at the others with solemnity sitting on his face, stiff as a graven image. His head nodded slowly.

The aperture was small and I squeezed through. A stone, about the size of the opening, was pushed aside. I cast the flashlight beam inside. It was a cave at least ten feet deep and over six feet high. I caught an unlit lantern, then a second one, a pile of books on a small block of stone, some bottles, some cans on another stone. The light leaped back at me from a small mirror wedged in the wall. It was dry as bone in there. On one side wooden boxes must have been reassembled, for they stood as a unit almost three feet high. On the other wall, to my left, was a canvas cot with the three sets of crossed legs. On it lay the old man of the benches partly hidden in a sleeping bag. He was colder than the inside of the cave. A slip of paper was a chance semaphore beneath the cot.

Tom—I saw the light go on before you did. I know you'll not be long. Please leave me here. This is home and the celebration will be ours. I have no more family in the whole world. It was my pleasure talking with you. Guido Poti.

PS: You can have my books, but leave Sandburg, leave the Grass. I'll try again.

We left him there in the middle of Breakheart Reservation, socked down into that tomb. No pharaoh, but fair. Nobody will ever find him. I've gone back a number of times. Once, late of an August evening, stars tumbling over my shoulder, a breath of a breeze, I carried a bucket of water from the Second Lake and set some cement in place, a few more rocks, as if I were just visiting at Riverside Cemetery. A number of times I dropped a wild flower or a found stone or an orange leaf from the cliff top, just to change the look of the terrain I suppose, or to make a comment.

Once, in the near darkness, I saw the lights of his eyes coming back through the trees, as if he'd been off someplace for part of the day.

I don't tell the guys about those visits, and they don't ask.

A Toast to Skink

Four stout memories continue with me today of the year 1938, when I was ten years old, blond, looking for the next size boots, positive in my thinking. The summer was warm and soft and languid most of the time—a riverbank laziness, bare hook in water, mouth of a breeze at my ear, grass like a spread comforter. I was hungry much of the time; a handful of salt was often more than a threat. Roosevelt, the Okies, and the dust bowl of America were not far from my palate. September's grand, memorable and utterly terrifying hurricane slammed against the side of our three-decker house as boisterous as an icebreaker working frozen Boston Harbor. I thought it would turn the building over on its side, leaving all of us huddled and exposed on the first flight of steps in the front hall. Terror has a fearful endurance all its own like bloody fists, broken noses, lost friends.

Lastly, Skink Hanscombe, eternal imbiber, errant but harmless citizen, began his wispy glide around the edges of my life.

The hurricane, though, kicked itself off to the northwest, the hunger passed on via slabbed chunks of peanut butter on day-old bread stiffer than collars. Summer passed into winter. But Skink Hanscombe did not go away for the longest time. When that did happen, when he did go away from me, is difficult to bring back. Hazy and gray it was, as things can be when growing up. The way special moments secret themselves, play hide and seek with your mind, the game of life itself. Perhaps one day, the day and the hour declaring themselves openly, they will surface clearly from their hideaways.

In the beginning was a mystery on what attracted me to Skink. He was the town drunk, homeless and adrift save for an occasional gift of bed. A fact of tragedy he was from one fateful incident, who never raised a hand against anybody, or, for that matter, his voice. During my morning paper route, tossing *Boston Globes* and *Travelers* and *Records* and *Posts* onto a hundred or so porches and front steps through the center of town, I had seen him so many times being slipped out of the police station. The duty sergeant might have eased a shoe horn to his bottom and nudged him from official sight. Skink was one of those few people who could count on a warm night in the police station. His consignment would have been any empty cell, a bare mattress, a bare pillow, at the back end of the station. Grudging or misplaced respect or consideration, one might have termed it. To enough eyes, though, he was the most harmless tenant of all. Skink was what one might call *an upright drunk.*

But other things came to my eyes and mind about Skink. They've stayed with me forever, always there the way my Grandfather had aged but whose aging I never noticed because I saw him every day. Skink, the man, was long and lanky, over six feet even at a glance, and not many spare parts to him at first note. Gaunt he was much of the time if you want a better word, that Lincoln-esque quality I came to associate with old Abe and Raymond Massey and whoever else played the part. I'd heard my mother a number of times say that he was "rather consumptive looking." I took that to mean the mouthful of teeth that was no longer a mouthful. Enough of them were missing so that even a glance at the slightest grin or smile showed off the spaces like holes in a picket fence. His high cheekbones sat like the shiny halves of stickballs, the sunken cheeks saying he was always sucking on his gums. A darkness dwelled in his eyes much of the time, as though Skink was still measuring all his options, all the chances he'd had and hadn't used. It hit me later on that that was the terror part of it all. The long look down a long trail, both ways, and the sudden stop at those places where he found himself, like realization setting in glacier-cold, the whole mass of reality. It was a long time after these initial glimpses and resolutions before I realized Skink had made a much deeper impression in my life than was apparent.

Because of the booze, I suppose, these impressions leaped out much clearer than his reddish complexion boasting of long hours in the sun. His dark shaggy hair was that of a lost pup, with a swirling tress falling boyishly over his forehead from under the soft felt hat he wore continually. His thin bony hands twirled constantly, automatically, as if a tool was missing from their grasp. Like what really belonged there wasn't there, or some part of his space not fully occupied. And two other points of interest came to light. One was his adopted and peculiar gait, a partially delayed and deliberate reach of his right foot as he walked. He went toe-first, groping, reaching, lightly treading for something he knew would not be there. Later on I found out about that delicate step. And the second was a fact my father pointed out, that Skink always carried a paperback book of one sort or another in the inside pocket of his ill-matched suit coat. The small bulge was ever noticeable the way a holster might hang in place. Never was I able to spot a spine's title. I could picture him stealing a moment now and then to read a page or two, perhaps from a book of poetry or *The Call of the Wild, The Red Badge of Courage* or *Lord Jim.* The selections were dictated by the tastes that had come sweeping down the line to me in those early years.

At other times I had seen him slide out of a cellar window at ground level at the rear of the Town Hall. Marionette of a newborn colt, he'd climb bony and clumsily to his knees, to stand wobbly erect.

Perhaps another time he'd look like a shadow right out of Washington Irving, all six feet two inches or so of him. Off into the still-darkness he'd move, pointing on to his day, after absorbing all those free calories from the municipal furnace. The janitor, his head-turned host, interim landlord, was blind but to want. He knew the Board of Selectmen, the Town Manager, and the Town Accountant, jointly or separately, would frown on such hospitality, at least publicly.

But Skink was no ordinary drunk. My ultimate attraction to him took me down into myself, into those partial secrets and shadows I held off from my own being. It took me into the origins and routes of my genes, into testable memory, searching for what had granted him warmth when he first came reeling into my life. That feeling had been immediate, comfortable, acceptable, but not without its mystery. It was more than the boyish lock of hair hanging over his forehead pennant-like. More than his haunting eye-search that was so visible to me or his Indian-face complexion. And it was more than the very acceptance by other people, all older than me. Here was someone nothing more than a drunk, a wasted tolerance, it seemed, of another's life. Measurements, in my young life, had become reality.

Very slowly, with the caution a ten-year-old can somehow call upon only when fiercely determined, I began to search the labyrinths of my short history. I looked for reasons. I measured.

In time, after poking and sifting odd lots, after turning over smallest stones of the way, it said that Skink was a replacement. He was a substitute put into my life to take the place of someone who had been called away. That transaction was not announced. There was no drum roll to it, no blare of trumpets. It just happened. One day it was there. Such needs come about from loneliness, from a void scooped out of the middle of your existence, from search, from an unknown desperation playing with your soul. You're not ever sure what's eating at you at such times. But the need nourishes itself and you don't always have control of it. Skink was not the first, nor would he be the last, in my lifetime, several of these dependencies arising at different times, filling different needs.

Skink was obviously one of the stark and joined similarities in my life. A bit earlier for me there had been an old recluse and sot, face so full of character it made me shudder when close up. His features had been hammered out so memorable they might have been cut into stone. He had sprung out of nowhere to fill the void left by my paternal Grandfather. It was a void demanding that a patriarchal image, spirited but not necessarily hard and fast, be attendant on my life. So had come to me in my need the Grand Drinker, the stolid neighbor, the rugged and highly individual old face and slow walker and broad-backed hooch-dreadnought, Jack Winters. He was a standoffish but firmly footed friend, a no-nonsense elder clinging to life in his most rigid manner. He became a magnet for me, a youngster at loss. I knew one Grandfather to the core, but held fluctuating memories of the other. I had measured that loss even then.

Later a headlong crash of a small passenger plane into the frozen expanse of Lake Erie took my lone brother from me. His body was never recovered. One close friend stepped into the breach to fill the void left by that sweet prince. For over forty years we never raised our voices in anger, never gave the other any advice. We let territories be what they were, factions and factotums at their appointed places. And a lost son will never be replaced. But sooner or later other young men will rise from my shadows, from the mists of my past, and I will love them and my daughters will beam through their full days. I'd willingly settle for such rare accounting. Substitutes, as proved so many times, have a way of counting.

The comparisons in Skink's case were eventually convincing. After the self-mining, after spading up my small garden of memories, I came at length to my Uncle Johnny. Here was the last picture of a man whose indelicate warmth I had loved with abandon. Laid out icy and dirty and stiff on my mother's bed he'd been. An oil tablecloth hastily spread its blue pattern of tea pots and watering cans and desert canisters under him. The doctor hovered over him, and my father cut away the frozen laces on Johnny's boots so that they could be removed. His last breaths were noisy and significantly irregular, each of them countable and singular in that small room. It had tight walls high and thin, a bed slight in its expanse, a small chest of drawers standing like a delicate miniature. A narrow-slatted chair sat beside the bed. A bare-bauble string of rosary beads hung on a half-driven nail over the head of the bed. Such were the final, thin veneers of a corruptible and simple life. Death, right down to the dreadful aroma, lurked about us heady and defiant. Hades and Limbo and the River Styx hung by a thread of that defiance.

I was four years old then. I had sneaked upstairs when they carried Uncle Johnny in. He was nearly frozen to death, planked but discrepant, beard white as starch, tears frozen round as pearls on his cheeks. His mouth began to slowly fill with a subtle blackness, as if France and the Great War, in their broad and timeless sweeping, in their endless reach, had finally claimed him.

They had found him on the railroad tracks, close to the Malden City dump, where he must have been headed. There was the dumpmaster's little shed with its huge and hospitable cast iron stove. As many as six or seven drunks and homeless dregs would be able to put their frosted feet up on a thick cast iron rim and fight the night away, any night of the week, any night of the year.

Uncle Johnny drank, a whole lot for sure, but he had been kind to me and my brother and sisters and my mother, his sister. She said he had never been right since his return from France and the infantry in 1918, just the bones and clatter of the fine young man he had once been. Nothing much else was left of him but his innate kindness and thoughtfulness. "The gas, you know," she had said, tipping her head in a knowledgeable way. Johnny tipped his cap to old ladies and obvious mothers, to funeral corteges, to any member of the ministry, to any legless or armless man who might have been his comrade in "The Great Stink" as he called World War I. He didn't work, not a day that I remember. But he drank, easing his life down that corruptible and inevitable trail to the railroad tracks and the dread siding that final night. I had, without reserve, loved that romantic and pitiful soul the way a child loves a warm mystery. I was never sure of which questions to ask, so I asked none.

Somehow, for undeclared reasons early in the strange acquaintanceship with Skink, I had been irretrievably drawn to him. I found him warm, friendly, and trustworthy. He became, slowly but surely in place, Uncle Johnny's substitute, filling a void in my life that demanded to be filled. He was so much like the gentle and pained veteran who too carried measurement in his eyes, who was the host of small kindness and innate politeness. There were the boyish locks, those dark eyes at query, the innocent warmth that accompanied him. And the constant and observable bulge of his inner coat pocket.

Oh, I said to myself so many times, *The Red Badge Of Courage* hidden away, or *Lord Jim* lade in deep cargo, or Walt Whitman, at song, in noble and endless transport, America on the robust wing. The small parts of my life selected his meager library.

Never once in all the time I delivered papers, and made my collections, many of them loose or in envelopes inside storm doors, dropped in mail boxes or cast like dice under mats, had any of that minor coin ever been taken. And Skink had seen me time and time again extracting my few coppers from their appointed hideaways. I began to think of him as one of my morning companions who moved slowly and surely alongside me. There was the milkman and the bakery driver, and the foot patrolman. All of them eased their way through the grayness of early light the way I thought the Holy Spirit moved. Floating, footless, near soundless, they whispered of identity and dignity and all's well with the world. As did the uncle I had seen draw his last breath on my mother's bed. If ever I was to be attacked, to be robbed of my two cents a copy pittance, to be harmed in any way, I knew all of them, including Skink, would have come quickly to my side. Never a doubt of it, not for a moment, the edge of one fictional knife having slit each of our right index fingers in silent ritual, all our bloods becoming one, all that sworn redness around me in the darkness. All of them had my implicit trust. All of them occupied significant space in my mind. All of them glided at the edges of my life, dreamy creatures, costumed, almost touchable, and worthy.

Skink was then part apparition and part character of life, a source of measurement for me. I bet I had seen him a hundred times, in the grayness of evening or dawn's false light. It was the way one might see an animal, like a raccoon on tiptoes at a hedge, shadowy but as company, moving at the edges of my small journeys. He was countable, even though shadows moved on him, or he moved on shadows. Once I had heard him talking to a patrolman on the

171

night beat who had told him to head off someplace to get his sleep.

"Sleep only comes when you're trying to get away from something," Skink had said.

I can hear his voice now, soft, low, wet, tooth-defined, the words spilling out in the evening, saying something it took me almost forever to decode.

In high school Skink had been a remarkable scholar and athlete. Top of his class, strong-armed pitcher in baseball and a sure-handed and speedy receiver on the football team, Dartmouth had beckoned. He was set to make the quick journey north, the third of our graduates in four years so selected. Tall, thin, dark-haired, handsome in a traditional way, he spent the summer driving an ice truck. Up long flights of stairs he hustled huge cakes of ice stolen in January and February from Lily Pond.

Nothing's ever so cool for long.

A four-year old youngster had fallen under one of his rear wheels. Skink's foot slipped repeatedly off the rubberless brake pedal. Panic became the log forever lodged in his chest, the incurable mill dam at origin. From that second forevermore his foot went reaching for the elusive and slippery pedal. Existence and being at two levels went their awful and sundry ways. Neither of the two victims salvaged a moment of their prior lives. Skink's life, thus and forever, spilled itself in beer, rye, bourbon, whiskey, scotch, vodka, white lightning, wines from most continents and nearly every conceivable valley on earth. There was after-shave lotion whether icy blue in color or musky as an armpit in aroma. Which one didn't matter. More than once surfaced an almost final bout with automobile alcohol. He learned how to strain potent liquids through sand taken from children's play boxes or unsliced loaves of bread, dread chemist at laboratory work. The laborious seeping cleansed microbes, germs and death out of the dread fluids. His body and his mind had begun their long torturous descent, getting drunk, keeping warm, falling still further away from what had been. It came, eventually as he did, to a gray, neutral, convent-like yard stick trying to lay things out for me.

One time special I saw him. He was in the bowels of an old foundation of random fieldstones and patched-up red mickeys stiff in clay and pink geometry, well behind our one theater. The foundation sat smack in a cluster of alders. By chance I had come upon Skink and a companion at illicit laboratory. He wore what he practically wore all the time, a suit coat whose sleeves were too short. Hanging on him was a pencil-striped dark blue coat with one pocket torn and hanging, heavy salty-like stains on the shoulders. His pants were black with a red thin stripe, what the Salvation Army specialized in, thin, washed out, but still black at a distance. He wore a gray soft felt hat, the kind my father and every other man wore in those days. Probably a thousand years old from the looks of it. Perched sort of jauntily on his head, it tipped to the sun riding high above us. Made me think of one of Emily Dickenson's poems he did. The lock of hair hung below the wide brim, still boyish, still in trouble or at trouble, it seemed to say. His hands moved automatically as always, a flurry of nervous energy working in them. His eyes were dark as dead stars in his face, his long frame throwing the smallest of shadows. The harmless warmth of him hung in the air about me, touched at my shoulders, at the back of my neck. Though I spied on him, I felt no sense of distrust, of disloyalty.

His companion's dress was nearly duplicated, but he came off a smaller version of Skink. Just as nervous in his movements he was, but he had no warmth about him, no acceptance on my part. No substitute, I might have argued if I'd have been lucid at the moment.

Through a crack in the old wall I saw them and their assemblage of anomalous gear. Chemists to the end they were, reprobates for sure, but chemists to the bitter end. Arranged about them were odd bottles, at least half a dozen, full of pale liquid. A wide-mouthed piece of pipe, the kind used for lally columns, was at hand. And, incongruously, not laboratory stuff, a loaf of bread that might have been straight from a mother's oven, or her windowsill.

At first I thought they were going to make sandwiches. But Skink cut off one heel of the loaf with the ugliest of knives, tore it in half, and handed a piece to his compatriot. His chemist pal laughed a guttural and naughty laugh, a back room laugh I thought, one coming from the celebration of a dirty joke. "Chow down!" he yelled. They were Romulus and Remus at chewing, the seedy pair of them, the copy and the copied, in their continuity tearing and gnawing as wolves at each portion. Their few teeth were prominent as bars of a broken grille. Each gummed a goodly part of the bread, and slobbered words through spaces where teeth had been lost.

"Where'cha cop the pipe, Skink? From Fogarty's, I'm bettin', 'Im the slimy bastard 'e is! Makes ya puke, 'e does. Wouldn't stand you a drink on Christ day, our Plumber's Delight." Titter rode in his voice.

His words also wet in their coming, he tossed his head in condemnation, rolled his eyeballs so that his dark eyebrows also moved. Down to the torn pocket his jacket almost matched Skink's pants. Black it was with a faint red stripe, as though they had changed clothes like boys at a boarding school, hiding their meagerness, disguising the home pocketbook. A felt hat he also wore, brimmed, feathered, heavy with stains on the brim. A dark blue shirt was buttoned tightly at the neck. His fingers kept moving of themselves, itchy movements, twitching the way the telegrapher at the Cliftondale railroad station worked at the eternal signals.

"Don't spill any."

His voice faded in and out as he spoke, the sounds split by his few teeth, the words continually wet leaving his mouth, atomized. I could have sworn they were accompanied by particles due for ingestion. The two were an ugly lot, but warming in their own special way.

Skink pushed the decapitated loaf of bread down inside the pipe, gently nudging it deeper into the iron, much of his fist disappearing.

"Fogarty's not the worst of the lot," he said. "Fact is I think he saw me take it, and if not, didn't want to see me take it. He's like that. He knows that I know he talked to Sergeant Farrell about the usual accommodations at the station." The look on his face was at first sad as he continued, "But he's Fogarty. Wants me to know, fact is. I'm going to name him in my will, Dexter, and that's for sure."

He propped the length of pipe between two stones. Arranging a third stone in support, he set an empty bottle under the lower end. He uncapped one of the full bottles. Slowly he poured its contents into the pipe, onto the open heel of the loaf of bread, onto the lap of the Great Plains grassland.

"What'cha goin' to name him, Skink?" Dexter said. Simultaneously the titter and laugh almost escaped his broad mouth, his few teeth. An announcement, came, an acceptance, both a-twitter in him. He shook devilishly.

"Probably Asshole of All Assholes, maybe Ireland's Biggest Bung Hole since Peter plugged the dike."

Skink's laugh was silent, it seemed, as if he was alone in that dreary foundation, a laugh kept within himself for his own enjoyment. Like food particles at the gum line, savory if only token. At the crack in the wall, my knees pressed hard against a rough stone, against reality. Suddenly I saw old man Fogarty somehow and somewhere getting the scoop on Skink's will and final testament. I near burst a gut. A marvel he was, I thought, this swaying, braying, graying drunk of all drunks, this language master, this grand comic of the gutter. I figured, on the very spot, then and there, that I loved him. I figured I owed him. I figured he had a due in life. I figured Uncle Johnny was somewhere looking at me and his counterpart, with a smile on his face. "One for the books," he'd probably have said.

"Perhaps yet again," continued Skink, "we'll dub him The Continually Parted Anal Rose of the Outhouse Arboretum."

Dexter shook all over, *petit mal* of seizures, wheezing deep in his throat. His eyes rolled in ecstasy of the odd lot, and two teeth, still white, in the company of bread, capped his joy. He slapped his knee the way the burlesque guys did those summer weekends on Cliftondale's outdoor stage, great leg-breaking slaps, joints snapping, the grandest of revelry. I expected his hat to fall off—the gray, squeezed-to-death, worn-out, bandless, pin-decorated hat.

I expected him to fall down in that stone remnant of a house. I expected to remember it forever, the contrived and expected and libelous humor of the pair of them. Then, as if at one end of a telescope, the subject end, or under microscope, I felt Skink's eyes pierce the slot of my peeking. They passed clean through me. He must have seen me, must have seen my eyes, must have recognized me, as it turned out, for in the following days he began to call me Sneaky Pete.

It was not distastefully applied, that sobriquet. It would come lightly and offhandedly across a field, from a bunch of alders or maples whose purpose from the point of creation had been to contain childhood's secrets. Or it would come from behind a dark house set back from the traffic of the Center. It would waft on the slightest breeze, as if Skink were playing games with me, as if we were at recess and he was *It*. I was sharing, whatever it was, and Uncle Johnny was probably a lot closer than I thought.

I didn't realize, until much later of course, that one of Skink's survival mechanisms was the knowledge he had acquired in his slow and laborious travels, in the variety of his bed and board. And how he used that knowledge. Subtilely, of course. Summer nights he often sprawled out behind a tombstone in Riverside Cemetery. Those stays provided him the identities of three women who wrestled, each on their own time, in the front seat of the patrol car with Sergeant Farrell, long after midnight, long after the town went idly to sleep. They said that Skink had seen Lonnie Brown making love to both Curtingham sisters, twins at that, in the grove beside Rapid Tucker's Pond. All four had eventually come face to face, one fully dressed and three not. From one customer to another I heard that a big banker in town had confided a secret to his girlfriend, in her little un-repossessed house tightly set against the tracks. The only person in town he feared finding out about their covert business was Skink. Skink wouldn't tell, but Skink would use. I could believe that. Anything for a bed as night closed down.

Now and again, but not often, he would whisper to me, from a culvert or behind a bush or having set himself down behind a rock on my route.

"Sneaky Pete, do you have a dime I might use for a time?"

He'd wink at me, chuckling at meter and rhyme. Uncle Johnny would be all over his face, the eyes, the chin, the taut cheekbones as if being pinched from the inside, a sadness spilling from his eyes the way girls can poke it up at melodrama and pain. The need for a drink flushed royally on his face. I would shake my head in amazement and reach into a pocket.

As all that may be, I took the whole foundation scene away with me. I never stayed for the last pour. I never knew what they called their final solution, what it was, what it did for them. I could only guess that in its original state it might have poured white and hot and illicitly from the bottom of a Chevy or Ford radiator. Or a Reo or Graham or Hupmobile or Hudson or Packard or De Soto. Or it had been scooped under cover of darkness from a cabinet at the Hood's Milk Company horse barn. A liniment or antiseptic lotion it could have been, not toxic but heavy in its aroma. And to be passed through wheat and flour and yeast and brown crust thus becoming something else. Eventually, only Fogarty remained of the ashes, the embers of his assigned names, the laughter silent but real. As it was, Skink, through this and other incidents, made me a keen observer of all that went on about me. Not that it was to be traded for cot or bedding, but that it all could be put away for some other use. Perhaps to be related as fiction. Or some part of truth.

Teddy Quinlan's father was a night patrolman. He told my father one morning at the paper store that Skink had had a bad night at the station. He had cried a good deal of the night away. He had called out the dead boy's name a number of times. No one needed to explain *who the boy was*, now living on at the rear of the police station, crowding Skink Hanscombe, inevitably, to the end.

It was that way for a long time, his life in an endless circle. After a time his territory shrunk, his abodes becoming more formalized. Hedda Halsey tolerated him for a short run in her house near the theater. And then a sister eventually brought him in to the back room of her house, a battle won or lost. His looks never changed while he was there with her, always wanting it seemed. The message ran clear across his face, locked into his fingers loose as old gum wrappers the wind played with. Skink stayed put with her most of the time, just breaking out every once in a while, knocking down a few with old friends of the main as he might have called them. They were stout hearts, long livers who fought the importunate odds. The lot included tittering Dexter and like-consumptive looking Ike Wiggins and toothless Tony Pomfret and a few others. They whispered through old haunts, and talked to old friends, who could not leave Riverside, when nobody else would listen to them. Skink called me Sneaky Pete every chance he could, for I had dropped my morning paper route and gone big-time for Sunday's knockout punch of heavier cash. And then that too fell by the wayside.

At length I got new classmates in high school. We became teammates. We squatted down on the scrimmage line and held on for each other's souls. We spent our time and energy in concert and demanded much of each other. Little was left over.

And Uncle Johnny and Skink, caught in such bind, faded slowly on the horizon, over which one worldly and imperious day came my summons to Korea. Quickly, as if redrawn and re-endowed, new zones and new comrades circled the grid about me. Life went spinning away not many feet from me on too many occasions. Thunder was closer than ever before. Earthquakes were common every day. Nights at times were spent in recall on this side or that side of the 38th Parallel, pulling back pieces of our lives, telling tales when we were bunkered down, coming close at times to bombast and misrepresentation. We set what we thought was yesterday into place one more time. And we shared the ration of beer one warm night at the Puk Han River where Skink Hanscombe was given a host of new friends. We toasted him with raised cans lifted from the cool waters of the bloody river.

"A toast to a great name—to Skink Hanscombe and Duquesne!"

We toasted his longevity, his long-time passion that was our short-time vocation at the river's edge where bodies floated in the darkness. His unknown library we almost had a pool on, the tip of his cap we never let idle, saluting each other, raising drinks overhead.

There was mother, apple pie, a Ford or Chevy pick-up, America, all sitting square in the same aura with Skink Hanscombe, town drunk, tipper of caps, inveterate reader. Next day we forgot him in the most horrid firefight imaginable. There were no hangovers left over for us. None at all. But Skink Hanscombe had been a quick companion to a squad of infantry who had never met him. Some of them might have taken him off with them, into the long, long day. And into the longer night. He might have been, that gentle tippler, the last name spoken or the last thought provoked for some of them. Like Emily Dickenson's little man leaning against the sun.

But, quick as the passage of the old days and Aggie Jenkins' wink from her front door after her old man had gone off for the day, all of us were on the way to school of one sort or another. I was on a ship on the Pacific on a train on the rails across America on a bus into the heart of my town and walking the last two miles to our house. My duffel bag was shouldered light as a pillow. Chevrons were matching the new wrinkles in my face.

It was dark. The house erupted. Sisters leaped out of their blankets and dreams. My mother gave back more than a year of prayers in a moment of silence in her room. My father and I shared our first beers ever together. Sleep called. I sank onto the couch in the front room. My father began to watch late-night snow on the television, which was but months old. Too soon into sleep came the crash at the back door of the kitchen as if a battering ram had smashed its way through.

I leaped from the couch. The wide Sam Browne belt, its broad brassy buckle long a learned weapon to be contended with, found its responsive way from my Class A uniform pants to appointment about my fist. There was noise in the den as my father mobilized his own armory, a belt similar to mine stripped from his guard uniform. We crunched against each other at the door to the kitchen, unable to get through at the same time. Our shoulders banged together in concert and at target for the very first time in our lives. There in front of us was the dreg of all dregs, soiled, rotten, almost cadaverous, dripping wet from a sudden rain. Shaking to the last splinter of bone, eyes ablaze in fear, was Skink Hanscombe, my homecoming present. Still scattering from his long convulsive frame were shards and slivers of glass glittering to the floor. Screams rose from his throat as if he were being crushed by some malevolent monster—Uncle Johnny come back from the dead. The icy pearls of his cheeks come back in their shine. The air was full of a horrid odor, thick and ripe, expansive, leaving room for all of imagination and memory. I brought gangrene back from the war, the smell of it, finding Chinese bodies where latrines were dug, no flesh but bones hanging onto odors. I recalled a black and white movie of a soldier's toe being removed with a pair of pliers, breakfast being spilled all over the place in Yokohama's Camp Drake. It had been too early in the morning for a stomach to contend with.

Skink stunk to the high heavens. He cried and he screamed and then he begged for help.

"Jayzus!! Jayzus! They're after me! Jayzus was right! They come in the night! They come after me! The rotten little bastards of them, they're after me, they're being after me!"

And then directly to my father, a moment of lucid light crossing that most pained face, a bare pause at recognition, an eye flicker's worth of intensity.

"Ah, Jayzus, Jim, is that you? Is that you, Jim? I never hurt you, Jim. I never hurt your boy, and the bastards are after me!"

My father was a tippler, a fair wine merchant in his own right, a Marine out of Nicaragua and Guatemala. He had first hand knowledge of the DT's while in the Tropics and what it can bring down on a man. He shoved me aside.

"You've earned your sleep."

That's all he said. He pointed me back to my bed.

Skink drank black coffee. My father walked him back and forth from our house to the mill a half mile away. Again and again through the late night he walked him. Skink leaned on my father who remembered horned bull frogs at the end of his bunk on a ship coming out of Nicaragua with the Marine Legation aboard. The bows and arrows and booze had been put away in a final salute, a party to end all parties.

Skink, finally, lay his head on a pillow on a spare mattress earlier tossed into our cellar. All of it at my father's recommendation and urging, his Marine DI's voice reconstructed, re-armed. Skink slept. I tossed just above him in my own pass at sleep. I thought again about Fogarty and Dexter and Farrell's women hiking their dresses at least up to their hips in the cemetery, white thighs running off to forever. I remembered people who didn't like to pay the pittance for paper delivery.

My thirty-day leave went as quickly as vacation. The last day my mother said she had heard a funny noise in the cellar. I checked it out. A card table was set up with four chairs in place. Four odd mattresses lined the fieldstone walls. At least six cases of empty beer bottles sat like concrete blocks waiting for a stone mason to set them in place. On the air I could smell Edgar Allen Poe's Amontillado, and the bricks and the lime and the cement.

She yelled down the stairs.

"Is everything all right?"

I could picture one hand pressed to her cheek, one hand on the door, ready to help if needed, how her head would be cocked alertly waiting for an answer. Everything was observable and memorable to me, all the times and all the considerations, all the characters that had filtered in and through my life. There was Uncle Johnny and old Jack Winters, and the ghost that accompanied me on my paper rounds, my guardian of the spirits.

"It's okay, Mom. Everything's okay."

Skink Hanscombe, as always, wherever his hat hung, had been at home, Skink Hanscombe and company.

Eddie Smiledge, Houseman

He was the houseman and smoked cigars thick as Baby Ruth bars short as he was. He always wore green pants and red socks so people could laugh at him a little bit on the side. He'd pocket change while the laughter moved around The Rathole. We always knew something special was ringing in him, some other call or cause. There were times he would lend a guy a buck who had missed a great shot at billiards or One-Ball and was almost there, getting his dough back. Never did he charge more than a buck for a buck. He could listen as good as a bartender, talk like a barber, remember to the minute the start of each game at each table. He answered only to Smiledge, never to his Christian name, never to *hey you* or *houseman* or *you over there* by a newcomer. Smiledge, he'd say. Smiledge it was. It seemed to us that it was Smiledge forever. Then one day he was gone, but that's ahead of me.

The sometimes darker room of The Rathole was tucked below the Knights of Pythias Building, below street level of Central Street passing by into the center of town. It sat close beside the railroad tracks that were just starting to get rusty, 18-wheeler trucks and time passing that roadbed by. In The Rathole dramas came in different shapes and different tones. Sometimes it could be a scream, like a mother who'd just stick her head in the sub-street door and yell, like a banshee promising the truant the devil end of the world.

"Charlie! Charles R. Parker! You get your fanny out here this instant!"

She'd embarrass the kid for a month of Sundays as it would appear how long he stayed away living it down. They tried to say mothers never had any say in a pool room. Or there'd be the truant officer, acting on a tip, come looking for Nicky Haskins always skipping school. Or there'd come a cop looking for whoever left his car parked at the door and the rear end halfway out into Central Street. Swearing as he came down the stairs so we could hear him before he opened the door, so we'd know who was coming because he had grown up himself in this deep hole. Once, early in his tour of duty as houseman, Smiledge hid a kid under the last bench and draped a table cover over him so the cops couldn't find him. All the guys knew he really was on their side from that moment on.

There was a whole lot we didn't know about Smiledge. Secrets were private property with him. Like who lost how much and who won, who was on a winning streak and who was not, who was prone to cheat a little bit or a great deal. Cheaters would get a leg up on the table and the rake out for a long reach at the cue ball and the sleight of hand at a ball tucked against one rail beside that thrown leg. The ball could be eased into an easier shot with a pinkie or the aft end of the cue stick. Smiledge knew who was apt to use his mother's grocery money for that week after he'd scoff it out of the oatmeal box or the old coffee can hiding spot. Sometimes Smiledge gently suggested the money was not good for legal tender that day or any day soon. The one great sin he thought was a mother at the door calling out a kid who had scoffed the week's grocery money, or worse, a father bearing down on him, chest out, face red, demands known from the first step through the door.

But, where or what was his own family background?

In a sense we knew beans about Smiledge… nothing about wife, kids, or siblings.

Someone said he lived in a rooming house in the next town, near the factory district. But no address ever came up. He did get off the bus from that town, right in front of The Rathole, which was not a regular bus stop. A few of the drivers got to know him as a regular or had spent some growing time in The Rathole on their own. Like Ray Abercrombie, who had a stiff arm bent about in one position from a haywire band saw at the icehouse. To make change on the bus with that bent arm, Ray had to lean over the coin box, dipping the hand of that bent arm to get the coins. He was one of the graduates who had spent many hours in Smiledge's company. Ray would toot the bus horn nearing The Rathole, letting everybody know that Smiledge was due. Then he'd toot him goodbye as he drove away after dropping him off right at the front door.

What was known was Smiledge had missed only one day of work in something like thirty years. He could be coughing or gagging or looking plain putrid, but he was always there, being the house man for the owner. He said on the one day off he had gone to a funeral, but gave no name; not wife's, not sweetheart's, not comrade's or deep friend's. On local wakes for known players, he'd slip out for an evening visit at the funeral parlor. Each one was a will of the wish visit you could count on despite the brevity. You knew, being a regular, that if you went down for the count, Smiledge would at least come by to say goodbye, in that flighty and quick way of his. He never knelt though. Never looked like he prayed. Only looked like he might be remembering a good game, a great shot like a clinical massé, a brilliant billiards shot, to clinch a point or a match, a graduation of sorts. We knew he loved his pool and, in his own way, the players, us.

Some deeds made Smiledge out special in one way or another. For example, each Tuesday, payday at the local giant General Electric plant, he'd let Edward Joseph Wozniak (Edjo) sleep on a bench at the deep end of The Rathole. Edjo would rest his one good eye with that sleep while waiting on a couple of GE guys to come by with their paychecks and gently remove much of it from their separate wallets. Now and then

Smiledge would gently shake Edjo awake; "Eddie," he'd say, "294's here," 294 being the GE guy's badge number, his name never known. Nothing was known about him except his insatiable desire to get some of his money back or try lifting some of Edjo's money, which he never did. I'd swear, as would a few other guys, that Smiledge knew Edjo would start playing 294 or 376 without having a dime in his pocket, he had that much confidence in his game. Edjo was blind in one eye and needed that rest for the good eye. Smiledge once admitted that Edjo had the right to a slight edge in all matters pool. Edjo was one of the guys who could throw a leg up on the table and move a ball hidden by his leg that 294 or 376 never saw get moved into better position. Edjo did it with body English and not cue ball English. I suspect that Smiledge thought 294 or 376 should have known better.

Backing up in all of this, there were a couple of times that spoke reams about Smiledge; what kind of stuff he was made of, or something that would only add to the pile of questions we all had about him.

You know that money and pool rooms move together, as much partners as any business or financial matter. There were times a lot of money swam around that room of four tables, most all of it at Table No. 1, the lead table, the host table, the best table in the house. When it ceased to be so, it would be moved along the line and one table would be moved out. Smiledge kept No. 1 covered when it was not in use, kept it dry, kept it clean, kept it for the guys who had earned their way to that table. Its banks were lively. It was insanely level in that cellar of a room and the leather thongs of each pocket were wiped down a number of times each day so that they shone like saddle leather. The green felt was like the grass in Eden.

None of the poorer players could play on No. 1. They had to progress up the line until the time when

Smiledge, ever the watchman and calculator and talent judge, would throw them a cue and say, "Want to hit a few?" That was graduation of a sort, a mark of acceptance. Some guys celebrated the move a little too much and would move out of favor sooner or later. Some brought their game to a higher level mastering billiards or One-Ball by bringing clean and positive play into their arsenal of shots. Once in a while you'd see Smiledge nod or get off a small grin as if he were attesting to an earlier judgment.

And some brought a lot of money into that room, passed it over that table one way or the other. Tin Horne was one of them. Tin had owned his own table at a Port of Embarkation during WW II, someplace down in Jersey, probably right outside the gate at Fort Dix. Through that gate moved thousands of guys at assignment or reassignment. Many of them were would-be pool sharks, guys from the big cities like Chicago and New York and Boston, and way down in Houston; you know, the supposed pros. The table was in a private garage, a single table under a single bulb. Tin had bought it from another dogface who was shipping out to those affairs in Europe. Tin made a hell of a lot of money before his time to ship out came and he had to sell it off also. For a long while some of the dough he was raking in went back to a sergeant at Fort Dix, finagling Tin's name off replacement lists for a long time. Maybe it was a lieutenant. Or a major. He probably got shipped out himself and Tin's time was up shortly thereafter. But also a ton of that money found its way back home into Tin's bank account at the local bank a few doors down from The Rathole. That account established him as a gambler who belonged from day one on Table No. 1.

Tin was one of the elite, a crafty, cigar-smoking guy who knew both ends of the cue stick, at perfection and execution, or at trouble. He was tough as the proverbial nail and as cool as a glacier. When he lined up a shot, and moved slowly around the table, from one shot to the next, some opponents were unnerved. Part of his game plan, one might say. I can see him now, that cold gleam in his eyes, that dagger stream coming across the table as he lined up a shot. When he shot it was not until he had let out that long puff of smoke directly at his opponent. Many times it worked.

Tin was playing Frankie Dykstra the day the gun came out of a pocket of Dykstra's jacket hanging on the wall. Tin had made a great shot, an impossible shot, and was about to win the big game of the evening. The cue ball had hung perilously close to the lip of a corner pocket. One of the bystanders was a little anxious because he had bet some money on the outcome, like a whole lot of money. He bumped the table so that the cue ball fell into the pocket. Tin reached for it, to set it back on the lip, his shot having sat there many seconds while he planned his next shot before the bettor bumped the table.

Dykstra said, his voice cutting through the layers of smoke that rode the air like pages of a book, "If you touch that ball, I'll blow your brains out."

He had pulled a revolver or a pistol from his jacket hanging beside the cue rack. The handgun was leveled at Tin who had his hand in the pocket, his eyes on the gun, the beginning of a smile on his face. Tin must have seen what nobody else saw.

WHAM! Smiledge brought a cue stick, thick end first, down on Dykstra's arm so hard that the gun jumped in the air. The second sound you could hear was the bone breaking in Dykstra's arm. Some of the guys can still hear that bone breaking.

"Not in my hall," Smiledge said. "Take your shot, Tin, and somebody else get this son of a bitch out of here and down to see Doc Carter."

Dykstra never came back to The Rathole again; maybe he got cured of gambling by Smiledge.

One other time one of the guys who had just started dating a real good looker from two streets over, and who had just broken up with her long-time boyfriend, came into The Rathole just before closing time. It was late, the drug store down the street was long closed and the guy whispered in Smiledge's ear. Smiledge went to the cash register, reached underneath the small countertop and came back to Table No. 1. He threw a handful of rubbers out on the tabletop, the only time I ever saw any debris on the green felt surface, and said, "You guys never use your heads. You never plan anything. I don't know how the hell you ever got this far in life," for that guy being about 17 years at the time.

The whole place went into hysterics, but lover boy reached over and began to rake in the pile of rubbers as if he had just won a huge poker pot. Smiledge said, "One rubber, Romeo, just one." The whole place went bananas again.

But lover boy was smiling the next day, all day.

Anyway, me and my gang were standing in line for a history of our own, him watching us come along the way, Smiledge the houseman, racking balls, collecting coin, a judge with a hundred dollar bill in the side pocket. He smoked cigars thick as cue sticks or continually ate candy bars until his teeth stuck. We saw his hair thin, his face widen, his paunch grow a bit in the green pants, and his step slow. During those growth years he'd send us home abruptly when our eyes became hazy or midnight slipped like a footpad over the green felt on table No. 4. He did not lend us money, but let the clock work in our favor. At a nickel a game he didn't see the eight ball eight times in the side pocket, and he forgot to lock away all the nickel bags of potato chips. One night, the world suddenly topsy-turvy again, we played One-Ball-in-the-Side-Pocket past closing. Smiledge sat in a corner waving off the game costs. One day later we walked off under a September moon all the way to Korea. The night I came back, chevrons up and down, deep new wrinkles struck across my face, measureless but valid, reaching for my yesteryears, a skinny bald-headed man was racking the balls. He didn't know my name, who was home and who wasn't, who wasn't coming home, why Smiledge had drifted off the day after we left for the army.

We had seen it all before. When the older guys moved out, when they left us, we in our sneakers and innocence of baseball's bright summer days. When they went away from us with our big brothers, left us lonely and miserable on corners, and in cold fields with all the long ball hitters gone. We cried in dark cells of home for our brothers and bubble gum heroes, our young community of family. Oh, Dropkick's brother not yet home from someplace in World War II; Zeke's brother who owned the soul of every pitcher he ever caught; a shortstop the Cards owned, Spillane, I think, his name; and in that great silence out there Billy Centerfield left his arm in Kwajalein debris. Oh, brotherless we had played our game, no deep outfield, no zing to pitch, no speed, no power, loveless without a big brother to show our growing. And then, not long after the Boston Braves rode that mighty crest in '48, our turn came, and we left our brothers on corners, in cold fields, we long ball hitters.

If Smiledge only knew how much we *had* grown while we were away in the Land of the Morning Calm. For sure, he would have smiled, nodded his head, agreed with his own judgment on our talents.

But they said he went off the day after we left and never came back. I don't think I'll ever know what happened. But I know what didn't... he didn't forget us, not a one.

The Three Fishermen

There were three of them. There were four of us,
and April lay on the campsite and on the river, a
mixture of dawn at a damp extreme and the sun in the
leaves at cajole. This was Deer Lodge on the Pine River
in Ossipee, New Hampshire. The lodge was naught but
a foundation remnant in the earth. Brother Bentley's
father, Oren, had found this place sometime after the
First World War, a foreign affair that had seriously
done him no good. But he found solitude abounding
here. Now we were here, post-World War II, post-
Korean War, Vietnam War on the brink. So much
learned, so much yet to learn.

Peace then was everywhere about us. It was in
the riot of young leaves, in the spree of bird confusion
and chatter, in the struggle of pre-dawn animals for the
start of a new day. A Cooper Hawk smashed down
through trees for a squealing rabbit, came the yap of a
fox at a youngster, and a skunk noisy at rooting.

We had pitched camp in the near darkness, Ed
LeBlanc, Brother Bentley, Walter Ruszkowski, myself.
A dozen or more years we had been here, and seen no
one. Now we were into our campsite deep in the forest.
So deep that at times coming in we had to rebuild
sections of narrow road (more a logger's path) flushed
out by earlier rains. Deep enough where we thought
we'd have no traffic. Suddenly there came the sound of
a growling engine. Into the camp site chugged an old
solid body van. It was a Chevy, the kind I had driven
for Frankie Pike and the Lobster Pound in Lynn
delivering lobsters throughout the Merrimack Valley. It
had pre-WW II high fenders, a faded black paint on a
body you'd swear had been hammered out of
corrugated steel. The engine made sounds too angry
and too early for the start of day. Two elderly men, we
supposed in their seventies, sat the front seat. Their

slouched felt hats were decorated with an assortment of tied flies, like a miniature bandoleer of ammunition on the band. They could have been conscripts for Emilano Zapata, so loaded their hats and their vests as they climbed out of the truck.

"Mornin', been yet?" one of them said as he pulled his boots up from the folds at his knees. The tops of the boots looked as wide as a big mouth bass coming up from the bottom for a frog sitting on a lily pad. His large hands and long fingers I could picture in a shop barn working a primal plane across the face of a maple board. *Custom-made, old elegance,* those hands said.

"Barely had coffee," Ed LeBlanc said, the most vocal of the four of us, quickest at friendship, at shaking hands. "We've got a whole pot almost. Have what you want." The pot was pointed out sitting on a hunk of grill across the stones of our fire, flames licking lightly at its sides. The pot appeared to have been at war. A number of dents scarred it, the handle had evidently been replaced, and if it had not been adjusted against a small rock it would have fallen over. Once, a half-hour on the road heading north, noting it missing, we'd gone back to get it. When we fished the Pine River, coffee was the glue, the morning glue, the late evening glue. That was fact even though we'd often unearth our beer from a natural below-ground cooler in *early* evening. Coffee, camp coffee, has a ritual. It is thick, it is dark, it is pot-boiled over a squaw-pine fire. It is enough to wake the demon in you, stoke last evening's cheese and pepperoni. First man up makes the fire, second man the coffee. Into that pot has to go fresh eggshells to hold the grounds down, give coffee a taste of history, a sense of place. That means at least one egg be cracked open for its shells, usually in the shadows and glimmers of false dawn. I suspect that's where "scrambled eggs" originated, from some camp like ours, settlers rushing west, lumberjacks hungry, hoboes lobbying for breakfast. So camp coffee, ever since, has made its way into poems, gatherings, memories, a time and thing not letting go, not being cast aside.

"You're early enough for eggs and bacon if you need a start." Eddie added. His invitation was tossed kindly into the morning air, his smile a match for morning sun, a man of welcomes.

"We have hot cakes, kielbasa, home fries, if you want." *We have the food of kings if you really want to know*. There were nights we sat at his kitchen table at 101 Main Street, Saugus, Massachusetts planning the trip, planning each meal, planning the campsite. Some menus were founded on a case of beer, a late night, a curse or two on the ride to work when day started.

"Been there a'ready," the other man said, his weaponry also noted by us. It was a little more orderly in its presentation, including an old Boy Scout sash across his chest, the galaxy of flies in supreme positioning. They were old Yankees. The face and frame of them saying they were undoubtedly brothers. Saying also they were staunch, written into early routines, probably had been up at three o'clock to get here at this hour. They were taller than we were with no fat on their frames. Wide-shouldered and big-handed and barely coming out of their reserve, but they were fishermen. That fact alone would win any of us over.

Obviously, they'd been around, a heft of time already accrued.

Then a pounding came, from inside the truck, as if a tire iron was beating at the sides of the vehicle. It was not a timid banging, not a minor signal. Bang! Bang! it came, and Bang! again. And the voice of authority from some place in space, some regal spot in the universe.

"I'm not sitting here the livelong day whilst you boys gab away." A toothless meshing came in his words, like Walter Brennan working the jail in *Rio Bravo* or some such movie.

"Comin', Pa," one of them said, the most orderly one, the one with the old scout sash riding him like a bandoleer.

They pulled open the back doors of the van and swung them wide. There was His Venerable Self, ageless, white-bearded, felt hat also loaded with an arsenal of flies. He sat on a white wicker rocker with a rope holding him to a piece of vertical angle iron, the crude kind that could have been on early subways or trolley cars. Across his lap he held three delicate fly rods, old as him, slim bamboo, probably too slight for a lake's three-pounder. But on the Pine River, upstream or downstream, under alders choking some parts of the river's flow, at a significant pool where side streams merge and phantom trout hang their eternal promise, most elegant. Fingertip elegant.

"Oh, boy," Eddie said at an aside, "there's the boss man, and look at those tools."

Admiration leaked from his voice. Rods were taken from the caring hands, the rope untied, and His Venerable Self, white wicker rocker and all, was lifted from the truck and set by our campfire. I was willing to bet that my sister Pat, the dealer in antiques, would scoop up that rocker if given the slightest chance. The old one looked about the campsite. He noted our clothes drying from a previous day's rain, order of equipment and supplies aligned the way we always kept them, the canvas of our tent taut and true in its expanse. He saw our fishing rods off the ground and placed atop the flyleaf so as not to tempt raccoons with smelly cork handles. He saw no garbage in sight. Then he nodded.

We had passed muster.

"You the ones leave it cleaner than you find it ever' year. We knowed sunthin' 'bout you. Never disturbed you afore. But we share the good spots." He looked closely at Brother Bentley, nodded a kind of recognition. "Your daddy ever fish here, son?"

Brother must have passed through the years in a hurry, remembering his father bringing him here as a boy.

"A ways back," Brother said in his clipped North Saugus fashion, outlander, specific, no waste in his words. Old Oren Bentley, it had been told us, had walked five miles through the unknown woods off Route 16 as a boy. He had come across the campsite, the remnants of an old lodge at a curve in the Pine River. A mile's walk in either direction gave you three miles of stream to fish, upstream or downstream. Paradise up north.

His Venerable Self nodded again, a man of signals, then said, "Knowed him way back some. Met him at the Iron Bridge. We passed a few times."

Instantly we could see the story. A whole history of encounter walked in his words. It marched right through us the way knowledge does, as well as legend. He pointed at the coffeepot. "The boys'll be off, but my days down there get cut up some. I'll sit a while and take some of *thet*." He said *thet* too pronounced, too dramatic, and it was a short time before we knew why.

The white wicker rocker went into a slow and deliberate motion, his head nodded again. He spoke to his sons. "You boys be back no more'n two-three hours so these fellers can do their things too, and keep the place tidied up."

The most orderly son said, "Sure, Pa. Two-three hours." The two elderly sons left the campsite and walked down the path to the banks of the Pine River. Their boots swished at thigh line, the most elegant of rods pointed the way through scattered limbs, experience on the move. Trout beware, we thought.

196

"We been carpenters f'ever," he said, the clip still in his words. "Those boys a mine been some good at it too."

His head cocked, he seemed to listen for their departure, the leaves and branches quiet, the murmur of the stream a tinkling idyllic music rising up the banking. Old Venerable Himself moved the wicker rocker forward and back, a small timing taking place. He was hearing things we had not heard yet, the whole symphony all around us.

Eddie looked at me and nodded his own nod. It said, "I'm paying attention and I know you are. This is our one encounter with a man who has fished for years the river we love, that we come to twice a year, in May with the mayflies, in June with the black flies." The gift and the scourge, we'd often remember, having been both scarred and sewn by it.

Brother was still at memory, we could tell. Silence we thought was heavy about us, but there was so much going on. A bird talked to us from a high limb. A fox called to her young. We were on the Pine River once again, nearly a hundred miles from home, in Paradise.

"Name's Roger Treadwell. Boys are Nathan and Truett." The introductions had been accounted for.

Old Venerable Roger Treadwell, carpenter, fly fisherman, rocker, leaned forward and said, "You boys wouldn't have a couple spare beers, would ya?"

Now that's the way to start the day on the Pine River.

It's All in the Maul

It was *the* moment of pure silence before we would set the forest on its ear with the roar of our chain saws. The deep woods that morning glistened with long tracts of snowy and scary silence. Now and then it was broken by the creaking of a frozen limb swearing it would fall to earth. At best that fall would be a minor distortion, a minor distraction. Yet again, that creak sounded like a baby in the night, or a wailing or a keening, or, at an odder moment, like a voice given to what has no voice. At attention we stood, my friend Eddie LeBlanc and I, some twenty yards apart, some huge oaks apart. The ugly and monstrous oak arms clawed at early daylight.

The clarity stings the memory, carries this day that day's ambiance. Somehow, inexplicably, it is soul deep, has pine aromas, the acrobatics of light, known temperature touching my face the way I recall the stand on a lone Korean outpost.

Apart we measured each other. We had worked this forest for a year of weekends that would eventually prove to be a twelve-year run at cutting and hauling wood. A friendly prophet could have cast this duo; not one word of argument had ever crossed our lips, or one word of advice. That time span covered the years since we had met in a carpool heading off to our jobs some twenty-five miles away from home, another twenty years earlier. The other, each assumed, was old enough and wise enough to do his duty, share his energy, bring his tools into play, mind his own business of life. Oh, with zest we fished, played cards, drank beer, watched hockey games on TV because our own joyous hockey days were long past. We lent tools and energies to the other's needed tasks: car brake repairs, roofing jobs, electrical and plumbing needs and solutions. You name it and we did it, programming much of our lives around labor or the touch of tools. We could have formed a company. At least *he* should have had a small fix-it shop in Saugus Center with a big sign over the front door that said *I Can Fix Anything*. And he could. He was engineer, radioman, finish carpenter, cabinet maker, TV repairman, mechanic, heavy equipment operator of major incidence, on and on, through the stand-up 40-hour tasks of tradesmen bent to task.

Eddie, five foot five at best, animated, smiler, great story teller who broadcast with deepest sound effects and extraordinary hand gestures. In a maximum hurry he brought life to a quiet and subdued morning car pool. Some sleepy and gray dawns he'd hit us with the force of a blowout. Often he took me from night's reverie in a rush.

But we never argued and never gave advice. Pointing or hinting was clue enough, a nod, a shoulder shrug, a raised eyebrow, a look that questioned some thing almost animate in the field of us.

Now, in this deep forest fifteen miles north of home, the pre-formed silence penetrated each of us. Mystical in its impact it came, the deep cold making it so much clearer for a listener.

He stood on the crest of the hill just above me. Laden clouds billowed behind him. Long-time friend, carpool companion, fellow fisherman and logging buddy, Adrien Eduoard LeBlanc yelled down at me. He held his chain saw in the air, saluting the day upon us.

"Wood burns twice, you know."

He waved the saw as if it were a ladle from a well. "That's what they say up in Moncton and Memramcook, way up in New Brunswick, the wood-burning LeBlancs."

And he was right. Sweat ran on my skin though the temperature had dropped since our arrival in the forest. Droplets gathered speed until they hit an obstruction, a belt line, a bent elbow, a high ankle sock in a booted foot. If I stopped working, I acknowledged, my joints would freeze.

But the task was at hand.

It was a sudden December storm of 1971 and the energy crunch was on, oil prices escalating with frenzy. We were cutting trees and hauling logs, part of a State Forest Management effort, in the Willowdale State Forest in Topsfield, MA, not far from the Topsfield Fairgrounds. Being throwbacks to a time of early communal efforts, early time-sharing ventures, we had committed ourselves to conserve energy. Air-tight, cast iron, wood-burning stoves had been trundled into our homes. New chain saws and six-pound mauls were brought into our tool collections, our energies dedicated and fused: two saws, two vehicles, two temperaments at one task. And abeyance to one old adage, *Do not go alone into the woods with a chain saw.*

In my then-231 year-old house, one of the two chimneys that had serviced four fireplaces on each side of the house was completely re-lined to accept wood fires. In turn, Eddie had erected a new chimney on an outer wall of his house, which was a mile away from mine. We'd do battle our own way; *Saturday maul's splitting wood sounded like gunshots.*

For close to eight years the whole wood-burning routine was a snap, though the work was hard. Many of our Saturday mornings, and parts of Sundays, were spent here in this forest. The struggle versus the weather, now and then, was more difficult than the work. But we were a team and there were measurable goals each time out; fill each of our vehicles with logs ready to be split once we got them home. Then we'd pile them up for the drying process in cord lengths.

On the way home on the good days, the season right, the van and truck laden to brims, we'd take a break. Cooling down from the first heat of the wood, we would have a noon sandwich and a quenching beer. We'd fish placid Pye Brook or the Ipswich River for the elusive and phantom trout. The brook, sneaking under old Route One, ran slowly past our feet. The river was quicker, wider, in its journey, and housed a thousand birds about the air, about our ears. Now and then across the water we'd send a quiet nod at each other when the first nibble came or a hungry carnivore snapped at our floating flyline. At times, I'll swear to eternity, we were in Elysium. I've always believed that that feeling can only happen with keen and durable friendships; demands that are silently made are silently answered. On that account I have always been right. But it took someone like Eddie to make it happen.

And the harvested log, for that matter, still burns twice. I keep telling that to Eddie on the phone these days. Twenty years ago he moved to Orlando for a job opportunity and we talked every weekend until the computer chat room came upon us a few years ago. Then it was every night we spoke. He told me his old chain saw hangs above his mantelpiece, a hard trophy of our long and communal efforts. And these days I do not go to the forest alone with a chain saw. I manage to cut down a few neighbors' trees right in their yards. I hustle drops from the town tree workers. Now and then at the roadside I pick up logs piled for curbside disposal. Sometimes I scrounge through the Recycling Center at the town dump, often unloading logs from another vehicle right into mine.

Wood still burns twice no matter how you look at it, or how it comes to hand.

Mostly, for me these days, that other first burning is with the maul. The exercise is decent and productive in many ways, and for a number of reasons. It's an exercise for a patched-up ticker, and a yearning for the old energies and a moment of pure silence abounding. But I don't think I've ever swung the maul over my shoulder that I have not thought of my friend's downhill shout, *wood burns twice*. I know then the graces of brotherly efforts and am still haunted by the feeling that we were throwbacks to another time. So much comes out of concerted energy. So much gets done. So much is learned. About yourself. About others. Comes about you with knowledge and command and respect, a trust deeper than most friendships.

Eddie would say, as the wind started to rise, the chill coming on, "If you want to keep your feet warm, wear a hat." It was an old survivor's saying he'd picked up in Boy Scouts as a troop leader for half his life. Or "Don't let your shadow fall across the water when fishing."

For years he had fished with the legendary Artie Tash and Brother Bentley and Ray Costanza Exel. He'd get his limit every opening day on the Saugus River, beside one of the fairways of Cedar Glen Golf Course. In a manner of speaking, that river's gone south these days, as far as the trout are concerned.

Eddie's there too.

Yet my maul still has a swift arc, the logs crack apart some days like OK Corral gunshots, and neighbors mark the energy. The stacked pile climbs higher in my back yard, starts to run lengthwise along a fence, gathers bees and an occasional squirrel. My sweat rushes and rises and is cast off in vapor. I look at the growing cords of wood and the coming winter, and make no assumptions. More first-time heating is needed, so the second heating can drift inward, lift itself slowly and surely through this old house, can climb the steep stairs. It is a most welcome tenant when the Montreal Express beats at these outer walls.

The arc, swift, accurate, concerted in its weight and momentum, catches silver from the sun on the maul's edge. The sun splinters itself into smithereens, joins my fusion. I move into another experience of my life and bring along what I have learned:

Wear a hat if you want to keep your feet warm.. Don't drop shadows on top of trout.. Wood heats twice (or more) if you have to cut and haul, and split it. Spending time in Elysium with a friend does not have to pass away from being. The maul in my hands, like any good tool, does wonders for the soul, for old and gracious statements made by my body even if hesitant, for respect and friendship anchored by sweat and good service to one another.

Once I cut up a neighbor's old apple tree at evening's rush into November. I did it as a favor for the neighbor, and as a ruse to rouse and send the singularly redolent winter apple smoke above our houses. Words came running through me like music. I said then about the apples from this tree soon to be burning, and it keeps coming back to me:

They have all gone now, the fire engine-red Macintosh, under batter with cinnamon, gone to day school on yellow buses with brown-baggers, or bruised to a freckled taupe and plowed under for ransom and ritual. Some will have the life crushed out of them for Thanksgiving cup. Standing on the stiff lawn downwind of winter, I drop the first cold moon of November into a fractured wheel of apple limbs and hear the bark beg away. A pine ridge, thicker than a catcher's mitt, grabs half the wind riding off Vinegar Hill and squeezes out wrenching cries that hang, like wounded pendants, on the necks of far, thin stars. Deep in the Earth, in a thermal tube of its own making, an earthworm grows toward a rainbow trout sleeping under ice and waiting to be heard, or the last of an apple's pips black as tar pavement but still on this side of the grass.

It all ends up, most generously, in a letter to Eddie continually ringing in my ears these days as winter plows through him. He is beset with Parkinson's, inoperative at the computer, my prayers continually beside each of us:

All day this December cold is a secret of my fleece-lined jacket and the bottom of my mittens. The senseless wind, without any direction and purposeless, gets hung up in the muffler I wear as some corrective device, thick and woolly and itchy, around my neck. It's the one you left in my van the last winter we cut wood in Topsfield and waded through that white tide until we fell exhausted. You used to laugh about wood heating twice. Now you've gone south, and I can hear the cry of the gnarled and aged oak as it lets go and throws the Earth out of kilter, the topmost branch brazenly and suddenly at hand, an old nest scattered to its beginnings. I walked quietly there yesterday, snow thrown like paint everywhere except on the sun side, and half-gray birches, like stalkers sly and half-white in the wind. They made me think of Finnish ski troops the Russians didn't like around or our own Kasabuski brothers of the 10th Mountain Division rampaging 1944's northern Italy. I suppose there are pieces of the battlefield left down south, but I bet you think of Topsfield when a cool wind grabs your neck, an old jacket lets out secrets, your fingers remember wood's endless caress, and all across a sunset sky falling downhill to your ears, a chain saw's evening prayers.

I swear to you, Eduoard, I can feel it all in the handle of the maul. It's like this: A three-beer push on the maul handle. My shoulders shooting nerves into fibrous white oak, elm never letting go its fibers, maple reporting splits clean as firecrackers, one time good wood lets go. Out and beyond, an Arab watches me through the eye of a coin hung on edge. I hear the flag sing in front of the house, my own drummer beating high on a hill, and, in strange field, crevice and creek bed, from here to foothills of the Montanas, gunshots of the maul, chain saw's deep roars, Howitzers booming in the everlasting fray.

The Ghosts of Lily Pond

Our old pond, long-gone Lily Pond, comes up
odd mornings of memory like a hobo rising from his
varied nights. Such a serious master of colors it was,
Persian red, coin gold, yellow of a wheat or a blonde,
autumn in the traces, ignition's flare. Or there'd be
April-May at explosion about that wide saucer of water,
Turnpike to dam, cliff-face to Prohibition cabins now
taller with cellars plunked beneath them.

Diamond-faced Lily Pond, our old Lily Pond,
the pond of the '30s and '40s and '50s, had many faces.
It had sleek and choice cuts, facets that still shine a kind
of brittle memory, a storehouse of vignettes. Tales are
borne by it, small mysteries, undimmed personalities,
pieces that continually show us growing up and coming
this way. If you're careful, alert, patiently waiting, the
larder might spill itself, tell its own tales.

The man was raw-boned, sleek, could skate like
the wind that blew out of Canada on winter days around
the corner of Appleton and Summer Streets. Hair dark,
eyes holding stories, he wore a magnificent pair of
hockey gloves. Great, shiny black elegant things, tools
of the trade, the kind we'd not ever seen. Hockey
gloves! Like a policeman's badge, a fireman's helmet.
An image gained and kept forever. Who had money for
such things, such extravagance!

And his stick was always new. The blade was
daily wound with clean tape. His name, barely legible if
you wanted to stare closely at its small letters, was
burned where his fist closed high on the handle. His
neat Chinos, telling you he might be a veteran of the
war newly at silence, all Pacific quelled, were neatly
bloused about his bulky shin pads with rubber bands cut
from inner tubes. The bottoms of the pads curved
visibly and deeply red as they hunkered above white

skate laces. Only his mean skates were throwbacks into other wars of ice; scarred, ugly things, merely the blades of them shiny with the art of maintenance.

He was not from Saugus, not a Saugonian, and carried a few pucks of his own, never to be without. But two days during the school week, and every Saturday and Sunday in skating weather, which seemed to be forever, he was on the ice of Lily Pond. Waiting for a game, he'd fly about the pond like something out of Hans Brinker and Hans' miles of canals or a Canadian truant doing the canal at Ottawa. When a game started he was first into it, then, as the games grew in number and spread across the face of the pond, he'd slip off to one with better talent, a headier challenge.

For the games did grow, especially on a weekend and the skaters coming out of Melrose and North Revere and Lynn to enjoy the hockey on Lily Pond with us Saugus skaters. There'd be ten or twenty games at one time spread across the pond. Skaters flashed by the boat house where canoes and rowboats were put away. In the cove by Cliff Road where we've skated as late as May of the year in the shadows of the cliff. Out beyond Fiske's Icehouse. Up near the Turnpike. At the head of the Island. Over by Frank Evans' Beach on Lily Pond Road. Down by the dam beside Rippon's Mushroom House. Hockey was everywhere. Pond hockey. Wide-open hockey. Pucks sliding out of one game and into another. Often we raced to retrieve our one last puck after we'd lost all our others down in watering holes where all the day we quenched our thirsts.

That's what brought the dark man with the great gloves. They said he once skated with the Boston Olympics, had been hurt in the Boston Garden, once was a Bruin for a cup of coffee. But he'd shift into gear easily in a game with Lonnie Green, Brother Parker, Jackie and Charlie and Googie Prentice, Neil Howland,

Eddie Ayers, Jimmy MacDougall, Mike Harrington, Billy Falasca, Randy Popp, Red Parrott, and Dickie Weeks. Fifty or sixty friends played out of East Saugus and Cliftondale and Saugus Center as the games grew and multiplied. They spread to all ends of the pond like a precursor to an Olympic Village in Lake Placid or out in Utah, building up in dreams.

If and when it snowed, we'd shovel rinks out of the snow, and Lily Pond, from a distance, from a hill, would look like a battlefield filled with square or rectangular bomb craters. Rocks or logs would be our goal posts. Occasionally, in early spring, the ice still on the pond, you'd have to be alert for old goal posts having sunk part way into the surface. Once an old pair of ankle-high boots lasted until the spring thaw took them down, past the last goal scored. Were they volunteered for their post, I wondered, or confiscated from a shore-line log? Did someone leave in their stocking feet?

But when the pond was free and clear and the ice good, there'd be hockey all of daylight. Then at night, under the stars or the moon pressing inevitability down on us, came trysts in the making, life-long friendships being developed or remembered forever. There'd be a whip with fifty or sixty kids holding hands. The one on the end better be a good skater because he or she would be snapped off to the winds, a solid rush of breath into lungs, speed momentarily paralyzing a pair of legs. Later there'd be cocoa and doughnuts at Frank Evans' pond side camp or a game of hide and seek. That's when you and your girl could be hidden for a while, away at the dark edges of the pond, the owls hooting at your daring, your hand slightly cupping one of the new graces.

But younger, when the pond began to be a building block in my life, friends and I would walk to the pond on a Saturday morning. Our skates were slung onto the blade end of hockey sticks, shin pads slipped over the other end and paired up with inner tube bands. We'd walk up Appleton Street, the ever-wind against us, anxious to see the ice condition, hurry in our pace. Dryness sat in our throats as we generated our own excitement. We'd pull on and lace up skates, play hockey until noon. My father would come oftentimes with a sandwich and cocoa in the back seat of the car. He'd loosen my skates, rub my feet, turn me loose in half an hour, and come back at supper time with the same deal. As he left he'd say, "Be home before midnight."

Trust was in the air, flowed about us as fully as the wind on the pond. Those were the days when a sleep was a sleep. And the dark skater with the great new gloves, almost as thick as boxing gloves, dreams in themselves, would be there. Just as he is in today's memories, flying across the ice with a puck on the blade of his stick, and never looking down at it. Never once.

The man with the beard, glasses, an old felt hat, would come in an old Chevy with his canoe tied across the top. He'd bring his gear to the edge of the pond near Fiske's Icehouse, put it on the bank or on a rock at water's edge, go back. Like some gymnastic creature, he would slide the canoe off his car and carry it overhead to the water, dropping gradually the prow to water's touch as he swung it counterclockwise from a stiff-arm tier.

When his gear was loaded, he slipped easily into the middle of the craft and slid off from shore. On his knees, a few paddle strokes took him straight as an arrow out toward the deeper water. Before you could time him he'd be fishing. It appeared as if he did not want to lose a minute of fishing time, or leave too much unfished water in his wake. His deft hands would swing and switch a rod's line out in front of the canoe. You could see where the lure plopped into the water, where pickerel and bass abounded you were sure, just as he was. He never came back empty-handed. Some mornings the envelope of silence was broken by that single lure hitting water. I can hang my hat on it today.

Other canoes would leave, during all parts of the day, and rowboats too. They moved out from the gray rental shack that now would be located below the Knights of Columbus gate, and behind Eldon Sweezey's place. People would come from East Boston and Revere and Lynn to boat and canoe and fish at Lily Pond. Sweet tooth for the carp roiling on the surface. They'd come by bus on the old Hart Bus Line or the Rapid Transit. I'd envision them getting transfer after transfer to get here, carrying their rods folded or knocked down on the bus, their tackle boxes as noisy as change makers. Or they'd come and park Hudsons and Grahams and Packards and DeSotos and Chevys and Fords where Shadowland Ballroom's cement block pile supports were still exposed after the fire. You never knew their names. You might never see them again. But you'd remember now and then their faces, their laughter, their gaiety as they came to share Lily Pond with us. The sun flowed new and shiny and warm on the skin, and the sky was blue all the way past the Turnpike. Saturday or Sunday at hand, and our Lily Pond swelling its ranks of lovers.

From the sloped rock face on the Island, southwest side, in the afternoon sun in the middle of Lily Pond, the girl in a blue two-piece bathing suit arced gracefully through the air. She was sylph-like, smooth, curving her body a little bit more as she reached the apex of her dive, and slipped easily into the water of the pond when she straightened out. We'd watch her graces, my friends and I, as we lay back on warm rocks, the sun beating down on us in its July fashion. Her name was Shirley. She was the first graphic torture for many boys, left their mouths dry.

You couldn't beat Lily Pond on a good day! That's for sure.

Canoes would slip past the island the way the girl dove, just as sylph-like, smooth as creation, and silent. Rowboats, though, would clank into sight, the oars banging in the oarlocks like messages of labor. Passing our place of swimming, fishing poles would be retrieved from water, lures pulled back. Nobody ever had to say, "Look out there! We're swimming here."

Of course there'd be more than one girl in a blue two-piece bathing suit, more than just Shirley. That's what swimming was all about. They'd come from Lynn and Revere and Malden and bring lunches with them and colored towels, and their combs. And there'd be our own classy classmates and schoolmates diving off the rocks, Hollywood on our own Island. There were the Stead sisters and Lila off the hill, and another Shirley all the way from Cliftondale, and Gracie, and a girl with the boldest message to her tan, who once swam in the Pit on Main Street after diving from a dead pine tree, sleek, tanned so daring, so daring.

At the other end of the pond, down by the dam and old Catamount Cove, as the historians call it, some sixty yards out in the water, was a rock that you could stand on and rest. A few of us would now and then pass an evening there with another swimmer, the moon directing conversation or directing the silent and hidden beat of correspondence. Along the shore on many days small boys would be looking for tadpoles and frogs, among other collectibles. They could see quiet flotillas of pickerel pressing hard against a banking, their tales barely twitching as they nosed into the shadows, digging into the work of life.

Every so often the boys would chase a butterfly or stop to listen to a bird singing it was a good day for hunting frogs.

Once in a while Dickie or Edson Evans' long, powerful blue boat with an in-board motor would cover the whole dam end of the pond with a roar. It was like in mid-winter when Dick Woods might fling his propeller-driven iceboat over the same route. The gasoline engine howled. A trail of blue smoke followed its cutting arc across the ice, the prop snapping at cold air. At a distance a pair of iceboats silently might show off their generous white sails with the elegance of grace.

Much of its surface reduced now, Lily Pond of our youth has gone into that other world. It was shrunken, fill taken for Logan Airport, the perimeter declining. At times in this short life there seem to be few mysteries. Other times they overwhelm you. But there was no mystery about Lily Pond. Except how it got away from us in one fell swoop.

Sometimes, in the dead of winter, Saugus frozen tightly, the pond face was smooth as baby's skin. We'd put remnant sheets on wooden crosses, as if Jesus was with us all the way, and sail on skates the length of Lily Pond. A number of times we'd done it, a number of days that winter, other winters, the cold plunge a solid being in itself. The cold was to be borne and survived only in total exuberance, there being no other way of "being about on the pond."

At times that ride bore breakneck speed, wind more the sole ally, as we blew away from Sawyer's Ice House. That's where innocently now and then, atop old strewn sawdust, orange I swear to this day, in the sweet cream of youth, in semi-darkness, we'd steal a light kiss or two from a dream girl. Kisses from those unfledged lips are to be remembered a lifetime later, or the first touch of a breast given to your hand. At the old tin shack where boats and canoes were rented out in another time, our sheeted flight would start down along a reedless shore. That shore climbed quickly to where gray cement blocks were all that remained of Shadowland Ballroom, long gone in fire. Skirt a hockey game or two we could or scream at a snaking whip of hand-holders that we were coming through, the tone of our voice depending on the wind's force. Past the channel by The Island we'd go, being sure to stay clear of thinner ice where water pumped below the surface.

Breaking out into the openness at The Point, Arctic bareness the challenge, a white almost never-ending expanse leaped ahead. The wind howled in our ears and at our backs, and we knew the practical certitude that our blades would not find a crack in the ice. And we faced the ultimate transition. Now pure speed became the entity. Sheer speed demanded that blades be light and controlled, knees slightly bent, arms the mast and tiller, eyes though air-struck on full alert. In a fraction of a second gauge all the other skaters on the pond. Calculate where paths might cross. Beware of mothers with babies in tow, doting fathers, the elderly, or the ankle-wearers who could not handle skates yet, who did not know this most savage of joys.

Keep an eye out again for Dick Woods' iceboat, roaring gray monster of the slick deep, with that wooden airplane propeller behind it pushing larger than life. Sometimes we surprised him! Swooping in silence out of the all-white shoreline, like a Finnish ski-trooper in the Pathe News at the State Theater or someone from our own 10th Mountain Division on the same screen. We had to be sure of residue rock goal posts between which players had the day before slung the black puck with both skill and vengeance. Sometimes they hit it so hard it could be picked up and carried unsullied and dauntless in another game, or fly clear across the pond.

On special occasions, in that Arctic waste, we had to be aware of other impacts. It was so at truancy from school, your sheeted cross the only sail on that vast sea of near-black ice. Or there'd come Buck Murray buzzing the pond in his Navy Grumman Hellcat, after he buzzed the Town Hall, after coming out of Quonset Point. The Truant Officer, in his car, might intend to meet you at destination, across from the White House Restaurant on the Turnpike. Other people might be reporting the capricious pilot. I've been there more than once on such occasion.

But past The Point, where the wind tunnel came to full effect, the exhilaration was the game. The free flight was near frictionless, almost a free-fall sensation. The Turnpike shore came riding to meet you. Cars and trucks hummed along out there on that black patch of road, commerce and usual care passing by in an endless Morse Code. And you were here on the pond, where speed and freedom counted more than anything.

To stop all you had to do was drop your cross.

Or have someone take down the dam, to grovel at gravel! Let Lily Pond float down-river! Past Salter's Mill and the old Scott's Mill. Past the foot of the Ironworks. Past old Indian burial grounds. Past the fleet of lobster boats at the end of Ballard Street. Past the red brick stacks of the General Electric, going all the way out of town. As if the Atlantic needed another droplet. Lose much of that great ice surface. Let loose all the swimming at The Island or at The Dam. Forget the winter donuts and cocoa or hot cider at Frank Evans' camp on the far side of the pond. Forget the midnight swims from there to the rock on The Island. Turn a goodly part of Saugus onto runways or extensions of Logan Airport, by the thousand truckloads.

All this was a conscious sadness. All this was savaged.

Generations of Saugus youth have missed that godly speed. It sits there now resurrected as Pranker's Pond, mindful, trying not to let go forever, the cut of the wind often sharp as honed edges, the spar and sheeted sail pulling at wrists, at shoulders, a cluster of skaters madly dispersing at your approach. It was all of time and memory being pulled along by a hidden wind.

Johnny Igoe, Spellbinder Remembered

My Grandfather Johnny Igoe was a little Irish man. He stood a mere five foot-six, but was a giant to me when his poetic voice rolled across the lamp-lit porch floor. He always wore a felt hat, a white beard, and often a pair of bicycle clips on his pant legs in the later years so he wouldn't trip himself. His blue eyes were excavations, deep and musical, caught up in other places you could tell, places where poems rang and memories, old names, old faces, and the geography of mankind dwelled. They held places he had left and feared he'd never get back to. Each of his canes knew the back of your knees, the rump, in a grab at attention. Older townsfolk, walking by, talked to him at the open kitchen window, the curl of pipe smoke rising between them, while Grandma was at her oven, her room full of breads and sweets.

On our summer porch at night, the fireflies hustling about in the near fields, my Grandfather read William B. Yeats to me when I was a youngster. He rocked in his chair, smoking his pipe, making music and rhythm in his life, and in mine. I was, at the first of Yeats, about six years old.

"Listen," he'd say, pointing his finger up. "Hear the music. Know the sound. Feel the grab."

Johnny Igoe, spellbinder remembered.

On that porch on Main Street, a mere mile out of Saugus Center, he and Yeats holding forth, his voice would roll into the field where fireflies lived and where Chuckie Shipulski's house now sits. His words, mixed with the fireflies waiting on my bottle, captured a sense of deeper darkness where they could further show off their electric prowess. The times were magnetic, electric. I knew what attention was.

Oh, I loved those compelling nights filled with
Horseman, ride by; Prayer for My Daughter or *old
marble heads*, captivating me with a sound so Irish I
was proud. *I will arise now and go to Innisfree*, oh, and
the deep heart's core. The lineage found me: I didn't
find it, and the echoes of those nights ring yet.

But other things come repeatedly for him:
Johnny Igoe only ate oatmeal in the morning, a boiled
potato and a shot of whiskey for lunch. By and on other
things he lived.

On the handle of a cane he would rest his chin,
his eyes on you making announcements you dared not
lose. He made Yeats's voice to be his own voice, that
marvelous treble and clutter of breath buried in it, *The
Lake Isle of Innisfree* popping free like electricity or the
very linnets themselves. Maude was like some creature
I'd surely come to know in my own time. Johnny Igoe
also wrote his own poems, and yielded me Mulrooney
and Padraic Gibbons as well out of the long rope of his
memory. The knots of that rope untied all those
Saturday evenings of his life and mine, on that porch.
He launched many of my own poems there, by the
dozens, and at the end, at 97, stained, shaking, beard
gone to a lengthy hoarfrost, potato drivel not quite lost
in it, he gave me his voice and eyes alive to this day,
sounding out in his own way.

Later, time hustling me on, in a Caedmon
Golden Treasury of Poetry record I heard Yeats read
his own material, three short poems. I swore it was
Spellbinder Johnny Igoe still at work.

But first things first: I quickly remember him as
the Dumpmaster at the City Dump in Malden,
Massachusetts where he ended up after his early travels
and began his family. He had been the first Irish sailor
of his family, sailing here alone, while his mother was
on her death bed. All those long days and nights at the
dump, the destitute came to him for warmth, for food,

for a place to put up their feet on a freezing night. They came to him, the drunks, the homeless vets still wandering loose from France and WW I, street people who then had no such name. They knew the welcome of his fire, the monger's stove to wrap around, hot curbing to prop cold feet, quick difference from the frozen air, wind-swept railroad tracks, bare entry ways, darkness where howling ghosts abide. Or, as often was the case, their last resort, the slim cardboard wrap.

He burned clinkers in a little shack he made of scrap. The lost, lonely birds came to him to roost. They flew in at dusk. He stoked the fire to stir up flames, dried their feathers off. Just as often he left his lunch about like tasty suet hanging in the yard. On Saturdays I brought his lunch, dense laminates of meat and bread, thick and heavy and coarse as sin, brown banana we would not eat, molasses-brown coffee in whiskey bottles wound about with paper bags. I never saw even one pint bottle finished off within his grasp. I rarely saw his small hand feeling inside a paper bag. His birds did the picking, had suet choice, hens dining before the cock.

That was as much his legacy as anything else he might have done or said. He cared for the downtrodden, those short-circuited by life, those who had paid their dues and somehow, through their humanity itself, had fallen prey to loss and deprivation. Mercy was what he preached, and that memory should be noble, and comfort to the aggrieved and succor for the pained should be a career. He made me observe the human condition. He made me look at man from the floor up, from his lowest grovel to his pinnacle, to realize that we end in dust before we move on, the manner of a man being God-like.

This kind and thoughtful man for years dreamed of his return to Ireland, but he never made that trip.

That lost dream trip pained him. His eyes said so, his voice said it too, in his own poem:

The Dream of the Roscommon Emigrant

There is a land though far away that's very dear to me, an island in the ocean most picturesque to see. As each day goes by I heave a sigh for those lovely native scenes:
Ah! Isle of Saints and Martyrs, I see you in my dreams.

I'm at the gate of Clooniquin, I hear the pearling stream now wend its way to Ross and then to far Culleen. I hear the thrush and blackbird in the holly and laurel tree; my soul says I must loiter in this fair locality.

I cross the bridge and up the walk and toward that lovely grove; with ecstasy my heart does bound as onward I do rove. From the countless pines a shadow runs to meet me on the hill where the pheasant and rabbit doth wander there at will.

Ah, solitude, thy charms are dear, to me how sweet they seem as I set me down and look around on Nature's lovely scene. The hills of Ross are beautiful, and so the lovely glen and meadows fair that stretch between those hills and dear old Elphin.

From Castlerea to Carrick I see the places all, from Roscommon down to Lulsk and to the Plains of Boyle. As I travel o'er that scope, with Nature's gifts so strewn, I stop halfway where I was raised now aided by the moon. I look around bewildered on all that I behold; the tree of ash, the hawthorn bush, now burnished in their gold.

219

*The cottage I was born in and raised by parents
kind, I enter with impatience but there I could not find
the one above all others whose love was dear to me.
She has gone to her heaven for all eternity.*

*Father, brothers, sisters, I join in fond embrace
as tears of joy and sorrow roll swiftly down each face. I
see the good old nabors, each remembered a pleasant
day, and shake each hand with affection as I did when
going away.*

*In harmony we all did join and traversed those
weary years since that eventful morning when I left
them steeped in tears. Now fond adieu to all my friends
around the dear old isle, though adopted by Columbia I
am Erin's faithful child; For the Stars and Stripes with
the flag of green will line in unity. Adieu again, old
Ireland, farewell my dear country.*

But others made the trip for him.

On our honeymoon in 1973, my wife Beth and I
visited at Elphin and the cottage where John Igoe was
born, where I saw the star peep through the thatch roof
and call his name, and where lived my mother's last two
living first cousins, Peter and Joseph Cassidy, since
gone. My mother, with four daughters, was able to get
over and visit there in 1987.

And in September of 2003, our children sent us
back for our 30th anniversary. The eyes are so pleased
at times that the heart sees. I told them the following
happened on our trip:

One Monday noon I stood in an Elphin,
Roscommon pub, a Guinness pint in hand, and said
aloud to the dozen men at the bar, "Gentlemen, do any
of you remember Peter and Joseph Cassidy, who 30
years ago, when we were here on our honeymoon, lived

outside of town near the statue to The Rising. They were well into their 70s then and long gone now, but I'd like to know if anybody remembers them."

All hell broke loose at the bar, eyes twinkled, smiles came galore, and one man leaped off his stool. "Eddie the Fiddler!" he yelled. "If Peter and Joseph were relatives of yours, Eddie the Fiddler is." He yelled to the barkeep, "Dermot, get Eddie on the phone!" Twenty minutes later I thought my Grandfather Johnny Igoe was walking through the door. It was a cousin of mine, Eddie Cassidy, in his sixties, I had never met and had not known about. We had a ball!

It was a great trip and Johnny Igoe was with us every step of the way.

He had bent his back in Pennsylvania and Illinois' mines and swung a hammer north of Boston, poled his star-lit way down the Erie Canal, and died in bed. But the tobacco smell still lives in this room. His books still live, his chair, his cane, the misery he knew, the pain, and somewhere he is.

His years are still with me in the wind he breathed and storms he stood against and earth he pounded with his fist to fill the mouths of his children and my mother. When he was lonely he was hurt and sometimes feared the pain he could not feel because he knew it and knew how it came. He said a man had to think hard and often to be wise and nothing was useless to man: not a sliver of wood because it makes a toothpick; not a piece of glass broken from a wine-red bottle because it catches sun and makes wonder. Neither a stray stone nor brick were useless because they were wedges or wall-part or corners like one, the first or the last, put to the foundation of the old gray house that clings to the light and had wide windows and doors that were never locked.

On snow-bound mornings he laughed with us when daylight sought us eagerly and in cricket nights of softness that spoiled kneeling prayers. Sometimes his soft eyes were sad while we laughed. We didn't know about the man down the street or the boy who died racing black-horse train against young odds. His prayers were not an interlude with God: they were as sacred as breathing, as vital as the word. And the politicians never got his vote because he knew the pain they intended and he hated hurt. Hated hurt. The floorboards creaked beneath him in the mornings and he brought warmth into chilled rooms and his coffee slipped its aroma between secret walls to waken us.

The oats were heavy and creamed in large white bowls, and "Go easy on the sugar" was the bugle call of dawn. His books had a message that he heard, alone, quiet, singing with the life he knew was near past and yet beginning. He pampered and petted them like he did Grandma, and spent secret hours with them and lived them with us rehearsing our life to come, and teaching us.

Then, a high-biting, cold spring day in 1955 I knew would be memorial, the sun shone but in snippets, ice still hiding out in shadow, winter remnants piled up in a great gathering, me bound to a shovel for the tenth day in a row. That's when I heard of Johnny Igoe's death so late in life.

Grass and buds and shoots and sprigs of all kinds were aimless as April. All vast morning I'd hunted the sun, tried to place it square on my back. But the breeze taunted, left a taste in my mouth. Sullivan Marino, brother-in-law, boss who loved the shovel, sweat, doing the Earth over, walked at me open as a telegram. Sicilian eyes tell stories, omit nothing in the relation.

"Your Grandfather's dead."

He was vinegar and oil and reached for my shovel. It would not leave my hands.

I saw Johnny Igoe at ten at turf cutting, just before he came this way with the great multitude. I saw how he too moved the ponderous earth, the flame of it caught in iron, singing tea, singeing the thatch, young Irish scorching the ground he walked. He had come here and I came, and I went there, later, to where he'd come from; Roscommon's sweet vale, slow rush of land, shouldering up, going into sky, clouds shifting selves like pieces at chess, earth ripening to fire. I saw it all, later, where he'd come from, but then, sun-searching, memorializing, Sullivan quickly at oil and odds, his hand out to take my tool away, could stand no dalliance the day Johnny Igoe died.

When he died they came by the dozen to grieve the savior of their awful nights; the drunken, besotted, brothered band who so often drained his cup. The mottle-skinned came, so soured of life, the pale host of them, the warred upon and beaten, they came to cache the little man who offered what was left of God.

The saga of Johnny Igoe is the epic of a nation. The root cell—Johnny Igoe at ten running ahead of the famine that took brothers and sisters, lay father down; sick in the hold of ghostly ship I later saw from high rock on Cork's coast. In that hold he heard the myths and music he would spell all his life. He remembered hunger and being alone and brothers and sisters and father gone and mother praying for him as he knelt beside her bed that hard morning when Ireland went away to the stern. I know that terror of hers last touching his face.

He might be housed in this computer, for now he visits, or never leaves. Yeats talks on record but the voice is my Grandfather's voice, the perky treble, the deft reach inside me, the lifting out, the ever lifting out. In the dark asides before a faint light glimmers it is the

223

perky pipe's glow I see, weaker than a small and struck match but illuminating all the same. I smell his old Edgeworth tobacco faint as a blown cloud in the air, the way a hobo might know a windowed apple pie from afar. I hear the years of literate good cheer, storied good will, the pleasantries of expansive noun and excitable verb. I hear his ever-lingering poems, each one a repeated resonance, a victory of sound and meaning and the magic of words. I hear his rocking chair giving rhythm to my mind, saying over and over again the words he left with hard handles on them for my grasping.

This Old House

For history and legend sakes, certain attributes, character traits if you will, have to be appointed here at the beginning of *This Old House (C. 1742)*, home for half a century of my life. To start off with, to walk these stairs, up or down, a signal for day or evening in the heart of an otherwise silence, is to hear sassy children underfoot. They are the underlings of square nails stretching their might, hanging on for two and a half centuries worth of treads and risers and hand-hewn stringers. Ah, *pingsnap*! Last night I heard one letting go, tired of the holding on. Without doubt, age talks back to you at night. *Pingsnap! Pingsnap!* Oh, hear that message, hear that voice.

Likewise, on a few major beams, newly exposed by my reach back into the house's beginning, some broadly a foot across, ax marks permanent as severe scars, bark on round edges clings in place, refusing to let go. That refusal boggles the mind to think these beams were slabbed out of trees closing now on three-hundred years of being, if not already there. Their span spans, their grip hangs tenacious.

A special window snugs close by the porch roof. How many times it has been the way in or out for generations of youth on to daughters or destinies we'll never know. That window is where my sons and attesting companions saw one Halloween night, stars mere, the moon absconded with light, the shadow of a man in a felt hat. A strange man, they swore and swear. So strong the sight that all these years later they step aside passing through the back hall, as if making room for the dusky *persona grata*, granting memorial space for the solitary and dark intruder. Though it's also sworn he wore the hat of a kind last seen hereabouts only on my father.

225

From a most personal confrontation comes another point of house lore. Standing by the twin windows of the bathroom one weekend morning, I watched two of my sons and a daughter at early play. The day bristled and crackled, leaves were at heavy spoilage and thick of pile, golden and myriad red Persians at a momentary standstill of their October march. My eyes trained on my own beginnings where an old barn, sloped at ridge beam and atilt, leaning forever, continued to loose energies and imaginations. In the barn rain hung on like old statements. Soft corners kept themselves wetter than rooting, heaved mushrooms out of droppings swept from stallions now but bone. Spider webs, taking up their dew, walked on railroad silver, aimed for stars locked at night where roofed pine knots fall, or the moon, needing a drink, dropped its straws down. It's wetter likely underground, but can't smell like this: old blankets out all night, dog's breath, leather still breathing hide work a mule threw off his brewed chassis barreling the field all day. My intent was to watch and marvel at children's play and hustle, to propose and endure love from a distance, tempest of the far heart.

Mysteriously, I was joined by another father who peered over my shoulder, sharing my intent. This man, this visitor, appeared out of the damp air of the room, a specter of comfort and custom, trying, I assumed, to take his place again, steal something back he had lost. I told him without looking back at him, sort of indirectly at first, and then most pointedly, that this time was mine. That father, and who knows how many others in conjunction with him in the same space, went quietly back to his eternal comfort. There were no tears, no ministrations or implorations, no wringing of hands, no fright wrought out of his visit, as though an inalienable right had been invoked.

For true appointment with time, accept this: this house was, in another heyday, in its infancy, the Oyster Inn, a stagecoach stop on the Boston-Newburyport run late in the Eighteenth Century. Put up or eat up, I'd suppose from clues. Part proof of that portrayal is the layer of discarded oyster shells. Every garden attempt in the backyard has revealed a thick white archeological stratum, most likely boasting both pre-Revolutionary and post-Revolutionary chalk. Such digs have uncovered old sump holes, dried and rock-throated wells gone harshly back to earth again, and leech fields and cesspools also bearing rock. All of them laying a way of drainage off to the river a quick 200 feet away, some almost as modern as me. Who knows where those fluids went? The theory is, after seventeen feet of such plunging, fluid purity is re-established, resurrected.

This is a house whose rafters and beams of its three floors are either 9x12 or 10x13 or 8x11 or thereabouts in its barn-body mix, leveled on the top for floor or the bottom for ceiling sighting. It is where ancient coin was deposited by carpenter or builder as a token fetish on a base sill thicker than a lineman's thigh. And where, inside one wall and atop one window coming down in constant maintenance of the years, came forth a child's high button shoe. The shoe was nailed with a square nail to a lintel as a carpenter's statement. The sole is worn extremely thin on one side as if that carpenter's child or builder's child had dragged one foot through a period of her early life. The shoe most likely is a fetish, a buttoned talisman or an amulet, or, as my father once pointed out from his worldly tours with the Marines, an *antinganting*, which a legendary Filipino had left impressed on his storied mind.

Oh, that child haunts me yet. She comes back each time I look upon the shoe. I have framed it in a recess of glass with a museum of house nails and clay marbles exhumed from beam restoration or foundation gravel. Each night dousing the last kitchen light, emptying out day, so much like a shopkeeper at the till, I think she might be the daughter of the other father who looked over my shoulder that day in the upstairs bathroom, where my territory, my time, was invaded, with a quiet retreat following. Honor among parents, perhaps, or the Good Carpenter, Joseph himself, making a stand for his tradesmen.

A house it is where boards in the roof are sometimes thirty-six inches broad in their endless cover, telling me the local forests have gone through generation change. It's a house where a portion of one cellar wall is a single stone no horse of theirs could have moved during construction and instead became part of the house's lasting support. It is where archways of red mickey bricks out of a long-gone nearby kiln stand as tunnels through the basement. Two and a half centuries later they continue to hold up for needed warmth all eight fireplaces, including two beehive ovens. Some nights alone, letting all my genes work their way into a froth of knowledge, or letting them free of baseboard or wainscoting, I taste the bread and the beans from those ovens, know the mud that sealed these domed cooking chambers, feel the kitchen work its magic.

This is, further, an abode from whose front yard I can, even today and bet the farm on it, throw a stone well into the First Iron Works of America, Cradle of American Industry. Waiting to sit again in that front yard, by the granite walk and steps, is a smooth granite hitching post, four hundred pounds or better, buried I'd guess for near a century in the backyard. There is a hole drilled through ten inches of that granite column, that snubbing post, that horse holder, where the wrought iron ring has fled back into the earth again. Though one

228

son, I know, will put both back where they belong, time coming, time allowed, tools at home in his hands, and history.

On the floor of the wainscoted front room, in front of another fireplace sitting on those red mickey arches, where my wife, as my young son said, "Mommy was kissing (infant) Betsy on the floor." Betsy, in the wrath of a momentary seizure, grand mal, and Mommy, RN, giving mouth-to-mouth to her daughter for the first of two times. The spot of that life-saving retrieval was, as it proved out, but feet away from the door where I met her sneaking back in at four o'clock of a morning in her fifteenth year, having slipped out her brothers' window, that route cover thought broadcast safe. "Oh, dad," she unflappably said, "you're up early." Now she has children she must watch!

But, all that aside, it is this room here that counts. At one and the same time, it is meager and plush, 11x15 in measure, a fireplace and hearth jutting off one wall, another wall lined with 60 feet of bookshelves. A quick look shows all the signed copies from Seamus Heaney, Galway Kinnell, Donald Junkins and Donald Hall among other Donalds, John Farrow's (sic) *City of Ice*, comrade James Hickey's *Chrysanthemum in the Snow*, some bound mementos of my own, and at least 60 sports trophies in hockey, football, baseball and softball awarded to my children. It has one window looking out on the Iron Work's original slag pile, Saugus River's salt basin plush with reeds and marsh grass, and telescopes towards Boston and the ocean a mere five miles away. It has three doors to front and back halls and a small bathroom. Without doubt it is the warmest room in the house with only one 11-foot wall an outside wall, the other three with camel's hair in the plaster mix all being inside walls. The floor is maple that I can't replace commercially.

The section of the floor, where a closet once sat, is now lumberyard oak, slightly off-color but in the mix. My original computer, an old Mac with a screen like a postage stamp, no longer humming late into the night or well before dawn, sits against one wall, beside the fireplace; here, where I work, a newer unit, chock full of ideas, aspirations, and memories, my own tonnage.

My Hometown: Saugus, Massachusetts

Ah, Saugus, the town I took to Korea many years ago, savored, brought back! Images strike here, deadly accurate in their mark. Metaphors, booted and buckled and loaded for bear, ride horseback through my town, holding forever in place. At times they ride roughshod or, taking a breath, saunter a bit, smelling new-cut hay over hill, or marsh grass caught up in light appreciation of salt about the air, all Atlantic talking.

Realization comes too. Times there were when our river was like an old man trying to get into bed, slow climb at banking, belt or pajamas astray, slight failures. Some springs, it would be caught up in flume's rush.

Water talks, the sea, the river, the pond.

The town talks. It is heard.

If you ask a hundred old-time Saugonians about our town, those that have moved about this world of ours, many still moving, the chances prevail that you'd receive many different approaches to the meaning of a town, Saugus, Massachusetts, 12 miles north of Boston on the historic North Shore.

It keeps exclaiming itself in the back of the mind, again and again and again. *Saugus* it says, in a way that never lets go. *Saugus* they say. They say it by poem and book, by disc or tape, in words and music, by a study of our old Indians.

From a corner of Cliftondale Square by Surabian's Store the recalls would spring, or from the old Morrison Drug Store on the corner of Smith Road or a house on Morton Avenue or Myrtle Street that somehow won't let go its grip even to this day. They'd come from a cliff-face up in the still woods of North Saugus or a late skate on Lily Pond or the Anna Parker when it used to be flooded for winter fun. Or from a game of playing tag on the rising form of the Post Office when it was being built in the Thirties.

All this reverie might begin with the ghost of a father's lilting voice calling across the cool air just after darkness started its descent. The tone of that voice, its song of airy stubbornness and care, settling its primal demand across a goodly piece of town, across Main Street to the deep end of a hay field near Gustafson's Florist. It would cross a section of the railroad tracks leaning from Lynn through the heart of the town to Revere on the Linden Branch. It would be a voice calling more than one person home, calling more than one person to memory. With sound there comes images, perhaps faint and distant, but ever real, freewheeling a stream of consciousness. The recallers might remember a summer cottage, and little more than a shed at that, in Golden Hills or high on Henshit Mountain, having a cellar constructed underneath, getting elongated, widened, being winterized, the walls becoming warmer, becoming home.

Sometimes, a clubhouse in those Thirties, in the tough times, became a full-fledged home, and stands in place yet, in part tribute to its young carpenters. Frankie Parkinson and the Petitto boys, among others, used to talk about their memberships in such clubs, how they came by their building materials, how they got into the real estate business in the first place. Those were marvelous stories of another time, of another liberty and another persuasion; the lumber floating across Lily Pond from a *special source,* or hauled by sled on mid-winter's ice, cover and darkness key words of the narratives. After a while taxes were imposed on these crude structures by the police chief, which forced the boys to move, to redraft plans, to rebuild, architects at the outset.

Among old timers, chances are a number of them might recall Blind Leonard living alone in his small shack near what is now Camp Nihan's waters, across from the North Saugus School. That is now a professional building at what is the newest traffic control point in town. Leonard would walk again for them along Water and Walnut Streets, the cane tapping its steady tap, coming from the bus stop, coming from Lynn, from music, from Danvers where he visited his brother, or from another relative's house where the lights were kept low. A survivor for the longest time, a marvel for getting done what could not be done, Citizen Leonard.

Too, some of them would remember an eleven-year-old boy at the wheel of a tractor on the family farm alongside Spring Street, where the Full of Bull now sits facing the Turnpike. It was dear friend Eddie LeBlanc, the sun beating down on him, sweat-generating, high August at its work. The old Ford tractor went off to war in 1942 as part of a pile of junk metal collected on the lawn of the town hall or the pile near the State Theater and the railroad tracks. The junk became Corsairs and tanks and LSTs pointing straight at Normandy or the sands of Saipan or Kwajalein, keeping Saugus boys company out there in The Big Noise.

Once, they'd remember, there was a freedom and independence and an initiative for the young to grow quickly, to do the manly thing, with whatever consequences waiting to happen. War does that, and the stretch of a town and its young people towards the next level of age. Citizens growing.

But, in all of these acts of definition, there would be a universal feeling underlining each approach. For the truth is you don't grasp Saugus outright. You don't jump in up to your knees and know right off what you've jumped into. You don't get to the heart of a town as if a rapid transit has dropped you at the heartbeat's center. You can see a hundred pictures of what we've been, what we've come to be. Lily Pond and the dam can leap out at you, as can the Sweetser School and the Felton and the Armitage and the Mansfield and the old North Saugus School. But, they're all gone in their initial sense. The old high school is gone. The State Theater. The Adventure Car-Hop. The Drive-In Theater. All gone. Tony Scire is gone and Reverend Gray is gone and Father Culhane. Dave Lucey is gone and Buzz Harvey and Hazel Marison and Walter Blossom and John A.W. Pearce. Albert Moylan is gone and Vernon Evans and William Smith. Art Spinney is gone and Doug and Bruce Waybright and Doc Williams and Jimmy MacDougall and George Miles and Charlie Cooper and Soupie Campbell. And Adlington's and Hoffman's hardware stores. And Graham's Market and Braid's and Sherman's and the Economy Store and Louis Gordon's Tailor Shop and Joe Laura's Barbershop and Ace Welding and Herb White's Diner and the Slop Shop and Warnie's Restaurant and Butler's Drug and Tony Cogliano's and the Rexall and Charlie Hecht's in the Center.

Bill Carter's Bar is gone and Chickland and Ludwig's Cleaners and Heck Allen's.

The perishable perish.

They're all gone, veered off the face of the earth, but we're still here.

For the time being.

We too shall pass on, yet in the meantime, in the moments of pure reverie of recall, we assess and measure and realize what we've become and what we came from.

We remember what we've taken out of a place.

Taken out of Saugus!

Through the gifts of Ellis Island, through the pouring out of people from Europe and all the continents, this little town on the North Shore in its day was becoming a little piece of America, a reflection of the larger mirror of this country. We, as a town, as a community in the truest sense, had become an amalgam at one time; but we were not complete. At the ports of Boston and New York and New Orleans through the terrible times of fever and along the cool St. Lawrence Seaway, the boats unloaded their cargo. The load of precious charges was destined to continue the rising of the New World. With them, of them, came the character upon which this town, as with many other towns along the North Shore, finally fixed its form and content.

The enclaves, of course, came into existence. Almost like estates of a sort, they were, like seeking like, economies of kinship, sea fares being paid, sponsorships coming into bloom, cousins coming from the Old World to help with the new farms along Walnut Street and Main Street and Vine Street and Whitney Street. They came to help in the shops and mills at the center of town and along Lincoln Avenue. The character of East Saugus developed beside that of Cliftondale. West Cliftondale bloomed in its own way as did Golden Hills and Lynnhurst, and North Saugus being molded in its near-sovereign outland independence.

Then, eventually, with charisma, with fusion, the edges were joined and the amoebae fully assimilated. We had, at some point, become Saugus.

Once the core of the town had come into being, once the character had been formed, and the energy flowing through it was live and vital, something else happened.

No longer was it what the people had given to the town. From its becoming Saugus, the measurement we had to make therefore came to be what we took from its being. What we took away from it when we left. It became much like looking back and trying to say what you carried away from a school you had attended, that school continuing long after you've passed through it.

All were pieces of Saugus carried away from her heartbeat. Like Lily Pond, as it was, gone! That those taken pieces keep getting regenerated is a marvel of township. It is why Saugus is loved by so many, and by so many more who have not yet found out what they carry with them, waiting to steal away in this lifetime. Old friends come back at me in many ways in the spell of time, often special in their wrapping or in their expression.

Don Junkins and Bart Brady Ciampa and Tim Churchard and Jim Smith and Tom Weddle correspond by letter or book or poem, CD or tape. All are Saugonians who had to go away to come home, now my mouth waters at correspondence and is full of Don's words, ("where have I been all these years?" from his latest book) and they say *Saugus* to me, all the way from the bull ring *he* writes about, all the way from a sweetened Iberia, all the way from the back of his head.

Don Junkins is in Deerfield, Massachusetts, retired but writing strong as ever, the metaphor saddled and ready. Bart Ciampa makes music in Vancouver, and puts it on CD's and sends them my way where they curl into soft and aging nights. So does the music and poetry of Tim Churchard in cool West Lebanon, Maine, where he teaches and coaches, the Irish drum and the guitar loose in the night. In far off Waldwick, New Jersey, Jim Smith writes letters full of music and intelligence and first choices of a select mind. They come five and six pages at a time, robust, explosive, wandering his tastes, sorting them out for me with gunfire delivery.

Now I read Don Junkins' new book, *Journey To The Corrida*, as I am surrounded by Bart Brady Ciampa's exquisite trumpet on his own CD from

Vancouver way, hearing his *Latinas Reflexiones*, and he does all the instruments, one atop the other, pretending it's about the Southern Desert, and all the time it's all about Saugus.

Bart and Don, what a pair! What a pair! And they level out with Tim Churchard and his music, and their long ties, and how they graced the same field as Tim and I did. And geologist Tom Weddle, unfailing communicator, writing elegantly of Tontoquon the Indian who roamed the banks of the Saugus River a few centuries ago. And we all, to a man, love Saugus for what she is and what she has been in our lives.

It was my son Timmy, whose home is in Franklin, Maine, who said, "So you and your pals are writing a book about Saugus in this past century. For example," he continued, "tell me about the Forties. What were they like? Why do some football players from those times write poetry? Or what in East Saugus made such music in the beginning that it now comes out of your computer, all the way from the West Coast? Or how do you hibernate in the night with an old teammate's book of poems, or another's sheaf of letters?"

It was not smugness on his part. But I did not know if that choice of his was spontaneous or specifically directed, as if he had in mind a period related to his own age, young, impressionable, bursting, a place where we all have been.

It was a catch in the throat, I said. I tried to explain it to him:

There was a time in the high school corridor when a girl turned away from me and walked elegantly off to her lifetime, smiling to this day, a raving beauty yet, mother-proud, bearing regal in her skirts just cut so, and the perfect edge of temperament. It was the time when I slyly tore open my brother's fragile V-mail letter from the wild Pacific before anybody else could get to it, its onionskin quality like a manuscript marked up by an editor serious at life. It was hearing my cousin's telephone voice from a Port of Embarkation hidden somewhere on the East Coast, for the lone single last time. I remembered how he'd call with that falsetto air to his brother while skating in the swamp near Siaglo's piggery on Longwood Avenue. He was mimicking Richie and Sumner Sears' mother calling out for them, the night late, the cold stealing down atop us mindless except for small joys.

Or it was seeing a neighbor's son heading home with one olive drab pant leg sewn much higher than the other one. It was watching newsreels, like *Pathe News*, at the State Theater on Friday nights, not really knowing what the gunfire and sudden combustion was all about, that gray mass of exploding sand or snow up there on the screen, now and then body parts in the mix, or hearing the high screech of shells or a plane diving off the clouds as if those sounds had been artificially appended to the film. Wondering if those sounds could be real. It would be early in the Fifties I'd come to know them for what they were.

It all came down eventually to my lost brother, locked up forever in my mind. There is a catch in the throat, a first order of breathlessness I remember behind my eyes with a clarity that could disturb some minds.

It was suddenly finding someone whose ear, like mine, could turn quickly to a cool jazz musician right after hearing Puccini at his very best (… that in New Jersey, Jimmy Smith would give anything to hear the trumpet and flugelhorn I'm tending on right this minute). Or knowing what Auden had to say about another poet, "In the nightmare of the dark/All the dogs of Europe bark," the words on the porch on Main Street falling from my Grandfather's lips. It was as if the old gent were reading from an Old World cairn, the Red Fergus put away or one more of the warring

O'Sheehaughns. The words were blessed and lovely, full of a music I vaguely could begin to hear, to recognize as my own. And a massive war about to begin that would change everything we knew or could feel, the measurements of that war forever at hand.

The catch in the throat became the names in thick black type in the local newspaper pages: Basil Parker, Larry Daniels, Tommy Atkins; boys who would never again make the walk along Summer Street or Appleton Street to Stackpole Field, a walk that I would make for four years in the same Forties they trod it. A walk that teammate Don Junkins would write about, the catch again in the throat, deeper, like a barbed hook had set, clutching what was soul.

The list of names came growing and running through the streets of the town; the Kasabuski brothers almost in one pained but exhilarate breath (them together forever), Vitold Glinski and his pal Alexander Chojnowski from East Saugus practically together again, Walter Barrett missing in the Pacific, Charlie Lenox killed in France, Al DeStuben wounded in Germany. The list grew and grew, the catch in the throat thicker, heavier, a weight coming with it, like measurement taking place, hand spans, arms' length of things.

My heart is forever locked into this town whose streets I walk the way I might one day walk another paradise. If there is one like this, if it is one I can earn my way to, where the river comes pale and palpable in its touch at East Saugus. If it is one where you can look across to Lynn, where old pilings and boats worn out by muscle and devotion continue their journey back into the earth. Where the marsh turns suddenly brown, then white, and where friends, the old and the new, the lost and the forlorn, herald every corner I turn, telling me they love what I still have.

Yes, Timmy, here is part of it, the Forties, the pain, the grace, the recall, the sound of another's words, another's music, coming to me at the same time. The images sound. Bart Ciampa's trumpet or Tim Churchard's banjo plays like one of Don Junkins' or one of Jimmy Smith's metaphors. There is no mouth, no voice, but a place…Saugus! God, I am still here, smack dab in the middle of it all.

Remarkable, Donny. Remarkable, Bart. Remarkable, Tim. Remarkable, Jim. Remarkable, Tom Weddle. Ah, yes, Timmy, remarkable, the Forties. For two years those Forties and all the years since ran through our minds as we set them down in our book, *A Gathering of Memories, Saugus 1900 – 2000*. For two years we garnered and gathered and placed them in order and ordered them in place, scribing a pass at a collection of memories. And it came about, after a total and consuming labor of love, an endless poke at the imagination. Saugonians from forty-seven states and places outside our borders have ordered the book. John Burns and Bob Wentworth and our committee prepared for them a true feast for the memories.

The book sold out in a few months, all 2,000 copies including the last five damaged copies, after doing our own warehousing, packaging, mailing for months of pure excitement. Five hundred more were printed and sold. A perennial scholarship stands, *The John Burns Millennium Book Associates Scholarship* for Saugus High graduates. It was a noble effort.

Perhaps, that too will be remembered as a piece of Saugus.

About the Author

Tom Sheehan writes from Saugus, Massachusetts, just north of Boston. He is co-editor of the sold-out 2500 copies of *A Gathering of Memories, Saugus 1900-2000* (2000), for which its committee borrowed $60,000 from the Saugus Bank to print a book not yet written.

His novels include *Vigilantes East (*2002*), Death for the Phantom Receiver* (2003) and *An Accountable Death (*2004*)*. Five more are completed and seek publication. His poetry books include *Ah, Devon Unbowed; The Saugus Book*; *Reflections from Vinegar Hill*; *This Rare Earth & Other Flights* (2003); and *The Westering* (2004).

Sheehan is a graduate of Saugus High School and Boston College. He served with the 31st Infantry Regiment, 7th Division, in Korea 1951-52, and is a member of Saugus High Hall of Fame and the New England Poetry Club.

His favorite pastimes include following Saugus hockey (three-time state champions), Saugus football and Saugus Little League (New England Champions, 2003).